This Grotesque Essence

AS SUNG AT THE

Principal Theatres

IN

England and America,

BY

Mr. T. D. RICE.

Theater poster for the original Jim Crow
as performed by Daddy Rice, 1833.

This Grotesque Essence

Plays from the American Minstrel Stage

GARY D. ENGLE

The minstrel show was the single most popular form of entertainment in America before the development of the motion picture. Through the image of the blackface clown the show inspired the nation's laughter. In the words of an English visitor in 1869, minstrels offered "a humor that was often genuine if always grotesque."

The essence of minstrelsy was the afterpiece, the finale that brought out the whole troupe in a combination of song, dance, and slapstick performed in an exaggerated dialect and studded with puns and malapropisms. *This Grotesque Essence* includes twenty-two of these afterpieces dating from the 1830s to the 1870s, minstrelsy's formative decades. Included are works by all the guiding personalities in this unique stagecraft, from T. D. "Daddy" Rice— "The Father of American Minstrelsy"—to George Christy, as well as representative examples of the major sub-genres in minstrel fare— Shakespearean burlesques, processional entertainments, extravaganzas, opera bouffe, farce, political satire, pantomime, and stage adaptations of non-theatrical humor.

Although the minstrel shows have all but disappeared from the American consciousness in the last decade, Engle argues that as an authentic folk art they provide rare opportunities for insight into the nineteenth-century American mass mentality. Students of American culture

GARY D. ENGLE, who received his doctorate from the University of Chicago, is assistant professor of English at Cleveland State University and film critic and contributing editor of *Cleveland Magazine*.

This
Grotesque
Essence

Plays from the
American Minstrel Stage

GARY D. ENGLE

Louisiana State University Press
Baton Rouge and London

Copyright © 1978 by Louisiana State University Press
All rights reserved
Manufactured in the United States of America

Design: Dwight Agner
Type face: VIP Baskerville
Composition: LSU Press
Printing and binding: Kingsport Press

Photographs courtesy of Hoblitzelle Theatre Arts Collection
Humanities Research Center, University of Texas at Austin

LIBRARY OF CONGRESS CATALOGING IN PUBLICATION DATA

Main entry under title:

This grotesque essence.

Bibliography: p.
1. American drama—19th century.   2. Minstrel shows.   3. Afro-
Americans—Drama.   I. Engle, Gary D   1947–
PS632.T47   812'.057   77–16617
ISBN 0–8071–0370–5

For Barbara Hawley

Contents

Contents

Illustrations

Acknowledgments

I would like to express my gratitude to Robert Rosenthal, director of special collections at the University of Chicago Library, for the encouragement he gave me at the beginning of this project; to William H. Crain of the Hoblitzelle Theatre Arts Library at the University of Texas at Austin for his assistance with the illustrations; and to Gwen Satchel and Sandra Coy of Cleveland State University for their assistance in the preparation of the manuscript. Special gratitude is due Hamlin Hill of the University of New Mexico for his excellent advice and personal support during the preparation of this edition.

INTRODUCTION

American Minstrelsy and Democratic Art

When America's position in the history of world cultures is finally evaluated, this nation will quite likely be remembered as one of the first great radical attempts to implement the ideal of democracy. Though America never has been a true democracy, it is nevertheless useful to discuss it in relation to that ideal; for it has been the spirit of democracy which has tended to distinguish American culture from its European antecedents, particularly during the nineteenth century. In a true democracy the will of the majority rules. This idea is axiomatic. It is no wonder, then, that American cultural historians are opening their eyes to the fact that the rule applies in all areas of a democratic society, including the arts. Because a ruling majority in a democracy cannot directly express its values and tastes in artistic creation, it expresses them indirectly by exercising the freedom to accept or reject any individual work of art. For better or worse, the characteristic art of a democracy is shaped by the will of the audience, not of the artist. Popularity becomes one measure of artistic value. It is reasonable, then, that as American society becomes more introspective through the efforts of its scholars, attention focuses more on the popular arts. A necessary part of that introspection is the task of salvaging the fragile remnants of early forms of American popular art.

Introduction

The plays in this anthology are representative examples of an art form which thrived during the nineteenth century. These afterpieces as they were called were an essential component of the minstrel show—that grotesque concoction of song, dance, and theatrical comedy organized around the thick-lipped, woolly-wigged image of the banjo-plunking, blackface minstrel clown.

In reference to America's treatment of blacks in the popular arts, Leslie Fiedler has said, "When *Uncle Tom's Cabin* was written, Uncle Tom became the first living image of the black man in the mind of the Western white world."[1] Acknowledging the importance of the Uncle Tom image, I nevertheless disagree. The minstrel clown was a part of the American consciousness long before 1852 when Harriet Beecher Stowe's novel was published. The image of the minstrel clown was indigenous to the growth of American culture. Minstrelsy had its roots in the decades surrounding the birth of this nation; and it died in the amateur productions of church organizations, young businessmen's clubs, Rotarians, and firemen's protective leagues in the first half of the twentieth century. The figure of the minstrel clown has been the most persistent and influential image of blacks in American history. It is interesting to look briefly at how critics of minstrelsy have dealt with that image.

The earliest view seems to have been a firm belief that the image was true. In reference to a performance in the summer of 1840 by T. D. Rice—the first great star of blackface entertainment—a critic for a New York paper wrote:

> Entering the theatre, we found it crammed from pit to dome, and the best representative of our American negro that we ever saw was stretching every mouth in the house to its utmost tension. Such a natural gait!—*such* a laugh!—and such a twitching-up of the arm and shoulder! It was *the* negro, par excellence. Long live *James Crow*, Esquire![2]

1 Transcript of *Firing Line*, taped November 15, 1974; aired December 1, 1974 (Columbia, S.C.: Southern Educational Communications Association), 8.
2 Quoted by George C. D. Odell, *Annals of the New York Stage* (New York: Columbia University Press, 1928), IV, 372.

Introduction

It was not until twentieth-century critics began analyzing the art form in its waning years that a substantial shift of opinion occurred. In 1930 Carl Wittke (one of minstrelsy's fairest and finest historians) acknowledged the essential falseness of the image. After a long and extremely accurate description of the minstrel clown, Wittke wrote, "This, in the main, was the Negro of the joke-book tradition, and more especially of the minstrel tradition, and undoubtedly he was a somewhat different individual from the one to be found in real life in the Southern states."[3] Yet the desire to believe that there was some degree of truth in the image persisted. Wittke could not resist the temptation to explain T. D. Rice's genius as residing in his "unusual powers as a delineator of Negro character."[4] The myth that the minstrel clown was more than sheer fantasy has died hard.

Part of the reason for the myth's longevity seems to have been the false belief that minstrelsy developed from plantation entertainments among black slaves in the South. A search for the records of those early black entertainments, however, reveals that they must have been rare and provincial things and could not have been a formative influence on the art.[5] A brief view of how minstrelsy did originate will show that the minstrel clown evolved out of the racial fantasies of northern urban whites.

The earliest recorded event that can be called a minstrel act occurred in 1769 in New York when a white actor named Lewis Hallam played the role of a black slave in a production of Issac Bickerstaff's *The Padlock*. During one show Hallam apparently snapped his fingers at professional discipline and went on stage in a state of almost total inebriation. The performance was extremely well received; and though Hallam cannot be credited with having caused the proliferation of such roles, his perfor-

3 Carl Wittke, *Tambo and Bones: A History of the American Minstrel Stage* (Westport, Conn.: Greenwood Press reprint, 1971), 8.
4 Ibid., 25.
5 See Richard Moody's discussion of plantation entertainments in *America Takes the Stage: Romanticism in American Drama and Theatre, 1750–1900* (Bloomington: Indiana University Press, 1955), 32 *ff*.

Introduction

mance certainly set the pattern for the American stage version of blacks in the last decades of the eighteenth century. By the 1820s blackface song and dance routines—based in part on the earlier stage roles but primarily on the mistaken assumption that blacks were in some strange way quite happy under slavery—were being consistently used as entr'actes and afterpieces in the formal American theater and were added to the variety entertainments of the medicine shows and circuses that traveled the frontiers. The earliest stars of this art (a few of whom were black) were men blessed with good voices and "natural rhythm." Such a man was Thomas Dartmouth "Daddy" Rice (1808–1860), the white man who brought minstrel entertainment to a position of status in America. Probably America's first entertainment superstar, Rice specialized in one-man blackface acts in which he sang semi-authentic black folk music (gleaned from his tours of the Ohio River valley) and danced grotesquely exaggerated versions of reels and hoedowns. He was, according to all contemporary accounts, an immensely talented performer deserving of the title "father of American minstrelsy." But Rice is important in the history of the art for other reasons. Specifically, he gave minstrelsy two of its primary and lasting elements.

First, he established the character of Jim Crow, the stereotype of the minstrel clown. Though the figure's name changed in the decades following Rice's career, his character did not. Whether audiences laughed at the antics of Cuff, Snowball, Jumbo, Juba, Sambo, Pompey, or Scipio Alcibiades Swash, the figure remained Jim Crow. There is a legend in minstrel history about how Rice "found" the character of Jim Crow. The legend is based on an event that occurred once upon a time (probably in the late 1820s) somewhere in the Ohio River valley—some historians say Cincinnati, some Louisville, others Pittsburgh. Rice, then a moderately successful itinerant performer, happened to observe a crippled black stable boy who was singing a nonsense song about a character named Jim Crow and trying to dance.

Introduction

Rice rearranged the song to fit the minstrel mode, copied the pitiful hitch-jump-stepping expression of happiness, and exaggerated the whole to the point of absurdity. He put this song and dance number into his act and gave the nation the character of Jim Crow—a figure full of childish emotion grotesquely cavorting across the stage. "Jumping" Jim Crow became Rice's trademark; and that single act carried him on an unprecedented wave of popularity across America and to Europe.

In addition Rice is credited with having put together the core of the minstrel show proper. In New York in the early 1830s, Rice began performing what he called Ethiopian operas. These were variety show finales using more than one performer in which the essential elements of song, dance, and slapstick antics were strung on a plot of childish simplicity, with the whole working toward a conclusion that had the characteristics of revelry. This classic entertainment structure became the pattern on which most minstrel show afterpieces were built.

The primary formula for the whole minstrel show was devised fairly soon after Rice developed his extremely popular Ethiopian operas. In 1843 at the Bowery Amphitheatre in New York City, a group of four white performers in blackface who called themselves the Virginia Minstrels put together an entire evening's entertainment consisting of standard entr'acte numbers arranged on a fairly simple structure. The group's leader was Dan Emmett; and it was apparently his idea to have the performers sit in a semicircle and put forth a medley of close harmony songs, instrumental solos, and comic dialogues. The show was climaxed with a walk around involving all the members of the group. From this elementary structure the minstrel show was born.

Several groups rapidly capitalized on the northern demand for blackface theatrics by following the lead of Emmett's troupe. Among these, E. Byron Christy's group has been singled out as one of the most influential. In 1846 the Christy Minstrels refined the blackface show and gave it the shape we tend to remember it by.

Christy divided the show into two parts. The first began with a rousing entry march after which the performers arranged themselves in a semicircle and responded to the command, "Gentlemen, be seated!" What followed was a lively series of songs, both comic and sentimental, blended with joking exchanges between the interlocutor, who served as emcee for the show and held center position in the line, and the end men called Tambo and Bones after the instruments they played. These end men were the essential minstrel clowns on the Jim Crow model whose rudimentary wit and childish antics constantly deflated the formal pretentions of the interlocutor. The second part, or olio, was a varied offering of specialty acts—such as plantation breakdowns, clog dances, and steamboat imitations—which were mixed with short skits and comic monologues called stump speeches that lampooned the American folk art of spread-eagle oratory. As a finale the performers gathered with full set and costumes and performed an afterpiece, which both climaxed the show and served as a curtain call by drawing on the combined talents of the entire troupe.

Taken altogether, the afterpieces which climaxed the shows based on Christy's model can be considered the essence of the minstrel art. Whether short farces, Shakespearean burlesques, or theatrical lampoons of contemporary fads, the afterpieces achieved their audience impact by combining the various theatrical forms that constituted the first parts of the show. Moreover, it was in the afterpieces that minstrelsy achieved its highest degree of genuine humor.

Though the minstrel show changed very little for thirty or forty years after Christy established its form, there was a period during the fifties and sixties when several of New York's more prestigious professional troupes dropped Christy's concert format and experimented with programs consisting predominantly

Introduction

of the blackface burlesques and farces. The success of these troupes (exemplified by the performances of Wood's Minstrels —one of only two troupes that Rice would perform with in his last years) is persuasive evidence of the importance of afterpieces in the overall minstrel art.

These, then, are the highlights of minstrelsy's origins; but they should be enough to indicate that minstrelsy and the minstrel clown were theatrical creations born on the stages of America's northern population centers. Early performers like Rice were from the Northeast. Rice himself was born and raised in New York City where he received much of his theatrical training. The first professional troupes to spread the art were white theatrical groups from the Northeast. In minstrelsy's most prominent period from the 1840s to the 1870s, the vast majority of its stars were of European immigrant stock, northern born and bred. The appeal of minstrelsy was based in its theatrical elements of song, dance, and comedy; and the heart of American theater during minstrelsy's formative years was in the Northeast. Whites had very little contact with blacks in that area at that time. As a result, the only relationship the minstrel clown had with blacks was that he was black, and a shiny burnt-cork black at that.

It is true, of course, that as minstrelsy radiated throughout the nation from its Northeast urban sources, some black performers and a number of all black troupes achieved tremendous successes in the art; but in doing so they were putting on a role created by whites.

Though minstrelsy had its roots in northern urban soil, it quickly branched out into every corner of the nation. Between the 1840s and the 1870s minstrelsy was the dominant form of American popular art. Within twenty years after the early successes of the groups mentioned above there were more than a hundred professional troupes in blackface. New York alone boasted ten resident companies by 1860, and professional troupes held forth at various times in Boston, Hartford, Washington,

Introduction

Richmond, Charleston, Savannah, Mobile, New Orleans, St. Louis, Cincinnati, Columbus, Cleveland, Chicago, St. Paul, and San Francisco. In cities where resident troupes did not have their seasons, traveling troupes took up the slack. Minstrel companies entertained passengers on the river steamers that plied the waterways of the Midwest; and as roads and railways cut into the heartland of the nation traveling shows visited every crossroads where the inhabitants could afford the few cents admission price. But the popularity of minstrelsy was not just defined geographically. The art was socially pervasive as well. Minstrels performed before every class in American society. In his autobiographical writings Mark Twain reminisced about the traveling shows which played the riverfront villages of the Mississippi valley during his childhood;[6] and as early as 1844 a group called the Ethiopian Serenaders played at the White House, thus inspiring a long-lasting love affair between America's presidents and its most popular entertainment form.

The tumultuous decades surrounding the American Civil War were minstrelsy's golden age. During that time minstrel shows became one of America's few cultural exports. Several troupes had profitable and enthusiastic receptions throughout Europe and as far away as Australia and New Zealand. But by the 1870s all creative energy in American popular theater was flowing into vaudeville, and minstrelsy was slipping into its very slow decline.

The economic depression of the 1870s forced professional troupes to retrench and engage in increasingly heated competition for the shrinking box office dollar. Consequently, the attrition rate among professional troupes was high. The hundred or so that flourished in the 1860s had by 1880 dwindled to around thirty, and by 1900 to less than ten. Those that survived during this decline were forced into competition with vaudeville, and

6 Bernard DeVoto (ed.), *Mark Twain in Eruption* (New York: Harper Brothers, 1940), 110–18.

Introduction

the result was stage spectacle rather than minstrelsy. But though professional troupes were disappearing, minstrelsy itself was not.

Shortly after the Civil War amateur minstrelsy became so popular that several mail order firms began competing to fill the amateur demand for minstrel literature—joke books, songsters, and acting editions of afterpieces. It was because of this commercial venture that we have any significant body of minstrel material to work with today. The pieces in this anthology were published during the years which marked the end of minstrelsy's golden era. Fortunately, many of the acting editions churned out to fill the mail order catalogs were transcriptions of material from minstrelsy's earlier days. Thus it is possible to get from a judicious selection of them a fair overview of this minstrel art in its strongest decades.

In its golden age, minstrelsy exhibited all the major characteristics of popular art. First, it was tied to the one true mass medium of its day. Before the marketing genius of firms like Beadle and Adams made the printed word in the form of the dime novel a truly mass entertainment medium in America, this nation depended on the popular theater for its fun. The power of popular theater was that it communicated entirely through sight and sound and thus shared a basic characteristic of such folk entertainments as singing, dancing, and telling tall tales. Popular theater became a particularly appropriate medium for mass amusement during a period when most Americans were seldom more than a generation away from their folk origins.

Moreover, minstrel shows were formulaic in nature. Like most mass arts, they were popular because they were familiar. Audiences participated in the shows because they generally knew what was coming next at any given point. The songs of minstrelsy were so patterned (or simply so familiar) that audiences frequently sang along with the performers; and more than one minstrel clown had the dubious pleasure of hearing the punch lines of his time-worn jokes shouted by an appreciative audience before he could deliver them. From its opening march to the final curtain, the minstrel show was only slightly less predictable than church ritual.

Minstrelsy was also a classic example of popular culture in the sense that it was an entertainment ultimately created by the people. One of the earliest notions that a critic of popular culture is made aware of is that mass arts tend to be highly anonymous—not entirely in the sense that a folk art is anonymous, its origins having been lost in antiquity; but rather in the sense that mass arts receive their inspiration from groups of people rather than individuals and are then shaped to the tastes and expectations of large heterogeneous audiences. Because of this, the traditional high-art critical approach of looking for the mark of individual endeavor in any single work of popular culture often leads to frustration. In minstrelsy several talents were required to put a show together. Musicians, choreographers, composers, playwrights, humorists, and actors all had to work in some kind of harmony to create a successful product. Thus, minstrelsy tended to be an art produced by committee rather than by individual endeavor. This phenomenon can be seen in almost all popular arts, whether in the production crews of television and film fare or the stables of writers and artists who churn out series of pulp fiction and comics.

The minstrel material printed for amateur use generally included cast information (usually for advertising reasons) and frequently identified authorship. But even in these instances credit cannot be clearly established. The name which appeared on an acting edition of an afterpiece, for example, was sometimes that of whichever performer or manager happened to serve as scribe for the troupe that originated the material.

The issue of credit for any work of minstrelsy is further complicated by the fact that minstrel shows were constantly shaped in performance. Within the limits set by its rigid structural formula, minstrelsy was a lively impromptu art. A performer might go on stage and, feeding off audience response, flesh out a bare-bones routine with jokes and extentions of jokes not in the original conception of his act. Seldom were any two performances of a single act, such as an afterpiece burlesque, totally alike. A piece in its acting edition form might run fifteen minutes, but when subjected to the constant energy of audience feedback it might run three quarters of an hours, depending of course on the talent and inventiveness of the performers.

As an impromptu art, minstrelsy was ultimately shaped by the audience. In an art which attempts solely to please rather than educate, the artist quickly learns to shape his product so that it conforms to the audience's will. In minstrelsy the power of the audience's will was freely and effectively exercised. When members of an audience got what they did not want, they gave the performers what *they* did not want in the form of vegetables, eggs, rocks, nails, hoots, small animals, and poor box office receipts. It was not unusual for audiences to literally determine an evening's program by calling for and getting their favorite songs and dance numbers, whether scheduled or not. Sometimes they asked for and received the same number over and over again in a single performance. There is a story that Abraham Lincoln, after hearing Dan Emmett's famous "Dixie" at a Chicago performance in 1860, stopped the show and demanded the entire entry march be performed again.[7] Even the verbal humor, which today appears so chaste in the acting editions, could be richly larded with sexual innuendo by the simple addition of gestures and vocal emphases; and frequently it was if the audience allowed it. When, for example, Daddy Rice sang a nonsense love ditty in which he asserted that after marriage "sassengers is riz," the audience generally understood that he was not necessarily talking about the price of liverwurst. The songs, dance numbers,

7 Related in Jesse W. Weik's *The Real Lincoln* (Boston: Houghton Mifflin, 1923), 75 and 85–86; and Albert J. Beveridge's *Abraham Lincoln* (Boston: Houghton Mifflin, 1928), I, 536 and 597–98.

and jokes were molded to fit the audiences' sensibilities and became the standard material of the minstrel show precisely because the audiences approved of them. Thus, in a very real sense the credit for minstrelsy was spread throughout the millions of Americans who patronized the art.

In every respect minstrelsy was a classic form of popular culture. Its primary value to us now is that it was one of the best reflections of America's democratic mentality to come out of the nineteenth century.

Russell Nye, in *The Unembarrassed Muse*, has suggested that minstrelsy was a thoroughly native American art form; and so it was. Like the nation which produced it, minstrelsy was a melting pot of numerous traditions. The art's ancestry can be traced back to the entertainments of European and African cultures from which America's population springs. The musical instruments associated with the minstrel performer—tambourine, banjo, and bones (a type of castenet)—were African before they were American; the songs were based in part on authentic black folk music but primarily on the folk melodies of England, Ireland, and Scotland;[8] the comic exchanges between the interlocutor and end men were derived from the exchanges between ring master and clowns in European circuses; and the burlesques and farces were descended from a long line of European popular theater running back through eighteenth century English burlesque to the commedia dell'arte, the harlequinade, the Elizabethan jigs, and the vulgar farces of medieval mystery cycles.

What America added to these entertainment traditions was that disturbing but genuinely funny figure of the blackface clown.

---

8 Music seems to have been the one area in which blacks had any influence on minstrelsy at all; but even this was minor. Wittke (p. 175) cites evidence to the effect that less than 10 percent of the minstrel songs were genuinely black in origin, and that, all things considered, whites did much more to shape black music in the nineteenth century than vice versa. Robert C. Toll, in *Blacking Up: The Minstrel Show in Nineteenth-Century America* (New York: Oxford University Press, 1974), proposes that significant black influences on minstrel music occurred only after the Civil War when black troupes added jubilee and gospel songs to the typical minstrel program.

Introduction

In order to understand what minstrelsy can teach us about American culture, one must understand that figure; and in order to do that one must understand that the figure had a double nature. First, the blackface clown was America's fool. As a fool, his main purpose was to comfort audiences by freeing them from their anxieties. This is, in some form or another, the purpose of all entertainment.

In the nineteenth century there were certain cultural ideals based on a democratic philosophy which helped to distinguish this nation from its European antecedents. Primary among these was America's attitude toward class. Though the American experiment in democracy did not eliminate class differences, it did make movement from class to class a reality. From this resulted the peculiarly American notion that all men could become socially mobile, could go from rags to riches, from obscurity to power in a lifetime. This pattern of belief was so basic to American thought that it came to be known as the American dream. The goal for which all Americans worked, if not practically at least ideally, was success based upon European aristocratic models —success defined by material wealth and social and political influence. This dream of mobility, though now viewed with cynicism by many people, was nevertheless a remarkable stimulus to human behavior. In America's most formative century the dream resulted in a vigorous national development which literally transformed the material welfare of the common man.

But the competition and struggle necessary to raise one's social status are directly related to a kind of cultural anxiety which might also be called a part of the American way of life. If a person's life is devoted to the perpetual improvement of social standing, that person is forever burdened by the fear of failure— failure to raise one's status and failure to properly play the role demanded by the new status once it is achieved.

In order to cope with this anxiety, nineteenth-century America quickly developed an obsessive taste for almanacs, etiquette

Introduction

books, and prescriptive grammars, indeed for any guidebook which could help to eliminate the insecurity of social mobility. But guidebooks were not enough. To cope with anxiety a person must be able to escape it periodically through some basic physical emotion like sentimental tears or laughter. Among a nation of people devoted to social mobility there is a constant demand for a scapegoat, a fool who exaggerates the contrast between what a person is and what he wishes or pretends to be until that contrast becomes humorously grotesque. By laughing at a fool, a nation can safely and beneficially laugh at itself.

, During the mid–nineteenth century the minstrel clown was America's favorite fool. The figure was a grotesque and cruel caricature of American blacks. He was intended by the white mentality that created him to serve as a comic representative of the racial minority which was forced to occupy the lowest class in American society. In the minstrel show the blackface clown played out his role as fool in two ways. First, he manifested the weaknesses which inhibit success in a socially mobile culture. He was lazy, ignorant, illiterate, hedonistic, vain, often immoral, fatalistic, and gauche. Secondly, the figure suffered in absurdly comic ways the indignities and embarrassments that can occur when a person's ambitions lead him into roles that he cannot adequately fulfill. When the minstrel clown recited what he thought was Shakespeare, when he donned what he thought were the most current fashions, when he pretended to be a doctor or soldier or great lover or artiste—indeed when he pretended to be anything more than chattel—America was entertained.

If this had been the figure's only function minstrelsy would have been nothing more than a monstrous and prolonged racial joke. Indeed it was that; but it was something more, for the humor of minstrelsy worked in two ways. When the blackface clown adopted any kind of highbrow pose, he not only made a fool of himself but somehow managed to taint the adopted pose as well. Thus, the perpetual effect of his presence on stage was the eradication of even the slightest hint of decorum. When for example he danced a simple *pas grave* in work shoes and tutu, sublimity vanished.

A tangible spirit of anarchy has always been one of the primary dynamics of American humor. The American common man, on whose behalf this nation's democratic philosophy was ostensibly developed, has persistently expressed in a kind of comic nihilism his essential distrust of the goals toward which the American dream has directed him. In the middle decades of the nineteenth century when minstrelsy was in its fullest flower, this distrust took the form of a generally playful hostility toward anything characteristic of the European cultural traditions from which America so chauvinistically wanted to divorce itself.

The anarchical spirit of burlesque was basic to the humor of the minstrel afterpieces. This can be seen in the significant number of Shakespearean travesties that for a period during the 1850s and 1860s dominated minstrel programs.[9] But an object of burlesque did not have to have the status of Shakespeare to be attacked. Fair game was anything associated with the formal American theater, which as an institution was a European cultural offspring. Melodrama, romance, opera, ballet, extravaganza, indeed any form which succeeded on the American stage quickly found a grotesque version of itself in minstrelsy. The blackface art was a theatrical creation which attacked its own parentage. It was, like the nation which produced it, thoroughly revolutionary.

The tradition of minstrel burlesque, however, was not just an expression of anti-European sentiments. It was one manifestation of a deeper psychological dynamic inherent in a democratic society. When a person is not convinced of his own personal worth regardless of his social status, he tends to develop a desire to annihilate any person, role, institution, or tradition that can

9 For a detailed analysis of this sub-genre see Ray B. Browne's "Shakespeare in American Vaudeville and Negro Minstrelsy," *American Quarterly*, XII (Fall, 1960), 374–91.

Introduction

conceivably be thought of as superior. The entertainments which such a person turns to tend to be, like minstrelsy, those which consistently deflate the "highbrow" and thus affirm the image of the common man. Early American humor, for example, made a hero of the type, in both the figure of the down-east Yankee with his wealth of mother wit and love of homely aphorisms, and the boisterous frontiersman who distrusted "book larnin." Even America's most beloved novel was the story of a roguish orphan who, choosing to follow the dictates of his untutored heart, set sail on a raft down the Mississippi in order to escape the yoke of "sivilization." It is significant that when Huck set out on his mythic journey his one true companion was Nigger Jim, a sympathetically drawn version of the minstrel clown.

The minstrel show was an integral part of this tradition in American humor. At its best, minstrelsy embodied the common man's refusal to be intimidated by images of success. The reason for this lies in the fact that the blackface clown was America's friend as well as fool. In his folly he dragged down to the common level many of the character types and artistic traditions which served as symbols of cultural achievement in America.

In the image of the blackface clown, then, minstrelsy reflected a basic complexity of nineteenth-century American democracy. Through its blatant racism it gave America a means of purging the anxiety which resulted from the pressure of the American dream. But at the same time it upheld the value of the American common man. Minstrelsy inspired the laughter of cruelty as well as the laughter of affirmation. It offered, in the words of one English critic who visited America in 1869, "a humor that was often genuine if always grotesque."[10]

10   John Ranken Towse, *Sixty Years of the Theatre—An Old Critic's Memories* (New York: Funk and Wagnalls, 1916), 86.

A Note on the Texts

The afterpieces in this anthology are reprinted from acting editions held in the Atkinson Collection of Ethiopian Drama in the Joseph Regenstein Library at the University of Chicago. Because these pieces were first published as ephemeral, mass-market items, they suffered from both a lack of original proofreading and from hasty production processes. This, compounded by the inconsistency of the dialect transcription in the material, has made it impossible to reconstruct perfect copy for any of the pieces. In preparing these texts I have corrected all recognizable typographical errors, which at times has meant silently reconstructing words and phrases made illegible by smeared type impressions. Nevertheless, I have tried to keep adjustments to a minimum and I have left the dialectical inconsistencies intact in order to preserve the sense of spontaneity and lack of sophistication which must have characterized this material in performance. In order to keep the editorial apparatus to a minimum within the texts, I have annotated only those slang terms and historical references which seem least accessible to the present-day reader.

This Grotesque Essence

Oh, Hush!
or, The Virginny Cupids

This piece was first presented by T. D. Rice on August 15, 1833, at the Bowery Theatre in New York. Although not the first of Rice's Ethiopian operas (*Long Island Juba; or, Love by the Bushel* was performed in January of that year), *Oh, Hush!* was the most famous and probably the best. It became one of the most frequently revived pieces in the entire repertoire of American minstrelsy.

The following version is by Charles White, who was himself a major force in minstrel history. In 1844 White founded the Kitchen Minstrels, one of the earliest professional troupes to spread the art. Over the next four decades he remained an active force as performer of merit, successful manager, and prolific writer and composer. At one time he admitted to having composed forty of the best "Negro" hits of all time.

The first recorded performance of *Oh, Hush!* by White's Sernaders occurred in 1855 at Barnum's Museum in New York. But the published cast list suggests this version may have reached the stage as early as 1850. In any event, White's version is important because it shows the structure and spirit of the original. The following text is reprinted from the acting edition published by Clinton T. DeWitt.

1

This Grotesque Essence

OH, HUSH!
OR,
THE VIRGINNY CUPIDS.
an operatic olio,
in one act, and three scenes.
arranged by CHARLES WHITE.

CAST OF CHARACTERS

SAMBO JOHNSON (a retired bootblack) . . . . Mr. C. White
CUFF (a boss bootblack) . . . . Mr. E. Deaves
PETE WILLIAMS (Cuff's foreman) . . . . Mr. W. Corriston
COLONEL BEN (an old polisher) . . . . Mr. H. Neil
MISS DINAH ROSE (a fascinating wench) . . . . . Mr. J. Huntly
KNIGHTS OF THE BRUSH . . . . by the company

SCENE I.—*Exterior, street*

THE CHARACTERS *discovered blacking boots, some sitting down.* SAM JOHNSON *sits on a chair,* R., *his feet resting on a barrel. He is reading a newspaper which he holds upside down.* ALL *laugh and begin to get up as the curtain rises.*

CUFF.   Pete, I hab been round to all the hotels to-day, an' I got so many boots to black by four o'clock dat I don't tink I can do it. Now, den, boys, if you polish dem by dat time, I'll gib you all a holiday dis ebenin'.

PETE.   Ah! dat's right, Cuff, we'll gib 'em de shine ob de best Day and Martin[1]—but, Cuff, gib us a song.

CUFF *(sings)*.
      Come all you Virginny gals, and listen to my noise,
      Neber do you wed wid de Carolina boys;
      For if dat you do, your portion will be,
      Cowheel and sugar cane, wid shangolango tea.

1   A brand of shoe polish.

2

Oh, Hush! or, The Virginny Cupids

FULL CHORUS.

Mamzel ze marrel—ze bunkum sa?
Mamzel ze marrel—ze bunkum sa?

When you go a courting, de pretty gals to see,
You kiss 'em and you hug 'em like de double rule ob free.
De fust ting dey ax you when you are sitting down,
is, "Fetch along de Johnny cake—it's gitting radder brown."

Chorus.—Mamzel ze marrel, etc.

Before you are married, potatoes dey am cheap,
But money am so plenty dat you find it in the street.
But arter you git married, I tell you how it is—
Potatoes dey am berry high, and sassengers is riz.

Chorus.—Mamzel ze marrel, etc.

CUFF *(turning round after the song discovers* JOHNSON). I say, Pete, who is dat consumquencial darkey ober dar, dat is puttin' on so many airs?

PETE. I don't know, Cuff. He stopped here a few minutes arter you went away, an' he's been reading dar eber since. Speak to him.

CUFF *(approaching* JOHNSON, *scrutinizes his person).* Why, it am Sam Johnson!

ALL. Sam Johnson!

CUFF. Yes, to be sure it am.

JOHNSON *(looking through his eyeglass).* Gemblem, is you distressing your conversation to me?

CUFF. Yes, sar, I is distressing my observation to you inderwidually, collectively, skientifically and alone. *(Seats himself on the barrel.)*

JOHN *(rising).* Well, sar, den I would hab you to know dat my name, sar, is Mr. Samuel Johnson, Exquire, an' I don't wish to be addressed by such —*(pointing to crowd)* low, common, vulgar trash! You had better mind your business and brack your filthy boots. *(He sits down again.)*

CUFF *(gets off the barrel).* I say, Pete, I'll tell you whar I seed dat darkey. He used to work in de same shop wid me for old Jake Simmons, but he drawed a high prize in de lottery, and retired from de 'spectable perfession of bracking boots. De last time I seed him he was down in old Virginny on a coon hunt. I'll tell you suffin' 'bout it. *(He sings.)*

3

'Way down in old Virginny, 'twas in de arternoon,
    Oh! Roley, boley!
Wid de gun dat massa gib me, I went to shoot the coon.

    CHORUS.
Wid my hiddy-co-dink-er—mi! who dar?
    Good-mornin', ladies fair.
Wid my hiddy-co-dink-er—mi! who call?
    Good-mornin', ladies all.

He sat on a pine branch, whistlin' a tune,
    Oh! Roley, boley!
I up wid my gun, and brought down Mr. Coon.

    CHORUS.—Wid my hiddy-co-dink-er, etc.

PETE. I tell you what, Cuff; speak to him in a more eliphant manner.

CUFF. Yes, I will. *(goes over to* JOHNSON *in his best style)* Johnson! *(no answer)* Mr. Johnson! *(no answer)* I'll fetch him dis time, Pete. Mr. Samuel Johnson, Exquire!

JOHNSON *(rises and bows politely).* Sar, I am at your sarbice.

CUFF. Excuse my interrupting you, for I see you am busy readin' de paper. Would you be so kind as to enlighten us upon de principal topicks ob de day?

JOHN. Well, Mr. Cuff, I hab no objection, 'kase I see dat you common unsophisticated gemmen hab not got edgemcation yourself, and you am 'bliged to come to me who has. So spread around, you unintellumgent bracks, hear de news ob de day discoursed in de most fluid manner. *(He reads out some local items.)* Dar has been a great storm at sea and de ships hab been turned upside down.

CUFF *(looks at the paper).* Why, Mr. Johnson, you've got the paper upside down. (ALL *laugh heartily.)*

JOHN. Well, yes, so I is. Golly! I didn't take notice ob dat. *(He starts with amazement.)* Oh, what do I see? has de perfession come to dis degraded persition?

ALL *(shout).* What is it?

JOHN. Does my eyes deceibe me! Bracking boots on de Canal street plan for free cents a pair!

ALL *(grab at the paper, which is torn in pieces, and cry).* Whar? wharabouts?

CUFF.   I say, Pete, I can't see nuffin' like dat here. *(to* JOHNSON*)* Mr.
Johnson, show me dat? *(holds the torn piece to him)*
JOHN.   Oh, I can't show you now—it's torn out.
CUFF.   It won't do, Mr. Johnson. Say, darkeys, don't you tink dat nig-
ger am in lub?
ALL.   Yes, yes! *(*JOHNSON *paces the stage in anger.)* CUFF *sings.*
Sam Johnson, why so solitacious?
Hah, hah, hah, hah, hah?
'Tis lub dat makes you so vexatious,
Sam Johnson, ho!

Does your lub lib in Philumdelphy?
Hah, hah, hah, hah, hah?
Oh! is she poor, or am she wealthy?
Sam Johnson, ho!

Now, gib him boots and make him travel,
Hah, hah, hah, hah, hah!
Oh, chuck dem at him widout cavil,
Sam Johnson, ho!

*(*JOHNSON *exits.* ALL *throw a perfect shower of boots at* JOHNSON *as soon
as he leaves, and begin laughing.)*

CUFF.   Dar he goes, Pete. I radder guess Mr. Samuel Johnson, Ex-
quire, won't trouble dis crowd any more wid his presence. *(He
sings.)*
De greatest man dat eber libed was Day and Martin,
Johnny, my lango la!
For he was de fust ob de boot black startin'.

Chorus.—Johnny, my lango la!
Did you eber see a ginsling made out of brandy?
Johnny, my lango la!
Did you eber see a pretty gal lickin' lasses candy?

Chorus.—Johnny, my lango la!
FULL CHORUS.
Ah, oh—ah! ah, oh—ah! oh—oo—o-o-o!
Ah, oh—ah! ah, oh—ah! oh—oo—o-o-o!

This Grotesque Essence

WATCHMAN (*crosses in front, or he may sing outside*).
    Past twelve o'clock and a cloudy mornin',
        Johnny, my lango la!
    Past twelve o'clock and de daylight dawning,
        Johnny, my lango la!

CUFF (*resumes singing*).
    Dat's de old watchman, we're going to fool him,
        Johnny, my lango la!
    If he stays outside, de weder will cool him.

        Chorus.—Johnny, my lango la!

    Now, cut your sticks, niggers, de daylight's dawning,
        Johnny, my lango la!
    We'll meet right here quite early in de mornin'.

        Chorus.—Johnny, my lango la!

(ALL *exit* R. *and* L., *singing very piano.*)

SCENE II.—*Exterior of Roses house. Dark stage. Stacato music.* JOHNSON *enters with banjo or guitar to serenade.*

JOHNSON.   Tank heaben! I hab got clar ob dem ruffian darkeys at last. I neber was so grossly insulted in all my life. Dey nearly spiled my best clothes, and—but let's see, I promised to gib my lubly Rosa a serenade dis ebenin', and if I can only find de house. (*goes up to house*) Yes, here is de house—I know it from a tack in de door. (*sings*)
        SONG.—"LUBLY ROSA."
    Oh! lubly Rosa, Sambo has cum
    To salute his lub wid his tum, tum, tum.
    So open de door, Rose, and luff me in,
    For de way I lub you am a sin.

ROSE   (*appears at window and sings*).
    Ah, who's dat knocking at my door,
    Making such a noise wid his saucy jaw?
    Ise looking down upon de stoop,
    Like a henhawk on a chicken-coop.
        So clar de kitchen.

Oh, Hush! or, The Virginny Cupids

JOHN.

 'Tis Sambo Johnson, dearest dove,
 Come like Bacchus, God of Love;
 To tell his lubly Rosa how
 He's quit his old perfesion now.
   So clar de kitchen.

ROSE.

 Oh, hold yer hat and cotch de key,
 Come into de little back room wid me;
 Sit by de fire and warm your shin,
 And on de shelf you'll find some gin.
   So clar de kitchen.

(She drops the key. JOHNSON *catches it in his hat and exits in house.)*

SCENE III.—*Interior of Rose's house. Table set—cups and saucers for two—two chairs.*

CUFF *(enters* R., *and sings)*.

   SONG.—"COAL BLACK ROSE!"
 I wonder whar de debil my lubly Rosa's gone,
 She's luff me half an hour sittin' all alone.
 If she don't come back an' tell me why she didn't stay wid me,
 I'll drink all de sassengers and eat up all de tea.

   CHORUS.
 Oh, Rose! you coal-black Rose!
 I neber lub a gal like I lub dat Rose.

ROSE *(enters* R., *and sings)*.

 Now, get up you Cuffy, and gib up dat chair,
 Mr. Johnson'll pay de dickens if he cotch you sitting dar.

CUFF.

 I doesn't fear de devil, Rose, luff alone dat Sam.
 If dat nigger fool his time wid me, I'll hit him
   I'll be—*(breaks a plate)*
  Chorus.—Oh, Rose, etc.

ROSE.

 Now, get you in de cupboard, Cuff, a little while to stay,
 I'll give you plenty applejack when Sambo's gone away.

This Grotesque Essence

CUFF.
> I'll keep my eye upon him—if he 'tempts to kiss or hug,
> I'll be down upon him like a duck upon a bug.

(ROSE conducts CUFF to the closet, puts him in, and closes the door.)

JOHN *(heard singing without)*.
> Oh, make haste, Rose, for sure as I am born,
> I'm trembling like a sweep-oh on a frosty morn.

ROSE.
> Walk in, Sambo, and don't stand dar a-shakin',
> De fire am a-burnin' and de hoe-cake am a-bakin'.

JOHNSON *(enters L., looks around the room, and converses ad libitum; he then discovers the table, starts with surprise and sings)*.
> From de chairs around de table and de two cups of tea,
> I see you been to supper and had some company.

ROSE.
> 'Twas de missionary preacher, dey call him Dr. Birch,
> He come to raise a 'scription to build hisself a church.
> Come sit you down, Sambo, an' tell me how you've bin.

(JOHNSON laughs.)
> Why, la bress you, honey, what does make you grin?

JOHNSON.
> I'd laugh to tink if you was mine, my dear, my lub, my Rose,
> I'd gib you eberyting dat's nice, de Lord above knows,
> Dar's possum fat an' hominy, and sometimes—

CUFF *(sings out from closet)*.
> Rice!

JOHNSON.
> Cowheel an' sugar cane, an' eberyting dat's—

CUFF *(sings out from the closet)*.
> Nice!

JOHNSON *(gets up, comes front and sings)*.
> I thought I heard a noise, Rose, it come from ober dar,

ROSE.
> It was de plaster fallin' down upon de chair.

JOHNSON.
> But it hollered out rice! as sure as I'm Sambo.

Oh, Hush! or, The Virginny Cupids

ROSE.

It was dat nigger Cuffy upstairs, dat jumps Jim Crow.

JOHNSON.

I wish I was a glove, Rose, upon dat lubly hand,
I'd be de happiest nigger ob all in dis land.
My bosom am so full ob lub—'twould soon find some relief,
When you took de glove to wipe your nose instead ob a handker-
chief.

        Chorus.—Oh, Rose, etc.

ROSE.

My love is strong, and of it's strength dar's none but you can tell.

CUFF.

Half past twelve o'clock and all's not well.

JOHNSON.

Dat's de old watchman took me up de udder night.

CUFF.

Half past twelve o'clock, dar's going to be a fight.

        Chorus.—Oh, Rose, etc.

ROSE.

Johnson, now you'd better go, for you see it's getting late,
An' missus will be coming home from de freminate.

JOHNSON.

Well, gib me one kiss, Rose—*(tries to kiss her).*

ROSE.

Why, Sam, what is you at?

JOHNSON.

Why, I'll hug you like a grizzly—what de debil noise am dat?

(CUFF *is trying to get down the gun from shelf, falls down and spills the
flour over him.* JOHNSON *gets up stage, brings* CUFF *down front and
sings.*)

Who is you, and from whar did you cum?

ROSE.

Oh, it am dat nigger Cuff—foreber I'm undone.

CUFF.

Ise been out whitewashin' an' feelin' a little tire,
I merely cum to ax Miss Rose for a shobelful ob fire.

This Grotesque Essence

JOHNSON.
> Tell me, you saucy nigger, how you do on dat shelf?

CUFF.
> I was pretty well, I thank you, pray, how do you find yourself?

JOHNSON.
> Come, no prevarication, or I'll smash dat calabash.

ROSE.
> Oh, Johnson, be advised by me—he's noffin's else but trash.

JOHNSON.
> Is dis your constancy, Miss Rose, you tell me ob all day!

CUFF.
> Why, de wench she am dumbfounded, and don't know what to
> say.

ROSE.
> I neber saw his face before—his berry sight I hates—
> I believe he am a runaway from de nullifying States.

CUFF.
> Say, tell me, Mr. Johnson, what dat nigger 'jaculates?

JOHNSON.
> Why, she says you am a runaway from de nullifyin' States.

CUFF.
> Dat's enuff to make a jaybird split his shin in two,
> For here's my free papers dat I carry in my shoe.

(shows his papers)

> *Chorus.*—Oh, Rose, etc.

> By dat darkey's peroration and his sarcarmastus grin,
> I'll bet he gets a lickin' afore he does begin.

JOHNSON.
> Be off, you common nigger!

CUFF.
> Not until we hab a fight.
> And, Rose, don't you interfere, I'll show dis moke a sight.

(clinches JOHNSON, and they fight)

10

Oh, Hush! or, The Virginny Cupids

ROSE (*screams, siezes frying pan, and strikes* CUFF *over his head, breaking the bottom*). Fire! help! murder, suicide, all sorts ob death!

JOHNSON.
Stand off, you common nigger, gib me time to draw a breff.

(PETE *and* OTHERS *enter,* D.F.)

PETE.
What's de matter, Rose, dat you gib dat Injun yelp?

ROSE.
Why, it's Cuffy killin' Sambo, and I was cryin' out for help.

PETE (*raises and supports* CUFF, *while someone does the same to* JOHNSON).
Cuffy, is you much hurt?

CUFF. Oh, no, I'm only drawing my last breff. You'd better take me to the hosspistol.

PETE. Why, Cuff?

CUFF. Oh, I don't know; but I hardly tink I shall live more dan twenty-five years longer. (CUFF *and* JOHNSON *have now regained their feet.*)

JOHNSON (*starts*). Why, Cuff!

CUFF. Why Johnson!

JOHNSON.
Rose, my love, pray tell me how this cum so?

ROSE.
Well, dear, I will, since you really want to know:
You see, he sweeps de street, and blacks de gemmen's shoes,
But when he gets de liquor in, he don't know what he does.

CUFF (*sings to* ROSE).
If I'd married you, Miss Rose, I'd surely had a curse,
I offered for to take you for better or for worse;
But I was blind wid lub, your faults I couldn't see.
You is a deal sight worser dan I took you for to be.

Chorus.—Oh, Rose, etc.

JOHNSON (*crosses over to* CUFF). Mr. Cuff, I ax your pardon.

CUFF. Mr. Johnson, dar's my hand. An Rose, I'm glad to find my head was harder dan your pan. But dar's no use to keep up grievances, since love am all by chance. So jest hand down de fiddle, Pete, and let us hab a dance. Come, darks, take your places and I'll saw the catgut.

This Grotesque Essence

(They form and go through a reel. CUFF *gets excited while* ROSE *and* JOHNSON *are dancing, and, jumping up, he breaks the fiddle over* JOHNSON'S *head.* ROSE *faints and is caught by* SOME ONE. JOHNSON *falls at her feet.* CUFF *stands with uplifted hands.)*

ALL FORM PICTURE

The Challenge Dance

As minstrelsy developed in the 1840s, the show's second part—or olio—soon developed small sketches, similar to theatrical interludes, which served primarily to set off certain specialty acts by providing minimal dramatic contexts for them. These sketches, represented by the following version of a challenge dance, differed from afterpieces in that they contained only the faintest suggestion of plot and setting and seldom used the entire troupe of performers.

Of all the dance specialists in minstrelsy, Dan Bryant was certainly one of the most famous and, if contemporary accounts are to be believed, one of the best. He was unrivaled at "shaking up a grotesque essence," in the words of one anonymous observer. Although the cast list printed with the following piece cannot be confirmed, there is evidence to suggest that a challenge dance was part of the program performed by Bryant's Minstrels in the spring of 1857 in New York. The following text is from the acting edition published by the Happy Hours Company.

THE
CHALLENGE
DANCE

A Prelude to Dance for Two Speaking Dancers,
Musician to Speak, and Instrumental Quartette.
as performed by

BRYANT'S MINSTRELS

CAST OF CHARACTERS

ILL-COUNT MCGINNIS (a Hibernian darkey) . . . . Dan Bryant

FARMYARD SAM (an Ethiopian exquisite) . . . . . J. Newcombe

MUSICIAN . . . . Henry Leslie

COSTUMES

MCGINNIS.—Blue pilot jacket, patched with light colored cloth at elbows and on the back—striped shirt, with large collar standing up—a large steel dog-chain from button-hole of vest into pocket of same—vest is of carpet stuff, broad flowered pattern—drab pants, patched with a dark strip of other cloth on one leg, just above the knee to the bottom hem—cap, with the vizor hanging by a few threads only—stripped stockings—heavy shoes.

FARMYARD SAM.—Dandy dress—grey felt sugar-loaf hat, with the brim tucked in all around, except for a hand's breadth in front, where it forms a visor—fancy pattern calico print shirt—no waist coat—light pants—coarse shoes, but not too coarse.

MUSICIANS.—As usual—evening dress.

SCENE *to full depth of a small stage to allow room for a walkaround. A garden or wood.—Entrances L. and R., open.*

FIRST MUSICIAN *and rest of* QUARTETTE *enter* L.U.E., *and place chairs for themselves in L.2E. They seat themselves and tune up.*

(Enter MCGINNIS, *R.U.E., singing.)*

MCGINNIS. "Den, walk along John, de piper's son, de work am finished, and" *(speaks)* How de do, boys? *(sings)* "And de day most done!" *(to C., shufflingly)*

14

1ST M.   We're all well; you seem merry, Count McGinnis—how do you feel?

MCG.   Generally wid my han's, when dar's anything grabable about. *(opens and shuts his hands significantly)* Why, what yer all a-doin' a-sottin' round heyah?

1ST M.   Oh, came to rehearse a little, against this evening.

MCG.   Does yer mean to say yer is gwin to deform at de ball to-night?

1ST M.   We are going to perform there.

MCG.   What! No nonsense! *(looking at the instruments)* Play in dem machineries? *(putting out his hand)*

1ST M. *(impatiently).*   Don't touch my violin.

MCG.   Who was wiolint—I was peaceable as a lamb.

1ST M.   If you were to get my violin out of order, there wouldn't be any dance-music to-night.

MCG.   Oh, dey'd bawl for de accordeon den. Is yer gwin' to play good moosic?

1ST M.   The best! *(Plays a few chords.* MCG *laughs and dances a step or two.)* You're rather spry, count.

MCG.   Slightually! I feel like a bird, Ned! like a —an ospr'y! *(emphatically)* I am gwin' to be dar dis ebening!

1ST M.   Are you, really?

MCG.   Didn't you hear nuffin' about de prize offered for de best dancer?

1ST M.   Oh, yes.

MCG. *(thumbs in his vest arm-holes, attitude, complacently).*   Dat's me!

1ST M.   It's a silver cup!

MCG.   Dey calls it a gobberlin in de bills.

1ST M.   A goblet, then.

MCG.   A silver gobberlin. I expectre win it!

1ST M.   Pooh! You don't stand the ghost of a chance!

MCG *(shuffling one foot before him).*   Who don't?

1ST M.   Why you, to be sure.

MCG *(faces the* MUSICIANS*).*   Look heyah! I'se gwin to take dat cup home! *(*ALL *laugh.)* Why not? Is some o' you going to challenge me? I tell yer ag'in I'se boun' to fetch dat cup home for my little brudder to play wid. *(*ALL *laugh—walks about saucily.)* Who's a-gwin to dance down dis chile? Dat—dat's all I want to know—

1ST M.   You needn't get excited in that sort of way. I know the little boy who *is* going to win that cup.

MCG. Who is? (L.C., *by* MUSICIANS)

1ST M. This little boy that I know.

MCG. What little boy?

1ST M *(looking over to R.U.E.).* Yonder he comes.

MCG. What, him? *(derisive laugh)* him? hur, hur! Why, dat's young Farmyard Sam. He can't shake a leg alongside o' me! *(looking off over to* R.U.E.*)*

1ST M. He can just walk you out of your shoes at dancing.

MCG. Kin he? Who says so?

1ST M. Why, I say so for one.

MCG. You'd better be car'ful!

1ST M. I do say so.

MCG. Dat's enuff. You hear him, fellers? *(to* 1ST MUSICIAN*)* P'raps you'd like to bet on dat?

1ST M. I ain't afraid to.

MCG. I'm easy! *(takes out pocket-book)* Would you go a five?

1ST M *(taking a bank-note from his vest-pocket).* If you like.

MCG. I'm easy! You'se witness, fellers! Lis'en to me, dis chief-engineer of de fiddle has a favorite comin'. Now, den, if dis pet of his turns out petter dan me, why—dat clinches de nail. But if on de country, I beat dis oder feller ('course I easy can!) why, I takes de money. *(takes note from hand of* 1ST MUSICIAN, *who was holding it out to be covered by* MCGINNIS'S*)* I covers it, *(lays his left hand on the note in his right)* and I walks off wid it! *(crosses to* R. U. E., *putting note in his pocket-book)*

1ST M *(rises).* Stop! hi! here!

(FARMYARD SAM *enters R.U.E., running against* MCGINNIS.)

SAM. Somebody's callin' you! *(catches* MCGINNIS *as he passes him by the slack of his coat behind him, and pulls him back)* May I prewail upon you to stop! *(slings* MCGINNIS *over to L. side)*

MCG *(adjusts his coat and collar).* I'll wale you if you toss a man about like that once more. (MUSICIANS *pantomine with* 1ST MUSICIAN *that* MCGINNIS *meant no harm in running away.*)

1ST M *(satisfied).* Well, Count, I suppose the bet's on?

MCG. Oh, yes, de bet's on! *(looks round, sees he cannot exit* R. *side, goes over to* R. *front leisurely, pulls a chair from* R. *wing to* R. *front, sits down —business of evincing contempt for* SAM*)*

1ST M.   How are you Sam?

SAM.   I am much de same, if not more so. My ole massa's gone at las' though.

1ST M.   Run away?

SAM.   No! Dead. It 'pears he'd got almos' used to livin' on a strictly wedgetarian diet (how he did walk into turnips!) when he was carried off de hooks in a werry unaccountable manner. *(wipes his eyes with sleeve-cuff)*

1ST M.   No doubt, you're sorry?

SAM *(solemnly)*.   Dat ole man was like a fader to me.

MCG *(half aside)*.   He'd a son to be proud of! (ALL *look over at* MCGINNIS, *who coughs and pretends to be brushing his coat.)*

1ST M *(to* SAM*)*.   Don't mind him. So, old Stevens was like a father to you?

SAM.   Yes! In de most confectionery manner, he'd cotch me by de frote when I axed for my meals, and dat's what he called gibin' me a collar-egiate eddicatium. *(Hands to neck—*ALL *laugh—*MCGINNIS *laughs, after the rest begin, in discord with theirs—*ALL *look over to* MC-GINNIS*—*MCGINNIS *smothers laugh, and is exceedingly solemn—*SAM, *to* 1ST MUSICIAN*.)* Who is dat imperent pusson?

1ST M.   Hush! That's Ill-Count McGinnis! the Italian refugee from Cork! the great dancer!

SAM.   Him a dancer! *(looking at* MCGINNIS*)*

MCG *(aside—sings)*.   "Oh, what shall we do when de comet breaks de world up, and scatters all de colored fokes aroun'?" *(Shuffles his feet, still seated.* SAM *taps his forehead meaningly.)*

1ST M.   He may not be all right about his head, but he means to win that cup to-night with his feet.

SAM.   He is? Why, I'm strikin' for dat same myself. My gal's set her heart on havin' it!

1ST M.   You can't both have it.

SAM.   Do you imagine dat anybody of his size can do dis? *(cuts a pigeon's wing)*

MCG *(looks around—aside)*.   He's woke up! *(Laughs and rises leisurely)* Ha, ha! *(dances, as if to himself, the same figure as* SAM, *but in a grotesque manner)*

1ST M.   You see that?

SAM.   I see dat, o' course. 'Taint much to see! If it was like *dis* he might talk! *(dances a few steps)*

17

MCG *(watches him—aside)*.   He's imperooving. *(Gathers himself up, and the moment* SAM *finishes, he brings down his foot and dances the same, breaking down at C. front—* SAM *crosses to R. to watch* MCGINNIS— MCGINNIS *finishes, and in returning to R., meets* SAM.*)*

SAM.   Ah! somethink of a dancer, I see.

MCG *(shrugs his shoulders)*.   On'y jess a-learning like! *(reaches chair R., with a little toe-heel "snaking")*

SAM *(to* MCGINNIS*)*.   Hear you are gwin' to de Ball to-night?

MCG.   Got an ap'intment wid de pint cup dar.

SAM.   Oh!

MCG.   Yes, oh!

SAM.   P'raps dar's some money goin' a-beggin' on dat same pint?

MCG.   Werry likely.

SAM.   Have you heerd on anybody what wants to bet high?

MCG.   I'm easy. You can come see me! *(business of taking out pocket-book which is too large for pocket)*

SAM.   I'll meet you to any amount!

MCG.   Got a thousand lying loose?

SAM *(aghast)*.   No! I've a ten-dollar-bill somewhar. *(by* MUSICIANS, L., *takes out money)*

MCG *(crosses over L.)*.   Post up your money. *(*1ST MUSICIAN *holds out his hand, and* SAM *puts out his note to give* 1ST MUSICIAN *to hold, when* MCGINNIS *lays it in his pocket-book, and draws back a step.)*

SAM *(surprised)*.   Here, I say—

1ST M.   Come, Count, what's all this?

MCG.   Why, I t'ought you understood de bet! Here's dis man, ain't he?

ALL *(nod)*.   Yes!

MCG.   And here I am! ain't I, or ain't I not? *(*ALL *nod.)* Werry well. *(pockets book)*

SAM.   But dis won't do!

MCG.   If you'd only pay attention!

SAM.   All de pay we will get.

MCG.   Don't be consultin' me, brack man! Ain't dis plain? Here you are, and here's me, gwin' to have a challenge dance, best two out of free, fair and square, walk-around and break down. You've put up *your* money, an' I—I've *put up* mine! *(slaps his pocket)* If I dances best of us two, 'course I let's de money remain whar it am at present speaking; on de oder hand, if you don't dance so good

18

as me, why de money is left at de indisposition ob de umpire, to await de judgment ob de referee.

SAM. *(shakes his head)*

MCG. I'm easy.

SAM *(to* 1ST M*).* It sounds all right, but is dis fellar safe?

1ST M. Oh, he's got some money of mine, too! I think he is. He looks honest. *(*MCG *assumes attitude of complacency by chair* R.*)*

1ST M *(to* SAM*).* Oh, you're sure to win. *(Tunes up.* MUSICIANS *tune up.)*

SAM. Dat'll do, since you say so. It's a bet den. *(to* MCGINNIS*)* Who's fust?

MCG. Toss for it! *(*SAM *throws up coin.)*

MCG. ⎫
        ⎬ Heads! *(together)*
SAM.   ⎭

MCG. What made you say what I did?

SAM. You'd no business to cry like me! *(*MCG *tosses up coin.)*

SAM. Tail! *(stoops over coin)* Ha! Knew I'd win! *(*BOTH *stoop to pick up coin—*MCG *gets it.)*

SAM *(holds out his hand).* Thank yer! *(*MCG *pockets coin, turns* R.*)*

SAM *(stops him).* You picked up dat penny!

MCG. Eh? oh, yes! It's wrong to leave money kicking about.

*(*SAM *goes up to* L.U.E.*, gets sand, takes off his hat, etc.—Music, prelude to the dance—He sprinkles stage with sand, shuffles it even—Music of walk-around to which* SAM *dances, and breaks-down.* ALL *applaud.)*

MCG *(Goes up to* R.U.E. *clumsily, gets sand, comes over to* C.*).* I knew he couldn't dance—didn't know how to frow de sand! *(Jerks sand out of cup, by twist of wrist, to make a snake of sand on the stage. Slow music to mark time—Shuffles slowly, to tread out the sand. Music, as before, dances, etc.* ALL *applaud.)*

SAM *(dances, etc. new steps introduced).* Rader tink dis'll fix his back hair! *(*L. *front to watch* MCGINNIS*)*

*(*MCG *takes off coat, lays it on chair* R. *front with his cap—tucks up his sleeves at the wristband, goes up* C.*, and dances, much more vigorously than before.—*SAM *goes up* L.*, as* MCGINNIS *dances down front, crosses, and comes down to* R. *front—kneels by chair and searches pockets of coat there.—*MCG *is concluding dance up* C.*, when he spies* SAM. *Business of inability to leave off dancing at so critical a point and of anxiety to stop the*

robbery. Misses step, trips himself up as he comes down, and falls full length toward R. front.—SAM *goes up and crosses L.)*

MCG *(takes up his coat, feels in the pocket—blubbers).*   Oh, oh! *(agony)* oh! whatever will my mudder say? *(Suddenly discovers that the pocket-book has slipped through hole in the pocket and down to the bottom of the lining at the hem of skirt. Change of countenance.)* I'm easy!

1ST M.   That's one against you, Count!

MCG.   Which one! *(gesticulating with coat in his right hand, and hat in his left)*

1ST M.   Why, you fell!

MCG *(in great wonder).*   Who fell?

ALL.   Why, *you!*

MCG.   'Cause of his fell-onious intentions. 'Taint fair—don't count!

1ST M.   I *do*, Count!

MCG.   Anyhow, I got one more chance. *(music as before)*

> *(*BOTH *walk around and dance, keeping at it as long as it "takes"—*MCG R.C. *gets gradually fatigued. Business of stumbling, recovering, finding he is going to lose, glancing sideways at* SAM L.C., *then working his way down R. for his coat, misses his footing, stumbles, catches at the back of chair, which comes off in his hand—He falls over chair.)*

> *(*ALL *shout.)*

1ST M.   You've lost!

MCG *(picking himself up, coat under one arm, hat in hand—to* SAM).   You've lost! Just decisium!

1ST M.   No, no, you fell! *(rises)*

MCG.   I neber touched de groun' oncet! (R.C.)

SAM.   Out with the money! (C.)

MCG.   Dis bank's breaking—*breaking* for de woods!

> *(Exit R. 1E. chair under left arm, the top of it in left hand, hat in right hand and coat on right arm—*SAM *follows him off R. 1E.—*MUSICIANS *exeunt L.)*

MCG *(appears R.U.E. to C., pause).*   I'm easy! *(exit L.U.E.)*

THE END

De Cream ob Tenors

Even olio sketches were subject to minstrelsy's spirit of burlesque, as the following piece shows. In form it comes very close
to *The Challenge Dance* except that here the specialty act is lost in
the broad comic interplay. The immediate stimulus for this piece
may very well have been the career of a black songstress named
Elizabeth Greenfield, who advertised herself as the Black Swan.
In the early 1850s she captivated New York audiences with her
recitals of arias and English ballads. But, though obviously using
Miss Greenfield as the butt of an in-joke, *De Cream of Tenors* is not
so much a specific travesty of her performances as it is a lampoon
of art-song recitals in general. The following text is reprinted
from the acting edition published by the Happy Hours Company in 1874.

DE CREAM
OB TENORS

An Ethiopian Absurdity,
in One Scene.

CHARACTERS

SANGUINETTO BLOWHARD (a tenor)
THEODORUS THOMASI (a conductor)[1]
FIVE MUSICIANS

COSTUMES

SANGUINETTO BLOWHARD.—Evening dress, very much shirt bosom and immense diamond pin (imitating the local celebrity of the day); one coat-tail to pull off and discover large red patch on pantaloons.

THEODORUS THOMASI.—Evening dress (caricatures the popular conductor of his locality).

MUSICIANS.—Ordinary evening dress.

SCENE.—*Interior in 2.G. Five chairs R. One chair R.C. One chair L. On flat a poster: "Renewed Detraction! Engagement of de Black Swan, that World-renowned Tenor, Mr. Sanguinetto Blowhard, in all his favorite songs ebery night."*

(Enter THEODORUS *R., followed by* MUSICIANS. MUSICIANS *take chairs R. Theodorus' chair R. As the* MUSICIANS *are arranging their music, they glance up at poster, chuckle and sniff derisively.)*

MUSICIANS.   Yah! *(yawning)*

THEO.   What dat mean, gemplemens! why yer not remember whar you am? Ise dislocated at sich low simpletons of dishapprobatiums as *(yawns)* Yah! 'Case a wocalist is not kerzackly twin-brother to a scalpaniny, am dat 'ar a good reason to go *(yawns)* yah, yah! at him? Why, when I was fust gong player at de Opera, dar was a belle—*(bell rings L.)* I mean t'oder kind ob bell—belle ob de ballet —*(bell rings L.—angrily)*—all right! I clean forgot de new tenor! Dat's just me, for when I was at the Summer-night's-concert *(the*

---

1   A caricature of Theodore Thomas (1835–1905). In the late 1850s and 1860s Thomas earned a wide reputation as a violinist and opera conductor. He later served as conductor for the Chicago Symphony Orchestra.

De Cream ob Tenors

MUSICIANS *stare at him)* I sold de progrums *(*MUSICIANS *fall back satisfied)*—a woman said she'd ring *(bell, same)* my nose if *(bell, same)*—hang dat bell! *(Beats time. Prelude of any ballad, not that* BLOWHARD *tries to sing.)*

Enter SANGUINETTO BLOWHARD L., *comes to* C., *bows, etc., sings.*

At de foot ob Bedfort hill,
In good cheer dar had grown
A miller—

Hold on, dar! Dat aint de t'ing at all! *(*MUSICIANS *cease playing.)*

THEO. *(calmly).*   What's wrong, pray?

BLOW.   Pray! enough to make a fel—gempleman sw'ar! Dat aint my cumpinament—folks what don't know harmony had better stay to home, and not make expedition of dar inkypassity.

THEO.   Folks what knows music always send me de right parts, sah! Dem's guv jist as dey come! *(*MUSICIANS *nod.)*

BLOW.   I dar' say; but dat air haint got eben de air of *my* air, dat are air!

THEO.   Not *your* air? *(amazed)* Den your air must be blowed away.

BLOW. *(dignified).*   My ballad, sah, was de celebrated "Foot ob Bedford Hill."

THEO.   Quite de hairistocrat! *(commences to search for music)*

BLOW. *(suddenly).*   What dat air *(points)* under your berry nose? *(Theodorus rises, and finds he is sitting on music.)* I t'ought I knew him by de edge—*kee*!

THEO.   I had no idea I was on yer ill foot, sah! *(Gives out the music to his musicians.)*

BLOW. *(impatiently).*   When you are quite ready, but don't hurry. *(gets chair L. and sits C.)*

THEO. *(offended).*   Not at all wulgar, dis man. Oh, you shall hab yer accompaniment. T'ink yerself clebber in taking de chair? oh?

BLOW.   Say, look yeah! *(rises)* I'll call again—in a day or two *(sarcastically)* when you is a little more at leisure. *(crosses L. with chair)*

THEO.   Stop! since you hab arrove, don't be a rover! *(to* MUSICIANS*)* He'll stick here all night 'less we play him out. *(aloud)* Ready gemplemen. You wid de flageolet, please don't fish for yer back toof wid yer implement! Attention, company! *(beats time)* One, two! *(music, prelude to Blow's ballad)*

BLOW. *(sings).*   At de foot ob Bed—*(sustains the note).*

This Grotesque Essence

THEO. *(sarsactically)*.   I'd long to hab sich a breff. *(speaks with* MUSI-CIANS*)*

BLOW. *(stops, furious)*.   When you have quite done gabbling togedder—

THEO. *(angrily)*.   Well, sah?

BLOW.   Gabble apart! *(sings very sweetly)* At de foot ob de bed—

THEO.   Poor fellow! Did um stop all night at de foot ob de bed—

BLOW. *(stops)*.   What dat you say, sah?

THEO. *(loftily)*.   Merely a scientific observation, not intended for de common ear—do go on!

BLOW. *(sings)*.   At de foot ob Bedford hill, in good cheer—

THEO. *(laughs)*.   He's slid off de bed into a good cheer.

> *(While* BLOW *is sustaining the note on "cheer,"* THEO *rises to get chew of tobacco of* MUSICIAN *up stage.)*

BLOW. *(singing)*.   Chee-ee-eer! *(stops)* 'Pose yer tink it perlite to go quid-hunting when I am warbling?

THEO.   Was dat warbling? You was in a good cheer—didn't want to upset you—dat all; dat all!

BLOW. *(admiring)*.   What exquisite perliteness! Quite de Chestnutfield!

THEO.   It doesn't please my party to spin out de tremble-o all dis time. *(beats time again)* Now, den, if *you* are *quite* ready?

BLOW. *(sings)*.   At de foot ob Bedford hill, in good cheer dar had grown—

THEO.   Dat am a groan! I say, your groan is too full grown!

BLOW.   Had grown a mill—*(loses breath, gasps)*

THEO.   His wind is all ground out—not a wind-mill.

BLOW.   Dar'll be anoder kind of mill heah pretty soon. *(sings)* A miller who plays—

THEO. *(disgusted)*.   Den he ought to go to work!

BLOW. *(glaring at Theo, but restraining himself, sings)*.   A miller who plays still—

THEO.   Still! Kee, he! Now, I tink him berry noisy! *(Lays down his bow and violin, and pulls out a newspaper, which he reads. Music ceases.)*

BLOW.   You're anuder! *(furious)* Will you take up your bow—yes or no, sah?

THEO.   Nebber! a big drum would blush to accompany you!

BLOW.   A big drum! A nice healthy pack of drumers you've got dar! Why, half dem is doing nuffin while I sing—look dar! *(Stoops to*

24

take up the bow to point with. Theo. spanks him with his fiddle.) Dar's dat gempleman—I'se had my eye on him—not a note ob dis does be blowed! And him, too! *(points)* Whateber I jerk out, deuce a bit will dat indiwiduable *trunpet!*

THEO.   Dat's right—dey's marking time!

BLOW.   Let time go unmarked! And dar's yer second fiddle—

THEO. *(offended).*   Violin! You do violinse to my feelings, sah!

BLOW.   Your second fid-olin! him wid de mustash! Why must he hash does and rays and roles like dat, hey?

THEO. *(handkerchief to his face, talking through his nose).*   De audience likes his *does* as buch as your'd! Why, I leave *(coughs)* it to any good *(coughs)* judge—you sing like a rusty hinge—

BLOW.   Nobody *can* sing to *sich* a band! Support me properly and I'll show you *(pauses)* for a dime a head!

THEO.   So we will, if you keep within balloon-shot of de tune. *(ALL prepare to play.)*

BLOW. *(returning to* C.*).*   I always do my best. *(sings)* At de foot ob de Bed—*(out of tune)*

THEO.   Too low! You are too low on de *bed*! You should rise on de *bed*!

BLOW.   How can a pusson rise on de bed and yet stay at de foot ob it?

THEO.   I aint heah to answer conundrums. It's *(sings)* "At de foot ob de Bed"—and not *(sings like Blow)* "At de foot ob de Bed."

BLOW. *(laughs).*   Call dat by de name ob—yah, yah, yah,—singing! Why, you don't half make enough ob de note—

THEO.   Spread him out on de bed, den! Thus—*(sings)* "At de foot ob de Beee—ee—ed——" *(stops)* But I'se not gwine to execute your singing, too—you kin murder him alone!

BLOW.   Sah!

THEO.   I mean, you sing it killingly.

BLOW.   I accept de apology. *(sings)* "At de foot of de Bed—"

THEO. *(applauds).*   Not bad, not bad!

BLOW. *(stops, surprised).*   I said Bed—not *bad*—

THEO.   Dat's it—*I* said not bad!

BLOW.   I knows yer did!

THEO. *(to* MUSICIANS*).*   Ky! he don't see dat!

BLOW. *(puzzled, sings).*   "Bedfort——"

THEO.   He's got a berry strong hold ob dat fort. *(aloud)* It's ford, sah, ford—

This Grotesque Essence

BLOW. I can't afford it—"fort."—*(sustains note to tremolo, kept up by orchestra)*

THEO. *(speaking through the music and Blow singing).* Dat niggah'll never get 'cross dat ford.

BLOW. *(stops singing).* If you keep on gabbling, de party will wear out dar dear little trembleohs! *(cease music)*

THEO. Dear, no! *(beats time)* Go to bed ag'in.

BLOW. *(sounding notes).* Do—oh, my! re! ha! ah! Whar was I? Oh, in de cheer! *(sings)* In good cheer dar had grown—

THEO. He's really splendid on de groan!

BLOW. Many tanks! But perhaps you wouldn't rebel in my opinion of you!

THEO. *(rises and bows).* From so courteous and talented a gemplemum ob color (BLOW *bows deprecatingly with a grin.)* any opinion would be welcome as (BLOW *grins and bows very low.)* worthless! *(aside)* Had him *dar*!

BLOW. *(angrily).* You're a fraudulent frost² ob de darkest dye!

THEO. Me a frost?

BLOW. Ob de frostiest kind!

(THEO. *lays down violin and bow, and goes up stage in a rage.)*

BLOW. *(to* MUSICIANS).* Kee! is de ole man offen took dat way? *(to first violin)* 'Spose you try de shake widout him! I'll bet it will go better. *(music prelude, sings)* At foo—oo—foo——

THEO. *(comes down).* Oh, I'm a foo-foo too, am I? *(kicks* BLOW., *who drops his music)*

COMIC DUO

THEO. A frost, am I? Nebber before but once in my life was I eber so chillingly treated. Dat was ober at Squampool, when I officiated at de picaner at Scudder Jack's Hotel——

BLOW. Eh, what? What dat? At Scudder Jack's?

THEO. Yaas. Dar was a tenor dar what dejected to my own song ob de Pigs ob Lead, and called me——

BLOW. A frost——

THEO. Dat woice! Why, don't say it was you?

BLOW. It were! De Brack Swan!

2 Theatrical slang for a failure.

26

THEO. You warn't dewalloped into a Swan den! De yaller gals called you a duck!

BLOW. And gabe me no peace. Yaas, dat's me! I is full-fledged now!

THEO. My old friend! *(They fall in, embracing, and remain seated.)* Why, gemplemen, you behold in dis young man de Cream ob Tenors!

BLOW. And you, gemplemen, am presided ober by de Champion Conductor.

THEO. Oh!

> *(They* BOTH *start to rise,* THEO. *catches hold of Blow.'s coattail which gives way, disclosing a gigantic red patch on seat of Blow.'s pantaloons. Musicians laugh heartily.* THEO. *apologizes to* BLOW., *in dumb show, who refuses to be mollified. During business, musicians exit* R., *and return with stuffed clubs and bladders, and with them beat them off stage.)*

CURTAIN

The Quack Doctor

The term farce can be used to categorize minstrel pieces like the following by John W. Smith, which had no recognizable object of parody. Like earlier European forms of popular stage humor, minstrel farces made use of stock comic types such as pompous savants, frustrated lovers, dandies, and dictatorial parents, and placed them in situations where pretention could be deflated and insincerity punished, usually to the accompaniment of graphically violent horseplay. What distinguished the minstrel farce from its European forebears was that each character type was a simplified version of the blackface clown.

In this stereotyped figure the language was as essential a feature as the burnt-cork mask, although what the figure said was often less important for comic effect than the way he said it. The fantastical minstrel dialect was totally consistent with a major trend in American literary humor during the middle of the century. Through dialect the clown figure could exploit that peculiarly American passion for comically corrupt speech. Malapropisms and puns were standard devices in minstrel humor; but beyond these the clowns created near chaos by wrestling with the phonetic and morphological dimensions of language in ways that rivaled the cacography and grammatical atrocities of such mid-century humorists as David Ross Locke (Petroleum Vesuvius

Nasby), George William Bagby (Mozis Addums), and Charles Farrar Browne (Artemus Ward).

There is no real evidence to support the popular notion that the minstrel dialect was a reflection of black speech patterns. In fact, the available evidence suggests that the language of minstrelsy was probably no more a reflection of nineteenth-century black dialects than the clown was a reflection of the black man. Certainly the language of minstrelsy bears little resemblance to the works of authors like Mark Twain or Joel Chandler Harris, who are generally acclaimed for the accuracy of their dialect transcriptions. Since a significant amount of the humorous slang used in minstrelsy came from theatrical jargon rather than black slang, and since the phonetic constructions in the minstrel dialect are highly reminiscent of the corruptions to be found in eighteenth-century English broadsheet satires, it seems more than reasonable to assume that the language of minstrelsy, like most of the other elements in the art, derived primarily from white entertainment traditions.

The following piece attests to the obscurity which attended many authors of minstrel plays. Little is known of John W. Smith. By all indications his professional career was brief and unspectacular. Smith probably received his training with various minstrel troupes in St. Louis; and he may or may not have been the John Smith who enjoyed a brief popularity among New York audiences for putting together an "Ethiopian Entertainment," which played on a variety bill at the Brooklyn Museum in 1851. The following text is reprinted from the acting edition published by Dick and Fitzgerald.

THE QUACK
DOCTOR

A Negro Farce
In One Act and One Scene
By JOHN W. SMITH

CHARACTERS

DR. SQUASH (the quack)
GINGER
JULIUS CAESAR
CROW
DINAH PRIMROSE
MOB, &c.

SCENE 1.—*Two chairs and a table, with large bottles and demijohns on table; a curtain upon which is painted:—"DR. SQUASH, NATERAL DOCTOR."*

(Enter GINGER *with his knee tied up, limping. He advances to the table and strikes upon it with his cane.)*

GINGER.   Hallo! Doctor! Whar de debbil are de doctor? Here I've walked more'n two miles, and my leg's so stiff and lame, I can't go a step. I wish I had the doctor set one of his sticking plasters onto it, so it couldn't move no how. Doctor! Hallo! *(Enter* JULIUS CAESAR. *with his eye bound up.)*

JULIUS CAESAR.   Oh, de lord! Whar's de doctor? Oh! my eye! my eye!

GINGER.   What de debbil is de matter wid you eye?

JULIUS CAESAR.   Matter? It's chock full ob matter, and nuffin else.

GINGER.   How you done it?

JULIUS CAESAR.   Why I was gwine down street t'odder night, and I met Ned Pepper, and sez he, Julius Caesar, what's dat I hear you've been sayin' about me? Sez I, hazzen't nuffin' at all to say to you—I don't 'sociate wid no sich half-price nigger as you be, no how. Wid dat he make a pass at me, and I hit him whar he live, and so we got at it, toof and nail. D'rectly I hear sumthin' drap, and what you s'pose it was?

GINGER.   I gub's it up.

The Quack Doctor

JULIUS CAESAR.   Well, den it was dis identical nigger. Den soon as I got up I made up my mind right off dat somebody'd got a mighty bad eye, and cum to look dat was dis nigger too. But whar's de doctor? —Doctor! (BOTH *pound on the table, and cry out for the Doctor. Enter* CROW *with his jaw bound up.*)

CROW.   Oh! oh! oh! Doctor! doctor!

GINGER.   Hullo Crow! Is dat you?

CROW.   To be sure it is—I wish it wasn't. Ow, ow, ow!

JULIUS CAESAR.   Oh, do hold yer jaw.

CROW.   Yes, I have to hold my jaw. If I didn't, it would bust out or drap off. Whar's de doctor?

(*Enter* JUMBLE.[1] JUMBLE *is a dandy nigger who as he enters is talking to himself and gesticulating violently, apparently in a great passion. He walks across the room once or twice before he discovers the other characters, and starts on seeing them.*)

JUMBLE.   Yes, yes, ob course; dar yer is, waiting for dat dam quack doctor. He'd orter hab his neck broke, he had.

GINGER.   What's de matter wid de doctor? He's cut you out wid Dinah Primrose. Dat's what ails him. Nuffin else.

JUMBLE.   You ignoramus niggar! you knows nuffin' 'about de merits ob de case. I tell you Dr. Squash duzzent know de fust principals ob de astronomical destruction ob de human frame.

JULIUS CAESAR.   Let me tell you, he will kill disease a little quicker dan any libing man 'bout dese parts.

JUMBLE.   Yes, he kill de disease, nigger and all, only gib him a chance.

JULIUS CAESAR.   It's nuffin' but jealousy ails you, and de doctor hab got you dar—You can't shine when he's about, no how. But whar de debbil is he? Doc—tor! (ALL *but* JUMBLE *pound the table, and cry out for the doctor.*)

JUMBLE.   Dar yer go agin! I s'pose you tink de doctor can do as much as ole Aunty Phoebe's plaster.

GINGER.   What did dat do?

---

1 Jumble was omitted from the list of characters in the acting edition.

31

This Grotesque Essence

JUMBLE.   I'll tell you. *(sings)*

AIR: "OLD SALUDY"

Dar was a wench libed down our way,
Who made a sticking-plaster,
And sold so many eb'ry day,
She got as rich as master.

CHORUS.

(All the characters join in CHORUS, *quick.)*

Sheepskin, beeswax, burgundy pitch and tar!
Debbil couldn't pull it off when you put it dar!

[JUMBLE.]

Dis plaster was so berry strong
'Twould draw a load ob cotton;
'Twould draw a toof wid seben prong
If your teef was gettin' rotten.

CHORUS.

Sheepskin, &c.

[JUMBLE.]

In a lottery 'twould draw a prize—
'Twould draw a bunch of roses—
'Twould draw the tears from white folks' eyes,
And de breff from out dar noses.

CHORUS.

Sheepskin, &c.

[JUMBLE.]

Aunt Phoebe, she one day went dead,
You mayn't believe my story—
But dey put a plaster on her head
And draw'd her up to glory!

CHORUS.

Sheepskin, &c.

(Enter DR. SQUASH, *with a pair of large saddle-bags, a codfish, a big loaf
of bread under his arm, and a chain of sausages around his neck. In bow-
ing to his patients, he drops the bread and fish several times, but at length
manages to deposit them on the table.)*

32

The Quack Doctor

ALL.   Here's de ole doctor now. Lord bress his soul. Doctor, how d'ye
do? We've been waiting for you.

DR. SQUASH.   Ah. gemblemen, how am de state ob your personal cor-
porosty? It gibs me great pleasure to hab de gratification ob aproxi-
mating to you on dis occasion, and I shall be happy to exasperate
my physical and intellectual faculties in your sarvice.

JUMBLE.   Physical faculties! I s'pose dat's what he carries in his saddle
bags. I'll put some powder in dar bime by, and blow his physical
faculties all to de debbil. (JUMBLE *walks up and down stage in a great
rage.*)

ALL.   Can you cure me?—can you cure me?

DR. SQUASH.   Ob course I can: I can cure anything. *(He sings.)*
AIR: "MY GRANDFATHER WAS A WONDERFUL MAN."
A doctor I am ob wonderful skill,
I can bleed, I can purge, I can cure, I can kill:
I can cut a man's leg off—his arm or his head,
I can kill off de living, and raise up de dead.

(Spoken) Yes, I allows dis chile is sumfin ob a doctor. To be sure I
don't know much about book larnin', but Ise got it in me nateral,
and dat's worth all de physiology, anatomology, ictheology, zool-
ogy, entemology, geology, or debbilology in all de books between
dis and California. So——*(He sings.)*
So come to me all you niggers what's ill,
For I am a doctor ob wonderful skill.

When a very small boy, my name I made big
By inwenting a squeal for an invalid pig;
And as I grew older, my science progressed
Till I turned out a doctor right square up and dress'd.

(Spoken) Well, I was an astonishing smart boy when I was little. I
invented a kind ob hair oil so powerful strong dat rub a bottle ob
it on a brick wall, and in a fortnight's time it would be kivered wid
a splendiferous coat ob moss. I'm always inventin sumthin new——
(He sings.)
So come to me all you niggers what's ill,
For I am a doctor ob wonderful skill!

I knows all de flowers dat grows in de field,
All de wonderful vartues dat roots and yarbs yield.

And all dat may try me will certainly find
I can cure all diseases ob body or mind.

(Spoken) Yes, I knows all de flowers dat grows in de field, and de
fairest flower ob 'em all is Dinah Primrose. Ah! she am a fullblown
rose, she am, and fragrant as de mornin' dew: and dis is de chile
what can pick her up—Hallo! Dere's dat dam Jumble watchin'
me. He tinks he can shine dar, but it's no use. His shinin' is all cold
moonshine, and it takes de warm rays ob my affection to make
her bud and blossom in all her glory. But I guess I'd better change
the subject—to——*(He sings.)*
So come to me all you niggers what's ill,
For I am a doctor ob wonderful skill.

I can cure de cholera, cholic, or cramp,
I can cure de worst fevers, coast, typhus, or camp:
I am death on de diarrhea, can physic off fits,
And can drive out de smallpox, widout leaving pitts.

(Spoken) Yes, I can cure all diseases flesh is heir to. I can cure her-
rings, I can cure bacon, I can cure de botts. I can cure anything
from pig's feet to Cholera Morbus and do it all on nateral principles. So——*(He sings.)*
So come to me all you niggers what's ill,
For I am a doctor ob wonderful skill!

Well, Crow, what's de matter wid you?

CROW.   Oh, sich a toothache, doctor.
DR. SQUASH *(examining Crow's jaw).*   Tain't de toofache.
CROW.   What is it den?
DR. SQUASH *(holding out his hand).*   Dollar!
CROW.   Dollar? I ain't troubled wid dat complaint.
DR. SQUASH.   Gib me half a dollar, and I'll told you all about it.
CROW *(gives him money).*   Dar!
DR. SQUASH.   Well, den, I wants you to substantiate on your under-
standing dat de occipital plugatorial bonum, vulgarly called a
toof, am not in and within its own individual functuation liable to
de fluctuations and sensations which you, nigger, am just now ex-
periencing in a highly antagonistical degree, but on the conterary
am entirely unperceptible to de warious contortions and lamina-

34

tions usually ascribed to it, in its localitory and indigenuous existuation. Darfore, I hold dat it am not de toofache. At de same time, I wish it to be extinctly understood, dat de ligamentary structuation, known as de narvous system, 'casionally penetrates itself into de exterior ob de aforesaid structuation, and effectuates de disagreeable ailimentary symptoms in medical phraseology denominated, achabus toothabus. (*CROW takes a seat in a chair;* DR. SQUASH *seats himself at the back of the chair, and produces an enormous pair of forceps, which he rubs with a great flourish.*) Stick back your cocoanut. (*The Doctor applies the forceps.*)

CROW.   Easy, doctor. Easy. Oh! oh!

DR. SQUASH.   Don't open your mouth so wide—I'm gwine to stand on de outside to pull de toof. It's a little hard a startin', but it's bound to come out, if de Lord give me strength. (*After a good deal of struggling and yelling, the Doctor hauls out two big wooden teeth with a jerk.* CROW *falls forward, picks himself up, and runs out: the Doctor falls back with the chair.*) Stop dar. Stop dar! you brack crow! come back and pay me for dat oder toof. I've got out two and you've only paid me for one.

JULIUS CAESAR.   Gorra mighty! I'se glad I ain't got de toofache—if dat's de way you cure's um. You can't pull de nigger's eye out wid dem instruments, though—so jess see what you can do.

DR. SQUASH.   Dat's a very wiolently excited inflamatery inflamation ob de obticular membrane superinduced by a highly irritated irritation.

JULIUS CAESAR.   Wall now, if I didn't tink dat was wot ailed me all de time. But you can cure me?

DR. SQUASH.   Oh yes. Terms invariably in advance: money down afore I do a ting.

JULIUS CAESAR.   To be sure. (*He pays the doctor.*) Now go ahead.

DR. SQUASH.   You will see——

JULIUS CAESAR.   Not out ob dis eye.

DR. SQUASH.   Shut up! What do you know about it?

JULIUS CAESAR.   Go ahead, Doctor. Ise a hark'nin'.

DR. SQUASH.   De trouble am jess here. (*gesticulating*)

JULIUS CAESAR.   'Tain't no sich ting—de trouble's in my eye.

DR. SQUASH.   You chuckle-headed nigger you. If you interrupts me ag'in, I'll take and break my arm across your jaw. The difficalty, I say, is jess here: dis inflamatory intimation is in consequence of its progressive and locomotive tendancy, maintains an active inclination to exaggerate itself throughout the cuticullary system generally, and by its own extraneous action, may produce the most serious consequences. Consequently, there is but one remedy.

JULIUS CAESAR. Lord a massy! You don't mean—

DR. SQUASH (*whetting thumb-nail on his shoe*). D'ye see dat thumb-nail? Yah yah!

JULIUS CAESAR. Gorra! gorra! Let me up, doctor. No gouging?

DR. SQUASH. Who said anything 'bout gouging? I'm merely gwine to perform a scientific operation in a natural manner. (JULIUS CAESAR *kicks, struggles, and yells, but the doctor keeps the advantage.*) You needn't kick so—it's no use, nigger—Ise got yer right by de wool. Whew.

JULIUS CAESAR. Oh dear! oh! oh! Murder! (JUMBLE *tries to interfere, but is restrained by* JULIUS CAESAR. *Both display much excitement while the struggle is going on.*)

DR. SQUASH. Now see how nice I'll do it. (*After a great deal of struggling, he succeeds in gouging* JULIUS CAESAR, *and holds up an eyeball on the end of his thumb.*) Whew! Yah? yah? Dar it is. Hold on a minit till I spit in your eye and clap on a plaster. (*He puts a plaster on* Julius Caesar's *eye, and both get up.*) Dem's um. (JULIUS CAESAR *flies around in great rage and pain, and finally exits.*) Dar's anudder wonderful cure. I'll get my name up afore long.

JUMBLE. Doctor, I wants to ax you a question.

DR. SQUASH. Well, ax me—ax me, why don't you ax me?

JUMBLE. And I wants you to gib your opinion as a medical man.

DR. SQUASH. Ob course, ax me—why de debbil don't you ax me?

JUMBLE. Den supposin'——

DR. SQUASH. Yah.

JUMBLE. Dat dar was a hogshead full ob whiskey, and at one end dar was a nigger at de tap a suckin' out de whiskey, and at de odder end dar was a bullgine[2] ob forty hoss-power pumpin' whiskey into de hogshead, a-n-d s'posin' dat de bullgine woodent stop pumpin', and de nigger woodent let go de tap—now, I wants to ax you, doctor, wedder in your opinion de hogshead or de nigger would bust de soonest.

2 A steam engine.

DR. SQUASH.   De nigger ob course, for under dem circumstances de colored individual was bound to hab a bust, anyhow. Yah! yah! Yer t'ort yer'd cum de suck ober de old doctor dat time, but you got sucked in about a feet, I recken. Yah! yah! Now, Ginger, I'll attend to your case.

GINGER.   Sich a stiff knee, doctor, it's awful.

DR. SQUASH.   I can cure dat easy enuff. Here, pint!

GINGER.   What?

DR. SQUASH.   Tip!

GINGER.   Oh yes. *(He hands him money.)*

DR. SQUASH.   Here's a box of my electro-magnetic pills. Take ten ob 'em eb'ry quarter ob an hour throughout de day, and in a fortnight or so, you will be better. Take a dose now. *(GINGER takes several pills with many wry faces.)* Dey's all down, am dey? Now you must take some exercise, or dey will neber operate.

(JUMBLE conceals himself under the table.)

DR. SQUASH *(speaking to GINGER).*   Travel! Slide! *(DR. SQUASH points for him to move off. GINGER looks first at the Doctor, then in the direction to which he points, and the Doctor kicks him a posteriere. GINGER starts off, limping, at full speed, and is followed by DR. SQUASH, who kicks him whenever he can. GINGER finally makes his exit, hastily.)* I reckon Ise got some ob de stiff out ob his knee. *(Enter DINAH PRIMROSE.)* Eh—m–m! Is dat you, honey! How you do to-day? glad to see you. I s'pected you'd be here, and dar's some preparations. *(pointing to provisions)*

DINAH.   Ah, doctor, I don't tink I'm quite so well to-day. I'm troubled berry bad jest now. I feel shocking here. *(She places her hand on heart.)*

DR. SQUASH.   You don't tell me dat? Den it's my indomitable 'pinion you is troubled wid an affection ob de heart. But I can cure dat. Let me feel your pulse. *(He feels her pulse, and then places his hand with DINAH's in it in his breeches' pocket.)*

JUMBLE *(looks up).*   Golly! I can't stand dat. I'll have to drap him d'rectly.

DR. SQUASH.   Say, Dinah, what you tink of dat Jumble?

DINAH.   Oh! bress me! He's just de most conceited imperent nigger I ever did see. Den he tinks he's good looking, too, and so he is— only he isn't—yah! yah!

JUMBLE *(greatly exicted).*   Dar now, he put dat into her head. Dat's sum ob his work, for she knows mighty well dat Ise de best looking nigger in dis whole county. He'll raise de debbil wid dat gal yet.

DR. SQUASH.   Dinah duck! *(He kisses her.)*

JUMBLE.   Dar, dar! I know'd it all de time. Jess as I s'pected. I s'pose he calls dat a scientific operation performed in a nateral manner, too. But I'll fix him out. *(The Doctor's saddlebags are on the table, and* JUMBLE *puts some fire-crackers in one side of them.)*

DINAH.   Oh, Doctor, you 'fessional gemmen hab such winnin' ways. *(*JUMBLE *touches off the crackers and conceals himself.* DINAH *faints in the Dr's arms. He drops her, seizes the saddlebags and sits down on them— bouncing up every time a cracker explodes.* DINAH *picks herself up, watches* DR. SQUASH, *shaking with fright.)* Bress me! How scared you be, doctor. *(She helps the Doctor up, and keeps her arm around him.)*

DR. SQUASH.   No, I ain't scared,—but I would like to know what de debbil got into my saddlebags. I'd tink it wer sum trick ob dat dam Jumble—but he's been out ob de way dis haff hour.

DINAH.   Yes, and he'd better keep out ob de way; nobody wants him here.

DR. SQUASH *(kisses her)*.   I must pay you for dat obserwation. *(*JUMBLE *runs up behind him, knocks him down, and conceals himself as before. The Doctor gets up, and looks around astonished.)* Oh, gorra! gorra! What was dat? Sumthin' hit me den. *(feeling)* I know dar did, 'kase dar's a big bunch on my head. I know somebody hit me. *(a great uproar behind the scene)*

DR. SQUASH *and* DINAH.   Good gracious, what's dat. *(Enter* GINGER, JULIUS CAESAR, CROW *and* MOB, *shouting.* JUMBLE *comes out from under the table. The more characters on at this time the better. The whole forming a* MOB, *with pitchforks and all kinds and sizes of clubs.)*

CROW.   Dar he is!

JULIUS CAESAR.   Knock his eye out!

GINGER.   Gib it to him!

CROW.   You've done it nice, you have.

JULIUS CAESAR.   Call yourself a doctor, do you? You've set up for a doctor free weeks, and killed more'n dan a dozen niggers in dat time.

DINAH.   I don't believe dat. De doctor's a gembleman.

CROW.   Den I suppose his wives is all ladies—and he's got more'n a dozen ob dem. He's a reg'lar ole rooster, he is.

JUMBLE.   Dar, dar! you hear dat, do you!

DINAH.   Yes, I do. *(to* DR. SQUASH*)* Oh! you willin'! you imposter! You ought to be rid on a rail you had—Say, Jumble, won't you forgive me?

JUMBLE.   I don't know 'bout dat. A little more and he'd a been the ruination ob you.

DINAH.   Yes, I s'peck he would. But I'm berry sorry. *(puts her arms around his neck)*

JUMBLE.   You won't nebber, nebber do so not no more?

DINAH.   No. *(They embrace and make up.)*

DR. SQUASH   *(grabs his saddlebags).* I am sorry to leab you, but I must go.

ALL.   No, you don't! *(* DR. SQUASH *tries to escape, but the* CHARACTERS *form a circle around him, and prevent him at each attempt.)*

AIR: "I'VE BEEN ROAMING."

CHORUS.
No you don't, sah, no you don't, sah!
No you don't get off so clear:
No you don't sah, no you don't, sah!
We've got business for you, here.
You ex-boot-black—
You rascal quack—
We'll make you pack
For de back track,
And neber show your face again,
Anywhere about dis place again.

CROW.   But, stop a minute—we ain't through wid you yet. I've come back to pay you for dat odder toof. *(* DR. SQUASH *tries to break out.)* Eh—ur! No yer don't.

AIR: "FIVE POUND NOTE."

CHORUS.
No you don't, sah, no you don't, sah!
No you don't get off so clear:
No you don't, sah, no you don't sah!
We've got business for you here.

(CROW *and* JUMBLE *seize the Doctor.)*

JUMBLE.   What shall we do with him?

GINGER.   Run him out!

JULIUS CAESAR *(tries to get at* DR. SQUASH*)*.   Gouge him, gouge him!

CROW *(gets out the forceps)*.   Pull eb'ry toof out ob his head!

JUMBLE.   Hang him!

DINAH.   I tell you something wuss dan dat. Gib him a dose ob his own physic.

ALL.   Dat's de ting! Dat's it.

JUMBLE.   And den we can hang him afterwards.

DR. SQUASH.   Oh, mercy! mercy! Hang me fust. (ALL *get him on his knees.)*

GINGER.   Gib us de die-stuffs! *(They open the saddlebags, and by pounding and cuffing make him swallow various kinds of medicines from the saddlebags, and bring the bottles and demijohns into operation.* DR. SQUASH *dies with a great deal of kicking. More doses cause him to revive, and he is raised to his feet, much exhausted, by two characters, who support him.)* Dat physic will neber operate in de world, widout gibin' him sum exercise.

DINAH.   Dat's it. Trot him out!

DR. SQUASH *(drops on his knees)*.   Gib me time to say my prayers!

(The CHARACTERS *form two lines and make* DR. SQUASH *run between them, hitting him as he passes. He then runs round the stage, followed by* JULIUS CAESAR, CROW, *and the others, "single file"; the foremost stirring him with a stick. He falls, and the others fall over him, but he extricates himself and runs out, followed by all the rest.)*

Notice. Fireworks may be rung in the finish to suit the fancy.

CURTAIN

Scampini

In order to confirm the importance of minstrelsy's verbal dimension, it is useful to compare a piece like *The Quack Doctor* with the following pantomime by Edward Warden. Although common on variety bills, pantomime never really became standard fare on the minstrel stage. This is difficult to explain in light of minstrelsy's habit of exploiting any and all popular theatrical forms, and in light of minstrelsy's dependence on high-impact visual humor. Part of the reason may have been the generally held belief that pantomime was a distinctly non-American art. The numerous troupes which specialized in the form were typified by the Ravels, a family of French performers who began putting together shows of acrobatics, pantomime, and ballet in the 1830s and remained a fixture in New York theater for half a century. Minstrelsy was essentially chauvinistic and tended to burlesque rather than emulate European culture. Pantomime, though, could not easily be burlesqued. Because of its necessary simplicity it rendered ineffective one of minstrelsy's primary burlesque techniques—over simplification. Pantomime could be the tool of burlesque but not its object.

What *Scampini* illustrates is that without its verbal dimension the minstrel afterpiece was essentially indistinguishable from other forms of low stage humor. That the playbook version of *Scampini* was intended for use by both minstrel and variety troupes is a further indication of its marginal status.

Edward Warden began his professional career performing minstrelsy and variety in the mid 1850s. During the 1858–1859 season when he was performing with Wood's Minstrels (one of New York's resident troupes), that troupe began experimenting with pantomime, perhaps at Warden's suggestion, in an attempt to bolster their sagging popularity. *Scampini* was offered by Wood's Minstrels in October of 1859 and again in December of 1861. The following text is reprinted from the acting edition published by Robert M. De Witt in 1874.

SCAMPINI
An Anti-tragical, Comical,
Magical, and Laughable
PANTOMIME,
Full of Tricks and
Side-splitting Transformations.
In Two Scenes.[1]

By EDWARD WARDEN.
Arranged for Minstrel and Variety Troupes,
By CHARLES WHITE.

CAST OF CHARACTERS
(Wood's Minstrels, New York, Oct., 1859)

SCAMPINI (the agile lover) . . . . Mr. E. Warden
DONUTINE (the opposing parent) . . . . Mr. C. White
BARBERIO (the shaving rival) . . . . Master Carr
WIGGERIO (an ancient visitor) . . . . Mr. J. Collins
VASSALLIO (a faithful runner) . . . . Mr. F. Boniface
LUCINDINA (the beloved bride) . . . . Master Eddy

1 The piece, in fact, has only one scene.

Scampini

MATRINO (a faded flower) . . . . Mr. M. Campbell
VISTERIO (a feminine fashionable) . . . . . . Mr. T. Vaughn
THE BLACK SHADOW . . . . Mr. A. Wood
Visitors, Attendants, etc.

THE ARGUMENT

A jealous parent opposing the union of true hearts, is exposed to a se-
ries of lovers' tricks, who (by the aid of a colored Cupid), laugh at lock-
smiths and such usual impediments, till they force the old man to unite
the destiny of
"Two souls with a single thought—
Two hearts that beat as one."
And thus ends this highly colored affair in a comic tableau of Love and
Laughter.

COSTUMES

SCAMPINI.—Red tights and shirt, straight-haired red wig, black trunks
and fly, slippers and belt, sugar-loaf hat.

DONUTINE.—White Pero dress; white wig.

BARBERIO.—White pants, striped stockings, short calico vest, fancy
neck-tie and white apron.

WIGGERIO.—A farmer's style of make-up.

VASSALLIO.—A country boy's dress.

LUCINDINA.—Fancy dress—Columbine style.

MATRINO.—Any extravagant old woman's dress. Large bonnet.

VISTERIO.—Very ludicrous female dress, overdoing the fashion.

THE BLACK SHADOW.—Full black tights and body painted like skeleton.

SCENE.—*Plain rustic chamber. Music.*

Curtain rises. LUCINDINA and BARBERIO discovered, also MATRINO at
table, ironing. LUCINDINA sewing on left, BARBERIO working at wig-
block. Bell rings. Old lady sends girl to door—she refuses, old lady goes
herself; in her absence the girl and barber have business. LUCINDINA so-
licits the barber to carry a note to her lover, he consents by having a kiss
granted to him. They then dance together, and he exits L. 2E.

Enter OLD WOMAN, 3 U.E. Resumes her work, first driving the girl
to her room. (*change of music*)

This Grotesque Essence

Enter SCAMPINI, 3 U.E.

Unobserved, he dances; sets down on table edge, gets burnt with iron; he dances again; sets down on chair by the table, gets burnt again; he makes love to old woman; she chastises him for his conduct, and leaves in search for DONUTINE, so he may punish SCAMPINI for his insolence. *(Exit R.U.E.)*

The girl then returns, discovers her lover, hears a noise outside, and secretes him under centre table, with his head sticking through. *(change of music)*

Enter OLD WOMAN *and* DONUTINE, L. 1E.

The latter with basket containing bottle of wine, tumbler, knife, bread and cigar. Towel over it all. They both go front; DONUTINE sets down his basket, hugs the old woman, and then goes and caresses LUCINDINA; after which he tells the old woman to send her to her room. The old lady does so, and takes her off. She hurries back and gets a kiss from SCAMPINI, unobserved by DONUTINE, then exits. The sound of the kiss attracts DONUTINE, who thinks she kissed her hand to him, on which account he instantly crosses and returns the compliment by kissing his hand to her. The stage now being clear, he prepares to partake of the content of his basket. So proceeds by pulling off his coat; after hanging it up, he goes front, takes basket and chair from the ironing-table and seats himself by the middle-table. Discovering dust on the same, he picks up the feather-duster from behind the ironing-table, and proceeds to dust off his own chair, the table, wig-block, etc. Then throws down the brush in its place, and seats himself all right and ready to enjoy the contents of his basket. He takes out the bottle and pours a half-glass of wine in the tumbler; then sets the same in front of the head which is through the table. While stooping and searching in his basket for bread, the head through the table has drunk the contents of the glass. DONUTINE being now ready, after cutting himself a slice of bread, reaches out for his tumbler of wine, and commences to soak his bread in the same, when, to his great astonishment, the wine is gone. After wondering for a moment, he pours out the same quantity again, and places it in the same place; he cuts another piece of bread, and commences to soak it in his wine. But again the wine is gone. He jumps up, searches about, sees no clue, and finally points to the double-bass player in the orchestra, who makes a heavy chord, which startles DONUTINE

44

back again to his place. He is about to go through the same process again with the glass, but alters his mind and drinks from the bottle as the safest remedy. While drinking, he stands on the front rung of the chair, and rubs his stomach as the liquor passes down his throat; after which he takes the candle from the ironing-table, and sets it down on his own table, and while looking in his basket for his cigar, SCAMPINI blows the candle out. DONUTINE reaches out for the candlestick, holds it up in front of him to get a light, when after a few pulls at his cigar, he discovers the candle is out; he sets the candle from where he first took it, and searches about for a light; seeing no other opportunity of getting one, he lies down on his stomach, and procures a light from the foot-light—which, as soon as done, causes the snare drum in the orchestra to give a quick, heavy roll, and that frightens DONUTINE back again to his seat, where he becomes sleepy, yawns, and sinks on his chair to take a snooze, his left arm lying across the table, with the cigar between the fingers of the same. SCAMPINI gets the cigar in his mouth, and puffs the smoke in the face of DONUTINE, which chokes him up, and causes him to advance front, R.E. coughing. He turns round, and discovers the table and head after him, and runs across the stage very much frightened. SCAMPINI kicks him as he crosses to the left, also as he crosses to the right, and then kicks him once more just as

DONUTINE *exits at* R. 1E.

SCAMPINI hears the rattle from the outside, and immediately sets the table off in one of the wings, 2 L.E., then hides behind one of the long barrels up the stage. Soon as done,

DONUTINE *runs in at* R.U.E., *with the rattle in his hand.*

Runs in a circle round the stage once, then stands in the centre of the stage, making his rattle go. SCAMPINI jumps over his head. DONUTINE turns around to see what it was that touched him, when SCAMPINI kicks him. DONUTINE immediately turns back again, and discovers SCAMPINI going down a round trap head first. DONUTINE immediately gets a club from the barrel upstage—goes to the trap. SCAMPINI puts his head through twice, and is struck at by DONUTINE. The third time, he puts the dummy head through, when it receives a blow from DONUTINE's club; it goes down again, and the trap closes. DONUTINE gets a board from R.U.E., brings it down, and crosses over to L.C. 1E., where he discovers a long white sack erect, which contains SCAMPINI. The sack is

45

about to fall—DONUTINE catches it, and puts it back again as he originally saw it; he turns, when the sack again falls over; DONUTINE places it right again, when suddenly the sack jumps. DONUTINE gets frightened and runs over on the opposite side. They then change sides—when DONUTINE takes courage, advances to the sack, and attempts to carry it off on his shoulder, turning once around with it. The person in the sack closes or shuts his body and legs on DONUTINE, which causes him to cry out. DONUTINE turning again, this process is done once more, whereupon the sack is placed upon its feet. DONUTINE turns away an instant, when the sack goes down crosswise, upon the stage. DONUTINE discovers this, and pulls the sack up the stage; he turns to get something, when the sack rolls front. DONUTINE stops it, and pulls it up the stage again, then takes hold of the hands of SCAMPINI and raises him up erect; after this he strips down the sack, gets it from under his feet, discovers it to be SCAMPINI, and lifts him up by the leg and arm, then lays him on the board. DONUTINE turns to get his sword; on returning with his sword uplifted, he is astonished to see that SCAMPINI has reversed from his back over on his stomach. He then throws down his sword, and goes to Scampini's feet as if to turn him, when SCAMPINI slides the length of the board forward away from him. DONUTINE pulls him back to his place again, when SCAMPINI slides again; DONUTINE pulls him back as before; then goes to the head of the board and raises it up; he is about to shoulder it, when SCAMPINI looks over the top and frightens DONUTINE, who is determined to carry him off on his back; he shoulders the board, and comes around front, where he comes in contact with SCAMPINI, face to face. DONUTINE, very much frightened, is not positive whether he still has him on the board or not, turns to look, when SCAMPINI kicks him; after which, DONUTINE carries the board off L. 1E.; returns; gets his sword, and makes seven cuts at SCAMPINI, stabbing him at the last one. The sword is in him so tight that he cannot pull it out by the handle, and therefore goes behind, and attempts to push it out by putting his hand against the point; he finds this won't do, and places his body against the point of the sword; he also sees his error here, and so goes in front, grasps the handle of the sword with both hands, then places his foot against Scampini's breast, and pulls the sword out. Both fall down on stage together in sitting posture. DONUTINE runs over to R., and tries to push SCAMPINI down flat on his back; he does so, when Scampini's legs come up. DONUTINE turns around, and by the same manner as before he tries to push Scampini's legs down; in doing so, he receives a push from behind, which sends him forward; on turning around, he discovers SCAMPINI sitting up as first. DONUTINE then goes and with both hands he straightens out SCAMPINI —when, on the instant, SCAMPINI flops over on his stomach. DONUTINE tries to lift him up by his slack, and the instant he grabs, SCAMPINI throws himself in a sitting position. DONUTINE, discouraged, determines that he will shoot him, and accordingly goes to 1R.E., gets loaded gun, and immediately returns, and discharges the same at SCAMPINI, who, on being shot, rolls and dies extravagantly. DONUTINE goes to him, steps crosswise over him, picks up his legs as if to feel his pulse in the heel of SCAMPINI. SCAMPINI pushes him away with the other foot. DONUTINE then places his hand on Scampini's breast, which swells out with a tremendous swell; after which, he pound's Scampini's head on the stage. *(Imitating the noise of head by stamping the foot)* DONUTINE, being now satisfied that he has subdued SCAMPINI, feels haughty, and proud of his triumph. Suddenly he reflects on the mischief he has just committed, *and pantomines that if known he will be hung.* He instantly falls on his knees and prays; after which, he runs to the bell-pull on the R. 1E., and rings for servants.

> VASSALLIO *and another one enter, R. 1E.*

One each side of DONUTINE, when they are instructed by him to take the body away. The SERVANTS do so immediately, and deposit SCAMPINI in a closet up stage; after doing so, they return for further orders, when they are instructed to bring table and writing materials—which they do. They bring table, two candles, inkstand, sand-box, quills, one clean sheet of paper, and one with black blotted spot on; after which, they retire to each side front. DONUTINE seats himself by the table, and the SERVANTS stamp and ask him if they are wanted any longer. DONUTINE stands up and tells them to go. They do so. Now DONUTINE sits down, and begins to write his letter.

> *One stroke of gong and lightning, which brings out the* GHOST *or* BLACK SHADOW, *who, with doleful music and thunder, seats himself at the end of the table where* DONUTINE *is writing.*

He touches DONUTINE on the cheek with his hand, which causes DONUTINE to shiver with cold. This is done once more when DONUTINE turns to dip his pen with ink; he discovers the GHOST, and comes front trembling. At the same time, the gong announces that the GHOST has disappeared through the closet. DONUTINE is about to leave, but summons courage enough to remain; he goes toward the table, discovers the chair which the GHOST sat upon, and removes it to the wing; then sits down again, and resumes his writing.

> *The* GHOST *comes out of the closet at the sound of gong, and sits on the back of* Donutine's *chair.*

While there he changes, by reversing, the inkstand and the sand-box—this is done twice. After writing all that is necessary, DONUTINE makes a mistake by dumping the contents of the inkstand on his writing instead of the sand. He goes front with the paper, and on looking at it, discovers he has blotted the whole thing with ink. During this time, the GHOST has crept under the table. DONUTINE goes to the table again, and completes his writing, when, pushing his paper forward over the table as he writes, the GHOST from under ignites the sheet, and the whole sheet of paper is in a flame; he goes front to extinguish the flame, and turns up stage, walking completely into the arms of the GHOST, who stands ready to receive him. At this, the GHOST disappears, and DONUTINE rings the bell for aid. The two SERVANTS appear, and tap him on the shoulder, but DONUTINE for a moment is still in fear, but finally falls in their arms exhausted. They support him to the front, where, on recovery, he tells them that he has been visited by a ghost, and slyly points out to them his secret hiding place *(viz, closet)*. The SERVANTS go and bring him out, but instead of the GHOST, they bring out SCAMPINI, and lay him down in front of the stage crosswise—one of them receives a kick. DONUTINE summons them to place the body on the top of a barrel which he himself places over the upper trap. They do so, when DONUTINE makes three cuts with his sword to music. SCAMPINI disappears through the barrel and trap. They carry the barrel front, and, to their surprise, SCAMPINI leaps over all their heads, which commences a chase after him. About the stage they run, when SCAMPINI goes through *(by leap)* the picture on the right side, which frightens DONUTINE to one corner. (SERVANTS *run off.*)

> *Enter* WIGGERIO *and* VISTERIO.

DONUTINE sees them, and readily runs to them with a shaking of hands, etc. He also invites them to partake of something; they consent, when DONUTINE leads them up the stage to table in front of soldier picture.

They both begin to eat, when, to their great surprise, the soldier picture consumes everything they take hold of. WIGGERIO falls with both arms on the table, when the picture grabs the wig from his head and eats that also as the other things, and then pushes the table over. DONUTINE and another bring SCAMPINI in with false red arms, etc., *(imitation of soldier)* and, by pulling him to and fro, his arms come off, and he gets away; they commence the chase after SCAMPINI. He comes in 1E. L., clears everybody, and goes through the clock. Chase still kept up. He enters again R. 1E., and plunges through the barrel, L. 2E. DONUTINE partially enters for him, and pulls out the long leg of SCAMPINI, which springs back through the barrel again very suddenly. DONUTINE enters again, and seizes SCAMPINI by the hand, who he pulls out of the barrel, and while doing so, SCAMPINI with a mouthful of flour blows the whole contents of the same in Donutine's face. DONUTINE staggers front, sneezing, etc., and LUCINDINA enters to join her lover SCAMPINI. They ask consent. DONUTINE acknowledges yes. The large table is instantly set, and all of the company sit down to dine. DONUTINE helps himself first, then his opposite man, and after sits down to eat; he finds his plate empty, which has been taken away by one of his servants, and in consequence of which makes a great noise. However, he resumes his eating again. Pours out a glass of wine first for himself, then for his friends; they rise to drink, but, as before, his cup is as empty as his plate was. He sits down with indignation, but, instead of seating himself on his chair, he finds himself on the floor. With anger he rises, and collars his servant —pushes him; the servant pushes him back again against the table, which upsets the opposite guest, who, on falling, pulls the whole table cloth completely from the table together with all the contents. All make picture. Large figure in the rear. Gong, red fire, and tableau.

CURTAIN

Old Zip Coon

The song "Zip Coon" (known today in instrumental form as "Turkey in the Straw") can be thought of as the epitome of nineteenth-century American popular music. Published in 1834, the song quickly became associated with the figure of the minstrel clown and was used innumerable times as a solo, a dance vehicle, and as the musical number around which minstrel finales were built. The following piece cannot be dated with complete accuracy. The playbook form was copyrighted in 1874, but there is neither cast nor production information available which could help to date the first performance of the piece.

Of particular interest in *Old Zip Coon* are the elements associated with Reconstruction attitudes. The sentimentalized plantation setting is typical of post–Civil War nostalgia, and the jokes created by the inversion of the antebellum social hierarchy illustrate the inherent racism of minstrelsy in its most vicious form. The following text is reprinted from the acting edition published by the Happy Hours Company in 1874.

OLD ZIP COON.

An Ethiopian Eccentricity,
In One Scene.

CHARACTERS

ZIP COON
CUFF CUDLIP
ITALIAN MUSIC MASTER
SALLY

SCENE:—*The common room of* Zip Coon's *house on the Old Planta-*
tion, opening on the verandah—the cotton and cane fields beyond—the
Mississippi in the distance.

(*ZIP, elegantly dressed, reading a newspaper and smoking a cigar, with his*
feet on a table on which are decanters and glasses. White boy presenting a
huge mint julip.)

ZIP.   Dere, clar you'self! (*drinks*) Dis brandy isn't so good as de last;
(*smacking his lips*) shall hab to discharge my wine merchant if he
don't improve, for sartin. Maybe it's my taste, but somehow 'taint
half so good as de ole Jamaica massa used to gib us to wash de hoe
cake down with. It's mighty comfortable to be rich, to be sure, but
it's debblish tiresome to hab to keep up de dignity all de time. O,
for one good old-fashioned breakdown, like we used to hab when
massa run de old plantation for us, and all we had to do was play
de banjo and loaf. (*looking right and left*) Nobody looking! Maybe
'taint genteel, but here goes for a try. (*walks around and sings*)
Long time ago we hoe de cotton,
  Grub among de canebrake, munch de sugar cane,
Hunt coon and possum by de ribber bottom,
  Past and gone de happy days—nebber come again!
Ho, hi! How de moments fly!
  Get up and do your duty
While de time am passin' by!

(*breakdown, throws off his coat*)

51

This Grotesque Essence

Dere we knock de banjo, make de sheepskin talk,
    Shout until de rafters to de chorus ring;
If de massa see us, make him walk his chalk,
    Trabel libely o'er de boards, cut de pigeon wing.
        Ho, hi! etc. *(Break.)*

(CUFF CUDLIP, *with a small bundle on his shoulder and in a ragged suit, peeps in and softly enters. Throws bundle down and joins in breakdown.)*

CUFF.

Hoe it down libely, dere's nobody to fear,
    De gate am off de hinges, no oberseer dere;
No one in de cornfield, all de coast is clear,
    Here de bell a-ringin', step up and pay your fare!

BOTH.

Ho, hi! etc. *(break)*

CUFF. Hy'a! it's no use talking—nigger will be nigger! *(puts his bundle on table and takes chair)*

ZIP *(slipping into his coat)*. I'd hab you know dere aint no niggahs now. I belongs to de upper crust. You'm makin' you'self mighty comfortable anyhow. 'Spose you couldn't be hired to refuse a drink?

CUFF. Don't press me. *(puts bottle to his mouth, takes a swig, spits it out)* Bah! What sort o' stuff dat? Hoss medicine?

ZIP. Hoss medicine, you ignoramus darky, you! Dat's de genuine Otard.

CUFF. If dat's "old tod" I don't want none of it. But, say, Zip, you look as if you took de world easy; can't you gib us a job.

ZIP. You wouldn't degrade you'self by workin', would you? Well, go out dere among de white trash, den.

CUFF. I say—I see a gran pianner dere, but whar's de ole banjo— whar's de ole cremonum?[1]

ZIP. O, dem ain't fashionable, now. You 'member when we lib in de ole quarter and I took a shine to Sal Beeswax, de master's cook? Hy'a! Well—de massa's goned away and I got his property and married Sal, and we got a darter—black one side de face an' white todder —an' she won't touch nuffin' short ob a piannum, and dat brings

---

1 Fiddle. A reference to Cremona, a town in northern Italy, the name of which was used to designate any of the exquisite violins made there by Nicola Amati, Antonio Stradivari, or Guiseppe Guarneri.

all de high-toned darkies round her, and—and de white trash dey
come round her thick as flies in a 'lasses hogshead.

CUFF.   Does any of 'em git stuck?

ZIP.   You bet! Here comes de gal; golly, look at dat hoof.

(Enter SALLY,[2] *with music and an Italian master.)*

MASTER *(sings).   O, dulce anima de mi con amore da poco.*

SAL.   "O dull seems the time unto me when I want to play poker."

MASTER.   *Casta Diva mi figelia, la croche se ha ben trovato,—*

SAL.   "Casta Diva." I'm sure I'd not sing if I wasn't "obligato." *(aside, seeing Zip)* My fader! *(puts her arms about his neck)*

ZIP.   My darter! *(embraces her)* Here's old Cuff Cudlip—don't you 'member Cuff! *(Cuff attempts to embrace her too. She curtseys and passes under—he embraces Zip instead, and is slapped.)*

SAL. *(sings).*

What magic's stealing o'er me, that mein, that noble brow!
    O, how my heart is thumping against my corsets now.
If this is what de crazy chaps call "love" in po*etry,*
    I's ready to frow up de sponge, for a gone coon am I!

(goes to piano with master)

CUFF *(sings).*

Now my heart with remembrance is wa'harming,
And lub all its outposts is sto-horming,
New hopes in my bosom am fo-horming,
    O, how like a belus[3] I sigh!
I feel like a chap-fallen lover
Dat a big garden roller's past over;
I'd consider myself in clover
    For to catch but a glance of her eye!

ZIP *(pulling on his kids).*

Put on your airs!
Here comes de company in pairs—

CUFF.

O, yes, by twos and threes they come;
I'll let them see that I'm at home.

2   It is probable that the actor who played Sally wore some form of pie-bald makeup—
a further indication of the grotesque visual extremes minstrelsy relied on.
3   A bellows.

This Grotesque Essence

(takes black coat out of bundle, and puts on coat and large white kids)

SAL. *(as enter company of both sexes, white and black)*
> Walk along, stalk along! Daddy's got de gout;
> Take him by de elbow, make him shake it out!

(sits at piano and plays to chorus)

CHORUS.
> Troll, troll! let de chorus roll,
> Him dat doesn't jine us, hit him o'er de poll! *(They dance.)*

AIR

CUFF.
> O, clar de kitchen, niggers,
> > Your music can't begin,
> Pull off your coats and spencers,[4]
> > Take your gloves off and sail in;
>
> Listen to de banjo
> > While de old ting am in tune,
> Incline your ears and listen,
> > And I'll gib you "Old Zip Coon!"

Taking banjo suddenly from bundle, plays—dance changed to the old melody—Sal leaves the piano and dances alternately with Zip and Cuff. She and they become more enthusiastic, all the rest nearly frantic, till Sal faints in the arms of Cuff, and

CURTAIN

---

4 A spencer was a short, close-fitting jacket.

Uncle Eph's Dream

By focusing on farcical elements it is easy to overlook the fact that minstrelsy was a very sentimental art form. The minstrel show's first part invariably included mother songs or pathetic ballads which helped balance the comic songs and exchanges between interlocutor and end men. Numerous performers were renowned for their ability to leave audiences weeping. Dan Bryant, for example, with his portrayals of starving slaves, is said to have been the only actor in America who could consistently move the great Edwin Forrest to tears. Even the afterpieces could indulge in the delicious pain of sentimentality as the following piece shows. Though the action of *Uncle Eph's Dream* tends toward slapstick, the subordinate elements—such as the setting, the background music, and the dream tableau—are evidence of the sincere though mawkish nostalgia with which a large portion of American society reacted to the harsh realities of Reconstruction.

The first recorded performance of *Uncle Eph's Dream* occurred on November 6, 1871, when Bryant's Minstrels added it to their bill at Mechanics Hall in New York. In the next three years the piece was revived four times by Bryant's and ran for several weeks each time. The cast list printed with this text is problematic. There is no record of these four performers having appeared together after 1863. Since Hart's name was the only one prestigious enough to have advertising value during the mid-1870s, it is quite unlikely that the list was devised for that purpose. The following text is reprinted from the acting edition published by Robert M. De Witt in 1874.

UNCLE EPH'S DREAM.

An Original Negro Sketch,
In Two Scenes and Two tableaux.
Arranged
By CHARLES WHITE.

CAST OF CHARACTERS

UNCLE EPH TOMPKINS (an old shade) . . . . . . Mr. Bob Hart
HANNAH TOMPKINS (his wife) . . . . Mr. Wm. Simpson
YOUNG EPH (their son) . . . . Mr. L. Simmons
MR. JONES . . . . Mr. T. Riggs
Two ladies and other characters by the company

COSTUMES

UNCLE EPH.—Grey wig and beard. Large overcoat. Loose pants and vest. Flimsy shirt collar. Loose, long cotton cravat. Large shoes, and wide brim hat.

HANNAH.—Old calico frock and handkerchief. Head tied up with a bandana hankerchief—old style.

YOUNG EPH.—Jacket and short pants. Boy's collar, gathered around his neck. Straw hat.

MR. JONES.—Light clothing—southern style.

TWO LADIES.—Light, airy, southern costume.

Other characters dress to suit climate and style.

Uncle Eph's Dream

SCENE I.—*Wood in 2d grooves, with bank on* R.

Enter UNCLE EPH R. 1E. *(with banjo and carpet bag filled with toys).*

EPH.   Dar's no use ob talking, old Eph is most broken hearted and can't get no 'teligence from nobody; no one can tell de old man where his wife and children am gone to. When I left here five years ago ebery ting looked prosperous, but now, look at it, ebery ting is gwan to ruin. I remember when I used to walk along dis road by de plantation, de field hands used to cry out to me, how does you do, Uncle Eph? Den I used to sit under de shade ob de tree and listen to de little birds sing and read my little bible; take off my hat to de white folks as dey passed by, and dey used to gib me silber; but it's all gone now! no birds sing, no white gemblem won't look at me.

Enter MR. JONES L. 1E. *(is crossing stage).*

EPH *(takes off his hat).*   I say, massa, can you tell me—?
JONES.   No, don't bother me. *(exits R)*
EPH.   Dat's de way wid all ob dem now; dey won't tell de old man nuffin'. *(sits down on de bank)* In dat carpet bag I hab a lot ob presents for de little ones, but I am afeared I will nebber see dem again; and dar's a banjo—Mr. Slocum gib me dat banjo for little Eph. I told him I was gwan to de old plantation to see my wife and children; den he told me to take dat banjo for little Eph. He used to be my massa once and a mighty good massa he was too—but we got no more massas now; de poor old slaves will hab to look out for demselves; but if I could only find my little Eph and gib him dis present from Mr. Slocum, I would be satisfied; he was always my favorite, and if I don't find him, I don't care how soon de green grass grows ober dese old bones. I must lay down here and get a little rest afore I go any furder. *(lays down on the bank and sleeps)*

Music $\left\{ \begin{matrix} \text{Old Kentucky Home,} \\ \text{Old Uncle Ned,} \end{matrix} \right\}$ *or any other appropraite melody*

(The flats draw off and discover tableau of plantation. HANNAH, YOUNG EPH *and all the children discovered. Red fire or calcium for the picture.* EPH *speaks in his sleep through picture. Scene closes again.)*

57

This Grotesque Essence

Enter YOUNG EPH L. 1E. *(seeing an old man).* By golly! Dar's a poor old man sleeping on dat bank. *(He notices the banjo)* Phew! my eyes, what a pretty banjo; how I would like to hab dat; I'll just see if I can play on it widout waking de old man up. *(He takes the banjo: goes to* C. *of stage; sits down on stage and plays* HOME, SWEET HOME; *after playing a little the old man wakes up, rubs his eyes and listens to the banjo.)*

UNCLE EPH.   My goodness! what a pleasant dream I had; I thought I was wid my wife and little ones. *(He looks around and sees young* EPH, *who starts and puts the banjo back again.)*

YOUNG EPH.   I wasn't goin' to hurt it, old man. *(and starts to go)*

UNCLE EPH.   Stop! look ahere my son—don't be skeered; come here —.(LITTLE EPH *advances)* Does you know many people 'bout dese roads?

LITTLE EPH.   Yes, sir; I know almost ebery body.

UNCLE EPH.   Does you? Well, I want you to told me sumthin'; did you know whar Mr. Mildman's plantation is?

LITTLE EPH.   Yes, sir; yes, indeed; I lib on dat plantation.

UNCLE EPH.   Does Mr. Mildman still lib dar?

LITTLE EPH.   No, sir; he was killed in de war.

UNCLE EPH.   Killed in de war? and his son William?

LITTLE EPH.   He was killed, too.

UNCLE EPH.   And dat good young man, Albert?

LITTLE EPH.   He was wounded, and died just a few days ago.

UNCLE EPH.   You don't tell me so? I suppose his wife and daughter still libs dar?

LITTLE EPH.   Yes, his wife still libs dar; but his daughter was taken crazy, just after Nan Alber died, and had to be sent to de Lunatic Asylum.

UNCLE EPH.   Dear me, de country and de people am all, all gone to destruction; too bad, too bad, too bad; but look ahere, my son; did you know any ob de field hands on de plantation?

LITTLE EPH.   Yes, sir; all ob dem.

UNCLE EPH.   Does you remember or know one among dem called Hannah Tompkins?

LITTLE EPH.   Yes, sir.

UNCLE EPH.   You did? Now, don't be in a hurry, but told me, is—is—is —I'm almost afraid to ask you—is—is—she alive yet?

LITTLE EPH.   Why, yes; ob course she is.

Uncle Eph's Dream

UNCLE EPH.   Glory to Zion! *(falls on his knees overjoyed)*

LITTLE EPH.   Yes, indeed, honey; why, Hannah Tompkins is my mother.

UNCLE EPH.   Eh! your mudder? and what's your name?

LITTLE EPH.   Eph Tompkins.

UNCLE EPH.   What, my boy Eph? *(He embraces him and dances with joy, etc.)*

LITTLE EPH.   Come, I say, old man, what am you going, is you trying to kidnap me?

UNCLE EPH.   Kidnap you? no, no; come to your father's arms.

LITTLE EPH *(staring at him)*.   I guess you is crazy; you ain't my farder, is you?

UNCLE EPH.   Yes, ob course I is; don't you know me?

LITTLE EPH.   No.

UNCLE EPH.   Dar's a child dat don't know his own farder; dat's case he ain't wise enough. Well, well, my goodness, how you am grown in de last five years. Den you don't remember de old man, eh?

LITTLE EPH.   No, ob course I don't.

UNCLE EPH.   Did you ebber hear mudder and de people on de old plantation talk about old Uncle Eph?

LITTLE EPH.   Oh yes, but he went norf about five years ago, and we spec he died dar.

UNCLE EPH.   Died? no, no, indeed, my son; he stands afore you alive and well.

LITTLE EPH.   Oh, is you my farder? Why, papa, how glad I is to see you; let's go right down and see mudder and de rest ob de family.

UNCLE EPH.   Eph, does de old woman wallup you as much as ebber?

LITTLE EPH.   Yes, indeed, she does; she licks me for de whole family.

UNCLE EPH.   Nebber mind, my son, she shan't lick you any more, de old man will be home now.

HANNAH *(calls outside)*.   Eph! Ephram! you young wagabone; where de debil is you?

LITTLE EPH.   Oh, farder, here she comes; now she'll gib me an awful wallupping.

Enter HANNAH *with child in her arms followed by all the boys.*

HANNAH.   You young rascal, come here till I kill you; I'll skin you alive.

ALL THE BOYS.   Give it to him old woman, give it to him. *(She starts for* LITTLE EPH; *he runs behind the old man.)*

This Grotesque Essence

UNCLE EPH.   Hold on! Hold on! old woman; don't touch dat child.

HANNAH.   What right hab you got to interfere?

ALL THE BOYS.   Yes, what is you intereferin' for?

UNCLE EPH.   What, Hannah, don't you know me?

HANNAH.   Eh! dat voice. Jim, hold de baby. *(Jim takes baby.)* Eph, is dat you?

UNCLE EPH.   Ob course it am.

HANNAH.   My goodness! Eph, how is you?

(She runs and embraces him; the children all embrace him; the old man has great trouble to extricate himself; this business is repeated several times, until UNCLE EPH *calls for help and drives them back to* L.C.)

UNCLE EPH *(out of breath)*.   Dat's worser dan a collision on de railroad, I declare; Hannah, I am almost squeezed to deff.

HANNAH.   Well, de children am only glad to see you.

UNCLE EPH.   Well, I am glad to see dem, too, if dey is gwan to squeeze me to deff. But who in de name of wonder does all dem mokes belong too?

HANNAH.   Why, dey all belong to you, Uncle Eph; don't you know your own children?

UNCLE EPH.   What, all mine! hush. Why when I went away five years ago I only had—let me see *(counts with his fingers and looks)*—well, I declare, I didn't think I had such a big family, I often thought some ob 'em might be dead.

HANNAH.   How is it you used to write to me regular, but we nebber heard anything 'bout you for a long time?

UNCLE EPH.   Yes, I ain't sent you a letter in two years.

HANNAH.   You telegram'd about a year ago, and I told you all 'bout de family.

UNCLE EPH.   You did? you nebber said anything 'bout dat little nigger yonder *(pointing)*. Well, nebber mind, I was only joking; come, children, de old man has got some presents for you all.

(He takes carpet bag and commences to distribute articles; they all crowd about him; he has some difficulty in keeping some of them off; he gives the dancing jack to LITTLE EPH, *and to others penny trumpets, horns, etc.; they all blow them together and make a terrible noise;* LITTLE EPH, *in* L. *corner, is playing with dancing jack, which* HANNAH *tries to get.)*

HANNAH.   Eph, let me have dat for de baby.

LITTLE EPH.   No, I want it for myself; I can make him jump.

HANNAH.   I tell you, Eph, I will hab dat for de baby.

LITTLE EPH.   No you won't—will she farder?

(HANNAH *tries to force it from him; the old man interferes, when a general row commences; some are on the old man's side, some for the old woman.*)

ALL THE BOYS.   Go in old man! Go in old man! Go in old woman!

(*The old man and old woman fight; all the rest crowd about; the old folks fall in C. All remains quiet till scene changes to Eph's happy home. One bar of music,* HOME, SWEET HOME.)

YOUNG EPH.   Say, mammy, if dat makes all de fuss take it. (*gives her the dancing jack*)

UNCLE EPH.   Well, dar, we won't hab no more quarrelin'; get in wid a dancing skirmish, dat's de best, den we'll go to bed happy and nebber fight no more, for Uncle Eph has come home to lib and die in peace. (*They all dance to some walk around music, and at proper time close in all lively, shouting, etc.*)

END

Desdemonum

By the mid 1850s the Shakespearean burlesque had become a dominant form of afterpiece. Though minstrelsy's spirit of travesty ranged freely over anything which found its way onto the American stage, it settled most frequently on Shakespeare for at least two reasons. First, Shakespeare's plays were constantly before the public throughout the nineteenth century. During the 1854/55 season in New York, to take a representative example, thirteen were presented in no less than forty-three separate productions not counting public readings and amateur performances. With such exposure Shakespeare was a natural target of burlesque. Moreover, the success of burlesque, then as now, was directly related to the distance between the object burlesqued and the treatment of it. Since minstrelsy and Shakespearean tragedy were opposite extremes of the theatrical arts, burlesque, by employing such devices as extreme foreshortening of plot, drag acts, slang, and dialect, could force the extremes together in a way which created the most grotesque comic effects imaginable, as in the following anonymous burlesque of *Othello*. The following text is reprinted from the acting edition published by the Happy Hours Company in 1874.

DESDEMONUM.

An Ethiopian Burlesque,
In Three Scenes.

CHARACTERS

OTELLER

IAGUM

CASHUM

RODERIGUM

BRABANTIUM

JUDGE

DESDEMONUM

Musicians, Officiers, &c., &c.

SCENE I.—A street in Wennice. House of Brabantium, with practical window R.H. *Night.*

(Enter OTELLER, *L., with tamborine, and musicians, who serenade and retire.)*

DUET

OTEL.   Wake, Desdemonum, see de risin' moon,
Ebrybody's snorin', nightingale's in tune;
Trow aside your lattice, show your lubly phiz;
Sing a song of welcome, while I go troo my biz!

DES.   *(at casement)*
'Tel, my duck, I hear you; daddy's gone to bed.
Fotch along your ladderum, I'm de gal to wed!
Since burnt-cork am de fashion, I'll not be behind—
I'll see Oteller's wisage in his highfalutin' mind.

BOTH.   De hour am propitious—come, my darlin' flame!
Dey say dat in de dark all cullers am de same.
(OTEL. *throws her a rope ladder. She descends. They embrace.)*

AIR

DESDEMONUM.

When my soldier returns full ob fame from de wars,
All cubbered wid honor and glory and scars,
Den how happy I feel, and his arms round me steal,
And as I feel his kisses my brains fairly reel.

63

This Grotesque Essence

OTELLER.

    Now sheathed be my sword,
        And to beauty
        Let duty, let duty gib way.
    Take de laurel from my brow,
        Wreathe it round wid roses now,
        And luff's go before de priest widout delay.

(They dance off L.*)*

(RODERIGUM *and* IAGUM *steal on* R.*)*

IAGUM.

    What's de matter, Rodereegum?
    Got de mulligrub?[1]
    Look so pale about de gills,
    Guess you are in lub.

ROD.

    She's gib me de mitten,
    And disconsolate I'm gittin';
    Great mind to go and drown myself
    In some old washing-tub.

IAGUM.

    Drown cats and blind puppies!
    Dere's fish in de sea
    Just as good as any
    In de market dat be!

ROD.

    (producing banjo). Yet one more dose my lub I'll gib?
    Uf dat don't fotch her, dam if I lib! *(sees ladder)*
    De jig's up for good—dat ladder tells de tale.

IAGUM

    (picks up Otel.'s hat). It's dat nigger Oteller. Let's kick up a
    gale! *(Rings door-bell fiercely, while* ROD. *pounds.* BRABANTIUM
    puts head out of window.)

BRA.

    Who dat makin' fuss dar?

ROD.

    Desdemonum's cut her stick.

BRA.

    Ring de bell and beat de gong,
    I'll make Oteller sick!

ALL.

    Ring de bell and beat de gong,
    Fotch your swords and guns along,
    While I sing a little song—
    My darter's cut her stick!

1   The blues.

Desdemonum

SCENE II.—*The Court-room at the Tombs. Judge on the bench. Crowd standing round. Hum of voices.*

JUDGE. Take off your hats, quit buzzin',
Fotch in dat hulky nig;
While de goose am cookin',
Guess I'll dance a jig. *(dances a breakdown)*

(Enter officers with OTEL., BRABANTIUM, *etc., R.)*

JUDGE. Brabantium, what's de matter, dat you look so blue?
BRA. Dat darky's stole my darter, but de act I'll make him rue.
JUDGE. To this what says Oteller?
OTEL. Judge, de fact am so;
De gal, you see, got struck wid me,
And would to parson go,
I ain't much on de talk, but when fightin's round I'm dere,
Knock de chip from off my shoulder, and for bloody
work prepare!
BRA. He's bewitched her, dat's de matter; come de Hoodoo
on de gal.
He's played de black art on her, and Iagum is his pal.
Let him gub me back my darter, gub my Desdy back to me,
And send him to de Island,[2] whar such fellers ought to be.
JUDGE. We'll hear de girl's opinion. See, she comes dis way.
Now, Desdemonum, what you got to say?

(Enter DESDEMONUM, R.*)*

SONG.—DESDEMONUM
When duty calls, de wise gib ear—
Dat principle I freely own.
My husband's claim in law holds good.
I owe my faith to him alone.

BRA. To dat Jamaica nig? Why, gal, you're blind.
DES. I see de feller's wisage in his mind;
Beauty's but skin deep anyhow, you know.
BRA. Well, since you've done de mischief you kin go;
But keep your eye peeled, Moor, nor cuckold be—

2 Probably Blackwell's Island (now known as Welfare Island) in the East River, New York City, the site of a workhouse and penitentiary in the nineteenth century.

This Grotesque Essence

She's humbugged her old daddy, and may thee. *(exeunt severally, R. and L.)*

SCENE III.—*A Chamber in the house of Oteller. Sofa, cushions, two chairs.*

(Enter IAGUM, *R., with a handkerchief.)*

IAGUM.   Now for de nex' 'ting on de peppergram.
Dis han'kerchum I foun' upon de stairs
Oteller gib to Desde. I'll convey it
Straightway to Michael Cashum. Then Oteller
I'll pump so full of stories he'll be jealous,
Sack Mr. Cashum, and I'll get his place. *(exit L.)*

(Enter OTEL., *L., meeting* DESDEMONUM.*)*

DES.   My dear Oteller, dinner's on de table.

OTEL.   *(aside).* How cool she takes it. Whar's dat han'kerchum dat an Egyptian to my mudder gib?

DES.   Bodder de kan'kerchum; come, git your hash.

OTEL.   De han'kerchum!

DES.   Your hash, I say, is ready.

OTEL.   I'll settle Cashum's hash. You gub it to him. Jus' now, I seen him wipe his mouf wid it.

DES.   It's no such t'ing! I drop it on de stairs.

OTEL.   Den say your prayers and die. De han'kerchum! De han'ker-chum! *(draws her, kicking, to sofa)*

SONG.—DESDEMONUM

Good-bye, husband; good-bye, dad,
       To go off this way's quite too bad.
Let's have one squall before I slide,
       And den to go I'm satisfied!

(He smothers her with cushions.)

OTEL.   Now, come in all;
For one last look
Ere black Oteller's life is took.

CASHUM.   Dere's some foul lie been goin' round,
Dis 'kerchief on de stairs I found,
And used it but my nose to blow.

66

Desdemonum

OTEL.   Den dere's an end to all my woe.
Fiddlers, scrape! and fifers, play!
For here's the deuce and all to pay!

(Stabs himself and falls on Desdemonum's body. The characters join hands and dance around them. OTELLER *and* DESDEMONUM *get up and join in. Tableau.)*

CURTAIN

Othello

Afterpieces seldom had distinguishing elements which helped to identify them with specific minstrel troupes. The pieces produced by Griffin and Christy's Minstrels in the late 1860s were rare exceptions. Much of the credit for this goes to G. W. H. Griffin, who served as scribe for the troupe and who can be called, more than anyone else, the author of the pieces. An analysis of the several extant pieces that can be attributed to Griffin suggests that he was more interested in the literary possibilities in burlesque than was generally the case in minstrelsy. The dialogue in the following burlesque of *Othello*, for example, contains as sophisticated a use of couplets as can be found in American humorous poetry.

Much of the success of the Griffin and Christy troupe depended on the performances and directorial skills of George Christy (whose real name was Harrington). Considered an excellent mimic and comedian, Christy was perhaps most widely known as the best of the female impersonators and, depending upon which historian one reads, is given credit for having established the "Negro wench" as a stock clown figure.

The period following the Civil War saw the breakdown of many previously definitive characteristics of minstrelsy, not the least of which was the art's straightforward presentation of the blackface clown as a caricature of the American black. As urban audiences showed signs of drifting toward variety theater (which in its heavy use of ethnic stereotypes prefigured late nineteenth-century vaudeville), minstrelsy responded by adding blackface Irishmen, Germans, Jews, and Orientals to the show. Even though there is some evidence of mixed racial and ethnic humor in minstrelsy as early as 1857 (see, for example, the description of Ill-Count McGinnis in the cast list of *The Challenge Dance*), this shift was primarily a post–Civil War phenomenon. By 1866, when the Griffin burlesque of *Othello* was probably first performed, audiences were being entertained by minstrelsy's overtly grotesque reflection of the impact immigration was having on American life. Griffin's decision to make his Iago an Irishman may very well have been motivated by a desire to exploit the bitter feelings between Irish immigrants and free blacks which periodically erupted into ugly race riots throughout the middle of the century. Thus, an essential character conflict in the original play is retained in the burlesque in a form meaningful to Griffin's audience. The following text is reprinted from the acting edition published by Samuel French.

OTHELLO;
A Burlesque,
As Performed By
GRIFFIN & CHRISTY'S MINSTRELS.
At Their Opera House, New York

CAST OF CHARACTERS

OTHELLO	G. W. H. Griffin
DESDEMONA	Geo. Christy
IAGO	Otto Burbank
BRABANTIO	C. Henry
CASSIO	Geo. Percival

This Grotesque Essence

SCENE I.—*Street.*

(Enter IAGO, *R., singing.—Air, "Low-Backed Car.")*

When first I Desdemona saw, I thought her very fine,
And by the way she treated me, I thought she'd soon be mine;
But she's cleared out and left me now, with a nasty, dirty fellar,
As black as mud—a white-washer—a nagur called Othello.
But I'll kick up the devil's own spree with her for
the way she served me,
And the way I'll plague her for marrying that nagur,
will be something amazin' to see.

(spoken)

Now let me see! how must the job be done?
First thing—I'll tell her father where she's gone!
And who she's gone wid. Hollo! Brabantio! here!
Try for a time to quit your lager beer;
You've lost your daughter, and your wealth and bags
Will follow it, if you don't see——

(Enter BRABANTIO, *L.)*

BRA. Bags, rags, rags!
IAG. Oh, damn your rags! come here; put down your hook,
And learn the step your lovely daughter took.
BRA. Mine daughter took your step you mean to say?
IAG. Took my step? No! I mean she's stepped away—
Cleared out—gone off—got married to a fellow
As black as ink—a nagur named Othello.
BRA. It is not possible! What! married mit a nigger?
IAG. Wid my own eyes, this morning I did twig her
Before the Alderman—and, 'pon my life,
She there and then was made that nigger's wife.
BRA. Ter dyvel! You're von humbug! It can't be!
IAG. A humbug, am I? Go yourself and see;
I've told you truth, and think you might be civil—*(going)*
BRA. Here, sthop a minit—
IAG. Oh, go to the divil. *(exit R.)*

BRABANTIO *sings.—Air, "Blighted Flowers."*
For nineteen years this has been a going
    About mine house, and of all things had share,

Mit switzer kase and bread, her bags out blowing—
  Den go to sleep in von large rocking chair,
I feed her up, to see if I could make her
  So fat to see her dat people would pay.
Just as I tink dat Barnum would take her,
  Dis nigger comes, and mit her runs away.
        (repeat last two lines, and exit R.)

SCENE II.—*A room.*

(*Enter* OTHELLO *and* DESDEMONA, L., *singing and dancing a walk around.—Air, "Dixie."*)

OTH. Oh, Desdy, dear, now you're my wife,
   I mean to pass a happy life—Away, away, &c.
   I'll never more be melancholy,
   But be happy, gay, and jolly.—Away, away, &c.
   I love my Desdemona, away, away,
   And hand in hand we'll take a stand,
   To spend Brabantio's money.—Away, away, &c.

DES. For you I've run away from pap,
   But I don't care a snap for that.—Away, away, &c.
   I love you and you love me,
   And all our lives we'll merry be.—Away, away, &c.
   With you I'll sport my figure, away, away—
   I'll love you dearly all my life,
   Although you are a nigger.—Away, away, &c.

   (*Enter* IAGO, L.)

IAG. Go in my darlin's—go it while you're young—
   Upon my sowl, you'll sing a different song
   Before the day is out—or I'm no sinner—
   Och! the darlins!

OTH. Now, love, get the dinner—*(exit* DES., R.)
   The wedding guests each moment may arrive;
   Why, here's Iago, now, as I'm alive!

IAG. You're right, ould stock—I'll always be in time—
   But dinner isn't all I've come for now;
   Her father's coming, and there'll be a row.
   He'll have her back!

OTH. Pshaw! let him do his worst—
   I've married her—he must undo that first.

IAG.   He'll undo you, for loud he swore and said
　　　 That when he met you, he would smash your head.
　　　 He's got Roderigo with him, too, a fellow—
　　　 Who all the time swears vengeance on Othello.
OTH.   Why, what's Roderigo got to do with me?
IAG.   He wanted Desdemona, don't you see?
OTH.   No, no! *(noise outside)*
IAG.   What's that? Upon my sowl there coming—
　　　 They'll murder both of us—come, let's be running.
OTH.   No, sir! I'll stand my ground and nothing shorter—

(Enter BRABANTIO *and* RODERIGO, L.)

OTH.   How are you, dad?
BRA.   You villain, vere's mine daughter?
OTH.   If for my wife—your daughter—you are looking,
　　　 You'll find her in the kitchen, busy cooking.
BRA.   Vat's dat you say! mine daughter is your wife?
　　　 You damn black rascal, I will have your life;
　　　 Go in, Roderigo, strike wid all your might.
IAG.   Whoo! murder! thieves! Here's a jolly fight. *(fight,*
　　　 and close of scene)

SCENE III.—*Chamber.* DESDEMONA *and* CASSIO *discovered playing cards.*

CAS.   By gosh, I'm euchered! Isn't it a shame?
　　　 I'm so unlucky, I can't win a game.
　　　 Do what I will, I'm always getting stuck—
DES.   Try again, you'll perhaps have better luck;
　　　 Here comes Othello—stop and play with him—
CAS.   No, if I should play all day, I'd never win. *(going)*

(Enter OTHELLO *and* IAGO.)

OTH.   *(to* IAGO.) What for you wink your eye?
DES.   Well, call again—*(exit,* CASSIO, R.)
　　　 (To IAGO) Why, what's the matter with you—say?
　　　 (To OTHELLO) My dear, why did you stay so long away?
　　　 I'm lonely if you're not by my side;
　　　 If Cassio had not called, I should have cried.

OTH. Well, well, go in—I'll be with you soon;
DES. He's crazy, sure—I wonder how's the moon?
      At your desire I'll go. I know my duty—*(exit,* R.*)*
IAG. Indeed you do. By jabers, you're a beauty!
OTH. What's that you say?
IAG. Say? Nothing!—but I think——
OTH. "Nothing!—but I think!" What do you think?
      You must mean something?—
IAG. Well, it's funny!
      That Cassio should be here with Desdemona
      So nate and cozy—as she says, all day,
      And when he sees you coming, sneak away.
OTH. I never thought of that. It does look queer—
      What do you suppose he wanted here?
IAG. That's not for me to say;—but "I don't want you,"
      That's plain enough to any blind man's view.
OTH. Do you think he comes in secret to my wife?
IAG. I don't think anything—but, 'pon my life,
      It looks suspicious when he leaves the room
      All of a sudden, when he sees you come.
OTH. I'll ask my wife about it. *(going)*
IAG. *(stops him).* Don't do that!
OTH. What for, I'd like to know?
IAG. She'd smell a rat!
      Women are mighty sharp, and let her find
      That to her game you're not exactly blind—
      She'd change her game and go on some other course
      That'll be no better and perhaps a little worse.
OTH. What must I do, then?
IAG. Nothing, now, but watch 'em—
      And so will I—between us both, we'll catch 'em.
      That she's doing wrong I don't pretend to say;
      But one small thing I noticed here to-day,
      Which raises in my mind a kind of doubt,
      That all—all things isn't right.
OTH. Well, spit it out!
IAG. Last week a handkerchief you gave your wife—
OTH. Well?

This Grotesque Essence

IAG.   Didn't she swear to keep it all her life?

OTH.   She did.

IAG.   Well, Cassio's got it.

OTH.   He has?

IAG.   I saw him *(imitates wiping nose)* then put it in his pocket.

OTH.   The devil!

IAG.   No, the handkerchief you gave her.

OTH.   If this be true, the devil himself shan't save her
From my revenge.

IAG.   Well, mind what you're about,
And don't say anything till you find more out.
Now I must leave you; but I'll soon be back—*(aside)*
    I've given that nigger a fine nut to crack.
    (exit, L.*)*

OTHELLO *sings.—Air,* "Canaan"
    Oh, if it was her plan, for to have another man,
        I wish I hadn't known a bit about it—
    For a man's dat's rob'd, dey say, and don't miss what's took away,
        Can very easy get along without it.
           Ho, ho, ho! it's wrong to use me so;
        I never gave her cause to be complaining—
    I'se done everything I could, day and night to do her good,
        But I'll send her to the happy land of Canaan.
    Oh, farewell the tranquil mind, since my Desde's proved unkind,
        Content my heart no more will be regainin';
    Farewell the fife and drum, Othello's occupation gone;
        And I'm going to the happy land of Canaan.
        (chorus and dance)

    (Enter DESDEMONA, R.*)*

DES.   Ha, ha, ha! well now that's funny!
Othello, dear what makes you——

OTH.   Desdemona!
But no, I'll have more proof before I tell her
I've found out that she loves another fellar;
and when I do find out, I'll make a crash, O!
I'll give particular fits to her and Cassio.

DES.   Good gracious! What's the matter? Ain't you well?

OTH.　Aye, well enough; but wish I'd been in hell
　　　Before I married. Then I'd have no woes—
　　　Your handkerchief—I want to blow my nose.
DES.　Here it is—
OTH.　Not that—the other—
　　　The one I told you I got from my mother.
DES.　I haven't it about me—
OTH.　Ah, is it so?
　　　Iago told the truth. *(aside)* Where is it, say?
　　　If you do lose it, lend, or give away,
　　　You never more will know a lucky day.
DES.　Oh! goodness, gracious! What is it you mean?
OTH.　My mother got it from a gipsy queen.
　　　It's full of charms, and so you'd better mind it—
　　　I want it quickly, too—so go and find it.
DES.　It can't be lost—I had it here to-day—
　　　But come to dinner, now—
OTH.　Away! *(gives slap, and exits* R.)

(Enter IAGO, L. *Sings.—Air, "Ireland the Place Is.")*

　　　Now, Miss Desdemona, I've got you my honey,
　　　　　'Twixt you and the nagur I've raised a fine strife,
　　　An' it is my intent, now, to make you repent, now,
　　　　　The way that you left me to become his wife;
　　　Be gob, it's curious, to see him so furious,
　　　　　And her standin' by him just ready to cry;
　　　And all the explainin' he gives of his manin',
　　　　　Is to up fist and give her a dab in the eye.
　　　　　(dances)

(Enter OTHELLO, R., *and knocks him down with whitewash brush.)*

IAG.　You damned black nagur, what are you about?
OTH.　I want to know the truth. Come, spit it out.
IAG.　The truth of what?
OTH.　That Desde is no good.
　　　I feel like tearin' things; Oh, blood! Iago, blood!
　　　I'll have some proof—

IAG. How will you get it, say?
　　　Would you go sneaking round from day to day
　　　To catch 'em in the act?
OTH. Damnation, no!
IAG. Oh, they're too wide awake for that, and so
　　　To catch 'em in the act they'll leave small chances—
　　　The only proof you'll get is circumstances.
OTH. Well tell me what it is you know about her—
IAG. Listen, and I'll tell you why I doubt her.
　　　Cassio, the other night, got on a spree,
　　　And being drunk, I took him home with me.
　　　Now, he's one of those men that down will lay,
　　　And in his sleep tell what he does all day;
　　　I listened to him—and here's what he said—
　　　Sweet Desdemona, how could you e'er wed
　　　　　That dirty beast, Othello.
　　　Then he'd hug me round the neck and cry,
　　　Oh, damn that nagur, don't you wish he'd die?
OTH. I'll tear her all to pieces.
IAG. Serve her right—
　　　And I'll cook Mr. Cassio's goose to-night.
OTH. And I'll cook hers. Here all remorse I quit—
IAG. You'll not forgive her?
OTH. No, I'll let her rip!

SCENE IV.

(Enter DESDEMONA, R. *Undresses herself and goes to bed. She has a black eye.)*

DES. I really think Othello must be mad;
　　　That was the hardest thump I ever had.
　　　Just one day married, and to cut this figure—
　　　But I'll have satisfaction on that nigger
　　　As sure as my name's Desde. Oh, my head,
　　　It aches like fury, so I'll go to bed. *(business.*
　　　　lies down and snores)

(Enter OTHELLO, L., *with lighted candle in bottle.)*

OTH.   Oh, there she is, I've got her now all right;
        But first and foremost I'll put out the light.
        How beautiful she looks—and yet I'll kill her—
        Not shed her blood—but choke her wid dis pillow.
        She wakes—

DES.   You villain! do you see my eye?

OTH.   Hush, Desdemona, you're about to die.

DES.   About to die! What do you mean by that? *(noise of cat)*

OTH.   List' to the squalling of that old tom cat.

DES.   Do you mean to kill me?

OTH.   Aye! dead as that old hat.

DES.   I won't die.

OTH.   Yes, you will.

DES.   I say I won't; and you can't kill me—

OTH.   Damn me, if I don't.

        (business with pillow, &c.)

THE END

The Ticket-Taker;
or, the Masquerade Ball

Griffin and Christy's *The Ticket-Taker* is an example of the processional format in afterpieces. In such pieces a simple setting was provided with a plot structure that allowed several performers (or as in this case one performer in several roles) to parade before the audience. The entertainment derived primarily from the quick succession of specialty acts or comic bits which made up the procession. This format was an extremely efficient way for troupes to work all performers into the finale.

Processions frequently consisted of very brief song or dance numbers, or a succession of various clown types (a variation on the mixed racial and ethnic figures seen in Griffin's *Othello*). Intelligence offices, hotel lobbies, and boarding houses were standard settings for such pieces. Common too were the processions which, like *The Ticket-Taker*, presented brief burlesque allusions to classic stage fare. Such processions echoed a common nineteenth-century theatrical tradition. Traveling troupes, which were limited in cast size, and amateur groups often presented shows which provided excerpts from several plays rather than a full rendering of a single piece. Shakespeare was frequently treated this way, a typical evening's production consisting of a few colorful tableaux, a soliloquy or two, and selected scenes of a sensational or sentimental nature such as the witches' scenes in

Macbeth or the balcony scene from *Romeo and Juliet*. The "Shakespearean Revival" by the Duke and Dauphin described in Chapters 21 and 22 of Mark Twain's *Adventures of Huckleberry Finn* is an accurate representation of such shows. A processional burlesque, like *The Ticket-Taker*, was particularly appropriate for audiences who could swallow their Shakespeare in such a piece-meal fashion.

The partial cast list printed with the following text is for a performance at New York's Fifth Avenue Opera House in 1866 or 1867. The first performance of an earlier version of the piece, however, occurred on January 14, 1856, when Christy and Griffin played with Wood's Minstrels at 444 Broadway. The following text is reprinted from the acting edition published by Clinton T. De Witt.

THE TICKET-TAKER;
OR,
THE MASQUERADE BALL.
An Ethiopian Farce,
In One Scene.
Arranged By G. W. GRIFFIN.
As Performed By
Griffin & Christy's Minstrels, New York.

CAST OF CHARACTERS

MANAGER (proprietor of a ball-room) . . . . . Mr. Frank Leslie
PREVIOUS DIFFICULTIES (comic character engaged as doorkeeper) . . Mr. George Christy

MASQUERADERS

CITIZEN . . . . _____
MACBETH . . . . Mr. G. W. H. Griffin

This Grotesque Essence

BANJO PERFORMER	———
RICHARD	Mr. G. W. H. Griffin
MAN IN BASKET HORSE	———
MOSE	———
BOGUS MOSE	———
HAMLET	Mr. G. W. H. Griffin
IRISH WOMAN	———

SCENE.—*A hall with set door* L. 2E., *leading to ball-room. Table and two chairs*, L.

(Enter MANAGER, L. 1E.*)*

MANAGER.   There now, everything is ready for the ball, I believe, except a good trusty doorkeeper, and him I must secure right away.

(Enter PREVIOUS DIFFICULTIES, R.*)*

PREVIOUS.   Good-morning, sir. I heard you wanted somebody to work around the hall, sweep out, pick up pocket-books, etc.

MAN.   You are not rightly informed, sir. I wish to engage an honest person to tend the door this evening, take tickets, etc., and if you like I will engage you for that purpose. Can you read?

PRE.   Yes, sir.

MAN.   Very good, sir. All you will have to do will be to sit at the door, and demand of each person who makes his appearance a ticket, five dollars, or the equivalent.

PRE.   All right, sir. I'll do it.

MAN.   Then take your seat at the door, and if you are faithful I'll give you five dollars for your services. *(gives him long sword)* Here, take this sword to defend yourself with in case you should get in trouble. Now, I expect there will be a lot of people here from the theatre, and they'll try every way to get in for nothing, so you must look out for them.

PRE.   I'll look out for them; there sha'n't anybody get by me without a ticket, five dollars, or the 'quivalent. *(Exit* MANAGER, L. 1E. PRE. *sits at table.)* Well, here I is got a good job, nothing to do but take tickets, and get five big dollars for it. *(looks* R.*)* Hilloa! here comes one of the fellers disguised as a gentleman.

(Enter CITIZEN R. 1E. *Goes toward door.)*

The Ticket-Taker; or, The Masquerade Ball

PRE. *(gets up and stops him entering).*   Here, sir; where you going?

CITIZEN.   I'm going into the ball.

PRE.   Where's your ticket?

CIT.   I don't need a ticket, sir. I belong to the *Press*.

PRE.   Well, you can't *press* in here. I want your ticket, five dollars, or the 'quivalent; that's what the man said.

CIT.   Well, sir. I believe I have got a ticket somewhere. *(looks all over himself, examines pockets, etc. finally pulls out enormous ticket from under his coat, "Admit One," offers it)* There, sir, can I pass on that?

PRE.   Yes, sir, you can pass. I sha'n't call you on this hand. *(CITIZEN goes into the ball)* I declare he's a nice gentleman. I wonder if they'll all treat me as civil as he did? *(looks R.)* Hilloa' here comes a fellow looks like one of them actor fellers, all dressed up like Macbeth.

(Enter MACBETH. Music—"Quick March.")

MACBETH.   So foul and fair a day I have not seen. How far is it called to Fox's?[1]

(Enter THREE WITCHES from different entrances, R. They wear long beards and carry long sticks. They come on suddenly and point at MACBETH.)

MAC.   What are these so withered and so wild in their attire?

PRE.   Three dead-heads,[2] I guess.

MAC.   That look not like the inhabitants of earth, and yet are on it. Live you, or are you aught that man may question? *(WITCHES put forefingers to their lips.)* You seem to understand me, by each at once her chappy finger laying upon her skinny lips. You should be women, and yet your beards forbid me to interpret that you are so. Speak! I charge you!

PRE.   That's right, charge them five dollars.

1ST WITCH.   Oh!

2ND WITCH.   No!

3D WITCH.   Go!

1ST WITCH.   No money here!

2ND WITCH.   For lager beer!

1   New York's famous Old Bowery Theatre was managed by G. L. Fox during the 1860s. Hence, it was often referred to as Fox's.
2   In theatrical parlance, a deadhead is a person admitted without charge to a show in order to fill an audience.

3D WITCH.   No ball, I fear!

PRE.   Yes, and they can't come here! *(*WITCHES *start mysteriously around the stage, followed by* MACBETH. *When they reach the door,* MACBETH *exclaims,* "Vanish!" *They all go into the ball, leaving* MACBETH *outside looking after them through open door.)*

PRE.   Say! here, do you pay for them goblins?

MAC.   Avaunt, and quit my sight! let the earth hide thee; thy bones are marrowless, thy blood is cold; thou hast no speculation in those eyes that thou dost glare with.

PRE. *(very much frightened).*   You can go right in, Mr. Mac., I don't want any ticket.

MAC.   What man dare, I dare! Approach thou like the rugged Russian bear, the armed rhinoceros, or the hyrcan tiger; take any shape but that, and my firm nerves will never tremble; or be alive again, and dare me to the desert with thy sword—if trembling I exhibit, then protest me the baby of a girl. Hence, horrible shadow, unreal mockery, hence! hence! hence! *(drives* PREVIOUS *to* R., *and rushes into the ball)*

PRE.   There he goes into the ball, and I didn't get any ticket. *(goes to table)* That makes four gone in without tickets. *(looks at large ticket, holds it up)* I wonder if this isn't a family ticket? I guess it is—I know how to fix it. *(tears four small pieces off large ticket, and puts them on table)* There, now it's all right; but I'd like to see somebody else get in without a ticket. *(looks* R.*)* Here comes a musician.

*(*BANJO PLAYER *comes in, playing a tune, and singing.)*

BANJO.   Here I go right down to the ball-er-um—down to the ball-er-um—down to the ball-er-um——

PRE. *(stopping him).*   No, you don't go down to the ball-er-um—down to the ball-er-um, without you got a tick-er-um. *(They have some business here; finally* BANJO *tells him if he stands up in a chair, he can make him come down before he tells him three times. They make the bet.* PREVIOUS *gets up in a chair.)*

BAN.   Get down.

PRE.   I sha'n't do it!

BAN.   Get down out of that chair.

PRE.   I tell you I sha'n't do it!

BAN.   That's twice, ain't it?

The Ticket-Taker; or, The Masquerade Ball

PRE.   Yes-sir-um!

BAN.   Well, now, you stay up there till I tell you three times! *(Sings, "Here I go," etc., exits into ball.* PREVIOUS, *finding he is sold, gets down, goes to table and tears off another ticket.)*

PRE.   *(takes sword from table).*   Now, I'd like to see any one else get in. Now I'm getting mad. *(flourish of trumpets and roll of drum)*

(Enter RICHARD.*)*

RICHARD.   Methinks there are six Richmonds in the field; five have I already slain instead of him. A horse! a horse! my kingdom for a horse!

(Enter MANAGER, *in a basket horse.)*

MAN.   My lord, here stands a swift donkey; time, 2.40. *(They rush* PREVIOUS *around the stage, then go into ball.)*

PRE.   There goes another feller in, and a horse. *(goes to table, tears ticket for* RICHARD, *and a very large one for the horse)* Now, I *am* getting mad. I'd like to see another one get in, that's all.

(Enter MOSE, *smoking cigar. Goes toward door and is stopped by* PREVIOUS DIFFICULTIES.*)*

PRE.   Where are you going?

MOSE.   I'm going into the ball!

PRE.   Where's your ticket?

MOSE.   I don't want any ticket, and I'm going *in!*

PRE.   What are you going in on?

MOSE *(bends his right arm, and points to muscle).*   I'm going in on this!
      *(*PREVIOUS *feels his arm and seems satisfied.)*

PRE.   You can go in, Mr. Moses. *(He goes in.)*

(Enter BOGUS MOSE.*)*

PRE.   Where are you going?

BOGUS.   I'm going into the ball.

PRE.   Give us your ticket.

BOG.   I don't want any ticket. *(showing very small arm)* I'm going in on this. *(*PREVIOUS *feels arm, thinks he is enough for him, takes him by the neck and kicks him out, then struts around very brave. Slow music, and then)*

83

This Grotesque Essence

(Enter HAMLET.*)*

PRE. Hilloa! that fellow looks like a broken-down actor.

HAMLET. To be, or not to be—that's the question. Whether it were better to suffer the slings and juleps to go by discarded, or to take up arms against the outrageous Excise Law,[3] and find myself ten dollars out in the jail; to drink——

PRE. No, thank you; I can't leave the door.

HAM. To get drunk——

PRE. That's rough——

HAM. Perchance to sleep——

PRE. That's snoozy——

HAM. Ay! there's the rub——

PRE. Yes, but you can't play the rub on me. I want your ticket.

HAM. *(takes him down front, and puts hand on* PREVIOUS's *head).* Hush! methinks I scent the morning air.

PRE. That ain't hair, that's wool. Say, Gimblet, ain't you getting hungry? Come, sit down and get something to eat. *(They both sit at table and begin to eat chicken or pig's feet, or something of that kind;* HAMLET *eating as though he was half starved.)* You ain't going in the ball without a ticket, are you, Gimblet?

HAM. Oh, no!

PRE. I'd like to see anybody else get in there without a ticket.

(Just at this point enter IRISH WOMAN *with basket on her arm. She makes an awful fuss and wants to go into the ball to get her husband home.* PREVIOUS *tells her he ain't in there. She gets angry and beats him with basket. In the meantime* HAMLET *has gone into the ball.* IRISH WOMAN *rushes in, leaving* PREVIOUS *sprawling on the stage. After awhile he gets up very angry, opens the door to ball-room.)*

PRE. Here, turn them all out; they haven't given me any tickets. Break up the ball! break up the ball!

(Scene changes to a wood or garden, and everybody rushes out. Music strikes up, and all join in Plantation Dance.)

---

3 A law passed by the New York City legislature in April of 1866 which attempted to regulate all liquor distribution in the city through licensing. For a fuller discussion of the controversial law see the preface to "Shylock."

Thomas Dartmouth "Daddy" Rice, *ca.* 1830. Rice, known as the father of American minstrelsy, developed blackface song and dance routines while touring the Ohio River valley in the late 1820s. He is credited with having established the character of Jim Crow, the archetypal minstrel clown; and his Ethiopian operas, first performed on variety bills in the 1830s, were the precursors of the minstrel show.

Charlie White, one of the most influential personalities in the history of minstrelsy, founded the Kitchen Minstrels in 1844—one of the first professional troupes to spread the art. During a career that lasted over four decades he earned a widespread reputation as a composer, writer, performer, and producer. At one time White admitted to having composed forty of the best "Negro" hits of all time.

A bone player in swallow-tail coat and fancy dress shirt, *ca.* 1860. The attire shown here is typical of the costuming used for the minstrel show's first part.

George Christy, *ca*. 1860. Born George Harrington, Christy "borrowed" his stage name from E. Byron Christy, founder of the original Christy Minstrels. Christy was considered an excellent mimic and comedian, and was perhaps most widely known as one of the best of the female impersonators. Depending upon which historian one reads, he is also given credit for having established the "Negro Wench" as a stock clown figure.

Dan Bryant, 1863. A superb dancer, Bryant broke into minstrelsy after achieving fame as an Irish comic. In the 1860s Bryant's Minstrels toured worldwide and set box office records that were not broken until minstrelsy evolved into stage spectacles in the 1880s.

G. W. H. Griffin, one of the better writers to emerge during minstrelsy's heyday, began working with George Christy in the 1850s and ended his career in vaudeville.

Rollin Howard (left) and Griffin, 1855. Howard's costume is indicative of the overblown elegance with which wench characters were presented in the afterpieces.

S. C. Campbell, 1861. Though many minstrel performers worked in other forms of popular theater, Campbell was one of only a small handful to make it on the formal stage. He had several remarkable years working with Griffin and Christy but is best known in theater histories for his highly praised work in grand opera.

DAN COLLYER

Aimé Dupont · 574 FIFTH AVENUE · NEW YORK ·

Dan Collyer, typical of the second generation stars, had moderate success in the late 1870s and 1880s, which he supplemented by transcribing afterpieces for the DeWitt Publishing Company, one of the largest mail order firms. Collyer's outfit here is characteristic of the spirit of exaggeration which pervaded minstrelsy's visual display.

Frank Dumont, one of the most prolific talents in minstrelsy's second generation, worked as a performer, composer, author, director, producer, and stage technician. In addition to hundreds of minstrel songs and afterpieces, he wrote melodrama, comedy, and farce for the legitimate stage as well as songs, jokes, and sketches for vaudeville.

Addison Ryman, who wrote for New York's prestigious San Francisco Minstrels during the 1870s. Ryman is best known for his spirited political satires such as *Julius the Snoozer*, which presents a fanciful account of the demise of Boss Tweed.

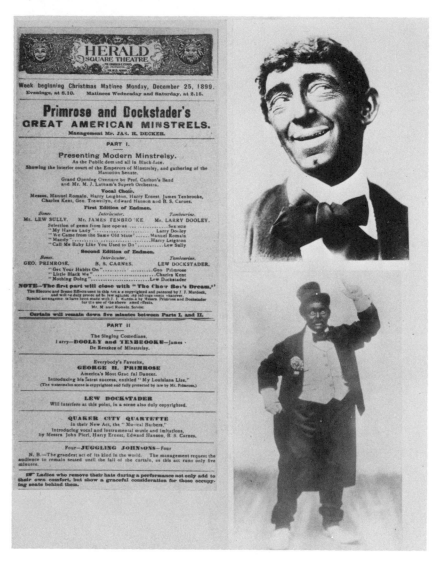

A program for Primrose and Dockstader's Minstrels, 1899. Unlike many troupes at the end of the century, Primrose and Dockstader's retained the original program format from the earliest years of the art. Lew Dockstader (below) was generally regarded as the most popular minstrel of his period, roughly on a par with such early stars as Daddy Rice, Dan Bryant, and George Christy.

Hamlet the Dainty

As early as 1843 *Hamlet* was being presented on the New York stage as a comic operetta in what was advertised as a "tragic-comico-illegitimate style." The first recorded performance of the burlesque in blackface occurred during the 1863/64 season when Wood's Minstrels added it to their bill. Minstrel versions proliferated soon after, one of the more notable of which is the following Griffin and Christy version which was first performed on June 18, 1866, at the Fifth Avenue Opera House in New York. The timing of this production was significant, for it occurred as the campaigns for the congressional election were getting under way. Throughout the country the 1866 election involved a fairly clear-cut choice between the conciliatory policies of the Copperhead Democrats and the harsh reform tactics of the Radical Republicans. At that time New York City was a center of conciliatory feelings toward the South. Just two years earlier, in a presidential election in which he carried all but three states, Lincoln lost the popular vote in New York City by a margin of more than two to one. In 1866 New York and Brooklyn sent Democrats to Congress while most of the rest of the nation did not. This perhaps explains why Griffin interjected sober political overtones in his otherwise ludicrous piece by associating the original play's revenge motif with the spectre of the defeated South. The following text is reprinted from the acting edition published by the Happy Hours Company.

HAMLET
THE DAINTY,
An Ethiopian Burlesque
On
SHAKESPEARE'S HAMLET.
Performed By
Griffin and Christy's Minstrels.
By G. W. H. GRIFFIN, ESQ.

CHARACTERS
HAMLET
HORATIO
MARCELLUS
OSRICK
LAERTES
KING
QUEEN
And members of the court (or alley)

SCENE I.—*A street.*

(*Enter* HAMLET, HORATIO, *and* MARCELLUS, L. 2E. HAMLET *is dressed in black tights, with tight fitting swallow-tailed dress coat, buttoned tight up to the neck, large black neck stock, a white hat with narrow brim, and black weed on it. The other characters are dressed in any comical wardrobe they may choose.*)

HAM.   The air bites shrewdly—it is very cold.

HOR.   I never saw a darkly half so bold.

86

Hamlet the Dainty

HAM. What is't o'clock?

HOR. *(draws out very large tin watch)*. Half past eleven, at most. *(winds up his watch)*

MAR. *(drawing out large round turnip)*. My watch says twelve. *(Clock strikes twelve.)*

HAM. Dry up! here comes the ghost.

(Enter GHOST, *dressed in shabby, ragged uniform, his face perfectly white with flour; he is smoking a long segar, and reading a newspaper.* HORATIO *and* MARCELLUS *are very much frightened. They fall against each other, then on the stage rolling over and doing all sorts of comic business.)*

HAM. He's from the South! Oh grace defend us!
Prythee! no more such frightful specters send us!
Be thou blacked up, or goblin damned!
Be thou with whiskey puffed, or old cheese cram'd!
Be thy intents indifferent, good or bad,
I'll speak to thee, thou look'st so like my dad—
In a trim box, so snugly was't thou lain,
Say! what the deuce e'er brought you out again?
I like a joke myself—but 'tis not right,
To come and frighten us to death at night.
Say, why is this, will you the reason tell us?
Why come to frighten me, Horatio and Marcellus?

*(*GHOST *puts his finger on his nose, then motions* HAMLET *to follow him.)*

HOR. He wants to speak a word with you alone!

HAM. Does he? Here goes then! Now, old pap, lead on!

MAR. You shall not go! *(They take hold of him.)*

HOR. Perhaps he means to kill you!

HAM. You'd better hold your jaw—be quiet, will you?

HOR. No, sweetness, you shall not go.

HAM. My fate cries out and gives me pluck—so mind
What you're about—(GHOST *motions him)*—Still am I called.
Paws off! The time does fly!
Let go your hold—or else I'll black your eye.
Hop off, I say! *(breaks from them. To* GHOST) Lead
on! I closely follow.

This Grotesque Essence

(to HOR. *and* MAR.*)* Wait here!
If I want you boys, I'll holler. *(exit* GHOST *and* HAM
R., HOR. *and* MAR. L.*)*

SCENE II.—*A wood.*

(Enter GHOST *and* HAMLET, R.*)*

HAM.   Look here, Mr. Ghost, this is played out—I'll go no further!
GHOST.   You had better.
HAM.   No!
GHOST.   Then hold your tongue and hear what I declare—
         I'm pressed for time—we keep good hours down there.
         Soon I must go and get an oyster roast;
         Then list; oh, list!
HAM.   Alas, poor ghost!
GHOST.   I am thy father's ghost,
         Doomed for a certain time to walk the night.
         I could such a dismal tale unfold—
HAM.   I knew he had a tale. Oh, Lord!
GHOST.   As would make your precious blood run cold.

         One afternoon, as was my use,
         I went to a gin mill to take a snooze—
         When your uncle into my mouth did pour
         A gallon of brandy smash, or more.

         Torment your uncle, for my sake—
         Let him never have a drink, asleep or awake.
         Your mother's plague, let her conscience be,
         Adieu! adieu! remember me! *(vanishes)*

         (Enter HORATIO *and* MARCELLUS, *running.)*

MAR.   How is't, my lord? What said the ghost?
HAM.   You'll blab.
MAR.   Not I!
HOR.   I'm silent as a post.
HAM.   He said I could not drink—then sneaked away—
HOR.   He thought, my lord, you had no stamps[1] to pay—
         That's all. He might have stayed then, in his bed—

1 Paper money issued during the Civil War to replace coin.

88

HAM. That's as he pleases—he comes in *dead head*.
   Here! I've a word to say before you go—
   Never make known what you've seen and know.
HOR. Not I!
MAR. Nor I!
HAM. Swear!
GHOST. Make 'em swear—that's right—
H *and* M. We will not tell the leastest little mite.
HAM. Dry up, secesh.[2] It's such chilling weather,
   Suppose we go and take a drink together.
   The world's gone mad—oh! cursed fate, that I
   Should live to see a ghost that cannot die. *(exit)*

SCENE III.—*Interior of palace—throne, chairs, &c.*

(Enter HAMLET *and* HORATIO.*)*

HAM. Horatio, I've not seen such scenes,
   Since I was in Boston eating pork and beans.

(Enter OSRICK, *dressed extravagantly, as a fop.)*

OS. *(to* HAMLET.*)* His majesty has made a match for you
   To spar with young Laertes, a rummy bruiser—
   And betted him the contents of his purse
   That you—young Hamlet—that you'll bust his crust.
   Laertes is quite ready to set to;
   They're all assembled, and but wait for you.
HAM. I'll fight him, sir. I ne'er felt bolder—
HOR. I'll be your second.
OS. And I'll be bottle holder. *(flourish of trumpets & drums)*

(Enter KING, QUEEN, LAERTES, *and others, and take seats to witness the contest.)*

KING. To put and end to all this muss and noise,
   (to H. *and* L.*)* Shake hands, and make it up, my jolly boys.
   (They shake hands and the gloves are brought in.)
   If in the two first rounds, Hamlet hits most blows,
   Or 'scape the third without a bloody nose—

2 Secessionist.

89

Let all the guns we've got make the discovery,
(drum)
The King shall drink to Hamlet's quick recovery.
(They put on gloves and make a comical fight.)
HAM.   A hit!
LAERT.   No hit!
OS.   An 'it. I'll bet a dollar.
HAM.   A hit or not, 'twas something made him holler!
KING.   Give me the beer. *(to* HAM*)* This Stoughton[3] is for you.
(pours poison)
Hamlet, your health—*(pretends to drink)*—You'd
better drink some too.
HAM.   Let's have this round—when I want drink I'll ask it.
I had him then, right in the bread basket.
QUEEN.   Hamlet, your health—*(drinks)*—ha! this is famous stingo!
KING.   Don't drink!
QUEEN.   I have!
KING.   The poisoned cup, by jingo!
HAM.   Another hit, Laertes, in the stomach. *(*LAERTES *down)*
LAER.   Then it's below the belt, you great big lummox.
*(*QUEEN *screams and faints.)*
OS.   Look to the queen! *(to* LAER.*)* How is't my lord?
LAER.   I'm dished! I'm whipped as neatly as I could have wished.
HAM.   How does the queen?
KING.   To see your bloody noses, her stomach slightly indisposes.
QUEEN.   No, no! I'm poisoned! Your old uncle, here,
Has mixed a deadly poison with the beer.
It's now too late—I took too many swigs—
He put the poison in, to kill off all you nigs.
(dies)

(They all attack the KING *with stuffed clubs, brooms, &c.; while they are all fighting* GHOST *appears; they all fall back upon the stage, and tremble with fright. Curtain.)*

THE END

---

3   "Dr. Stoughton's Bitters" was a widely used household remedy during the nineteenth century.

Shylock

Few afterpieces achieved the comic intensity that can be seen in Griffin's version of the following standard minstrel burlesque. There are song parodies, vigorous dance numbers, a racial and ethnic mix in the characters, and a blanket-toss revel at the end. But what dominates the piece is the way Griffin pushed the art of comic punning to its absolute limit. Some of Griffin's puns are truly witty, but most force together the barest echoes of sound and sense in a way that causes the language of the piece to hover on the edge of absurdity. The humor stems less from the individual bad puns than from their massive cumulative effect. At various points the frequency of the puns and their heavy emphasis become pacing devices for the dialogue and create a counterpoint rhythm to that of the rhymes in the couplets.

Though precise performance information is unavailable, *Shylock* was certainly presented in the spring of 1867, as is indicated by the numerous satirical references in the piece. During that time a political feud broke out between John A. Kennedy, the police superintendent for New York City, and police magistrate Michael Connolly. The feud was a direct result of the controversial excise law passed less than a year before by the city legislature. The law, aimed at regulating liquor distribution in the city, was highly unpopular primarily because of the righteously high-toned rhetoric of moral reform and suppression of vice used by the legislature to mask the law's real purpose, which was economic. Besides establishing uniform hours for retail operations, the law required all retailers to obtain city licenses. The ensuing revenue was used to finance the city police force; thus, vigorous enforcement of the law was assured. In February of 1867 Kennedy issued an order forbidding all police officers to take accused persons before magistrate Connolly. Connolly was a former tavern owner and had angered the superintendent, it seems, by sending two policemen to prison for over-zealously enforcing the excise law. As a result of his order Kennedy was sued for slander by Connolly and was subsequently called before a city review board, where he had a great deal of difficulty justifying himself. That the affair made its way into the entertainment of the period attests to the sensational nature of the controversy.

The following text is reprinted from the acting edition published by the Happy Hours Company.

SHYLOCK,
A Burlesque,
As Performed By
GRIFFIN & CHRISTY'S MINSTRELS.
Arranged By
G. W. H. GRIFFIN.

CAST OF CHARACTERS

SHYLOCK *(dealer in old clothes)* . . . . . . Mr. G. W. H. Griffin
DOOK . . . . Mr. Geo. Christy
ANTONIO . . . . Mr. Geo. Percival
BASSANIO . . . . Mr. R. Hughes
LORENZO . . . . Mr. Otto Burbank
PORTIA . . . . Mr. Fred Abbott
JESSICA . . . . Mr. W. W. Hodgkin

Shylock

SCENE I.—*The Rialto in Chatham street.*[1]—*Two hooked-nose gentlemen discovered* R., *walking up and down before a clothing-store. Enter* SHYLOCK, L.U.E., *to the air of "Old Clo', Old Clo',"from the orchestra.*

SHYLOCK. Aha! my frients; how's pishness dis cold day?
I've brought you vun pair pants, and lettle veskit, eh!

FIRST HOOKED-NOSE GENT.
Ah! Shylock, you are faulty with the rest,
You mustn't call it "veskit," call it "west!"

SECOND DITTO.
And "vun pair pants," too, how it sounds,
Whoever saw a *clown* in pantaloons?
You should say *trousers*, if you wish, my pet,
To rouse us from a breach of etiquette.

(band strikes up air from "Faust")
SHYLOCK *(advancing)*.
Sirs, I will not put up with it,
Sirs, I will not put up with it,
Sirs, I will not put up with it,
And if you don't shut up pretty quick,
I shall give you your notice to quit.

HOOKED-NOSE GENTS *(repeat)*.
And if we don't shut up pretty quick,
He'll give us our notice to quit.
(They all break out in a perspiration.)

(Enter ANTONIO, *in haste.—He advances toward* SHYLOCK.*)*

ANTONIO. Oh. she-ylock! dearest, best of men,
Oh, gentle Jew, pray lend me two pun ten?
To be without a cent is deep disgrace.
At Crooks' I cannot even "run my face."
At Simpson's,[2] to-day, I left my "ticker."

---

1 During the 1860s New York's notorious Chatham Street was teeming with brothels, at that time called concert saloons. Many tavern owners whose businesses were on Chatham Street were denied liquor licenses by the excise board simply because of their addresses.
2 Crooks' and Simpson's were two of the numerous Chatham Street concert saloons. Crooks' was one of the few Chatham Street operations granted a license by the excise board.

This Grotesque Essence

SHYLOCK. That's *watch* 'ure up to! all for liquor!
ANTONIO. Not so, my friend; this printed ticket means
        I popped my watch to get some pork and beans:
SHYLOCK. Faugh! how nasty *pork* must be!
ANTONIO. *Porquoi*? But, *bein's*, you say so, why, it be,
        But still it is a change; these hotels make
        A dinner out a *martyr* to the *stake*;
        Potato, too, as hard as any wood—
        Peut-etre, they think that, so they do you good;
SHYLOCK. You asked for cash, but you'll not get *assent* from me,
ANTONIO. Be *decent*. Jew! if you *dissent*,
        Why take my bond at ten per cent;
        So now, good Shylock, how about the cash?
        To have it I'm *itching*.
SHYLOCK.   Don't be rash!
        My landlord says he's bound to raise my rent,
        And if I lend it, why it's shent-per-shent!
ANTONIO. Oh, hang the terms, the money have I *must*,
        I'm bound to-night to spend it on a *bust*,
        Sculptures,[3] you see, induce my taste to roam,
        I'll pay you, Shylock, when my ship comes home.

(Enter BASSANIO.—*He advances to* SHYLOCK *and* ANTONIO.*)*

BASSANIO. Say, Tony! have yer raised the wind?
        Who's that old Bluebeard—how he grinned!
ANTONIO. And well he may, he's made a precious haul,
SHYLOCK *(aside).*
        Oh, how these *squalid* Christians talk of gold—
        In *my* opinion Tony's "badly sold!"
        If at the time he doesn't come and pay—
        I'll cut his *liver out*, the very day!
        If he's a liver then, he shall not prate,
        He must *die early*,so he shan't *di-late*!

(Orchestra plays "Tapioca."—The trio advance to the front and sing.)

---

3 As part of their entertainment many concert saloons offered nude or seminude models posed in representations of classical sculpture.

94

SHYLOCK *(impressively).*
    Whack fol de riddle rol de ri do,
ANTONIO *(mysteriously).*
    Whack fol de riddle lol de day!
SHYLOCK. Whack fol de riddle rol de ri do,
ANTONIO. Whack fol de riddle lol de day!
BASSANIO *(joyfully).*
    Oh, me! Oh, my!
ALL   *(with a will).*
    Whack fol de riddle lol de diddle lol de day!

(ALL dance off.—Scene closes.)

SCENE II.—PORTIA's *Room.—A lounge-table—and two chairs. Enter* PORTIA, *R.U.E., in a blue dress and a melancholy frame of mind.—She is reading a letter from* ANTONIO. *Music.— "The last rose of summer."*

PORTIA.   'Tis the last note from that bummer,
    And I can't say I like its tone;
  For his boozy companions—
    Will not grant him a loan;
  I'm dead broke, too, oh, how dreadful,
    To be wanting in cash—
  I must get some, or there will be
    A-a-bad-fi-i-nancial crash! *(crash outside)*
  With my tiddy fol lol de lol de li do, &c.

(goes to lounge and sinks into a sweet sleep)

(Enter ANTONIO, *by the window, C.)*

ANTONIO *(Looking at her).*
    Her eye-lids both completely closed she keeps—
    And as they say in melo drama "she sul-leeps."
PORTIA *(rising).*
    Don't be too sure of that my friend—
ANTONIO. Well, did you get my *note of hand?*
PORTIA. Your *note off hands* me very much—
    I'm deeply grieved that you should write me such
    A *letter* Tony—

This Grotesque Essence

ANTONIO. *Now let a* feller speak,
    I want the *spons*[4] the middle of next week.
PORTIA. You want the *spons, sir?* And you think
    I must stand *sponser* for your nasty drink!
    Go to that table, there, uns*table* man,
    And bury that big head in that big can;
    You say you're thirsty—and you have good reason,
    That table what *sees on*, you may *seize on*;
    Drink, drink your fill, and fill your drink to me,
    Get drunk at home, and baulk old Kennedy.
ANTONIO. Aha! hast heard the news? The Sunday News, I mean.
PORTIA. Five cents? sold by all dealers.
ANTONIO. Yes, they're Keen on *keno*, and they say just now
    That Kennedy to Connolly must bow!
    The judge has ta'en him by the *beard*, d'ye see?
PORTIA. Oh, don't *be-ard* with that *felo-dye-se*;[5]
ANTONIO. But soft! I'll tell you of this serious wrong,
    In verse, inversing an old song.

    (They advance to front.—Music—"Wearing of the Green.")
ANTONIO. Oh, Portia, dear, and did you here,
        The news that's going around:
    Another flaw in the Excise law,
        Judge Connolly has found!
    Old Superintendent Kennedy,
        Of New York he was king:
    Until the big Judge floor'd him flat—
        And thus broke up his ring.

    *(*PORTIA *leaves him singing—and exits softly.)*
ANTONIO. I'm left *alone*, but still without *a loan*,
    I really feel quite *lonely*, that *I'll own*;
    There are *two doors* to this room I conjecture,
    'Tis in the *Tu-dor* style of architecture;
    Or rather say the *Doric*, since I see
    That leading to the pantry there makes three;

---

4 Probably a shortened form of spondulics, a common nineteenth-century slang term for cash.
5 A pun on *felo-de-se*, a legal term meaning one who commits suicide.

Shylock

I wonder *who's in* this one, for I feel
My courage *oozing* out; I'll softly steal
Up to the door—Oh, goodness as I live!
There is Nerissa!—

(*Enter* NERISSA.)

NERISSA.   Don't be so inquisitive!
How dare you seek, mischievous blade
The *Mysteries* of your Mistress' waiting maid?

ANTONIO. Well, I'll to t'other door—

NERISSA.   I think you'd better,
For Shylock's hunting for his recreant debtor;

ANTONIO. Oh, lor! Oh, lor! that horrid *two-pun-ten*,
I shan't wish oft *to pun* with him again;
Oh, wretched *punster*, I'm indeed undone,
For he makes *pun stir* well as any one!

(*Enter* SHYLOCK, *door* R.)

SHYLOCK. Aha! my frient, this week your bond is *dew*,
Will it be missed?—

ANTONIO. You can't sue.
I'm under age, you villain of a Jew;
At all events pray wait until the day,
And then your dastardly demands I'll pay;

(*aside*) What shall I do? I have no bonds at home,
I think I'll take some from my friend Jerome.

SHYLOCK. If you don't pay, my knife I'll sharpen keen,
Upon my soul—

ANTONIO.   Upon your *sole* you mean,
Your *mien* is haughty—but your soul is *mean*.

(*Enter* BASSANIO, R.U. E.)

BASSANIO. Hallo, my tulips, *at it* once again!

ANTONIO. His *at it tude* on your part gives me pain,
We are not common-councilmen pray understand,
So at our heads pray throw no vile ink-stand.

SHYLOCK. Give me an *ink*-ling of it, it is quite *ink*-redulous!

BASSANIO. *Ink-redulous?* You surely mean *red-ink-ulous*;

NERISSA. Here, stop this *chaffing*, I am *chafing* nigh,
You quite forget a lady's standing by;

This Grotesque Essence

This *badinage* is simply my *aversion*,
I don't *a verse shun*, but I make assersion
That if you find *a verse 'un* than the one I sing,
Why you shall take the *medal*.
ANTONIO. This *meddling*
In our affairs, I don't half like—
(to leader of Orchestra)
Pray give the cue—strike upper C. good Mike.

(Orchestra plays "Dudah!" [6] *and characters sing "That's So.")*

NERISSA. The yacht race now has all cooled down,
The thing was really done up brown;
    That's so, that's so too!
CHORUS. We're bound to sail all day, to sail till all is blue,
I'll bet my money on the *Henrietta*
    That's so, that's so too!
ANTONIO. Old Barnum run for congress once,
I never thought he'd be such a dunce,
    That's so, that's so too!
He'd run some other day, but he thinks it will not do,
He'd better stick to his menagerie,
    That's so, that's so too!
SHYLOCK. Oh, Wall-street is a tick-lish place,
There's ruin in the golden race,
    That's so, that's so too!
When gold goes up all day, oh, that's the time to do,
CHORUS. I bets my monish on the bulls and bears,
    That's so, that's so too!
BASSANIO. Women's rights are all the rage,
Girls want to vote when they come of age,
    That's so, that's so too!
CHORUS. And then they'll vote all day—
Oh! Lord, help me and you,
I'll bet my money on the crinoline,
    That's so, that's so too!
ENSEMBLE. Then come, let us all take a "tod" or two,
We'll drink in spite of the Excise hue,
    That's so, that's so too!

6 Read "doo-dah." The following is a parody of Stephen Foster's "Camptown Races."

Shylock

We're bound to drink all day, hang old Kennedy's crew,
We'll drink bad health to the excise board,
     That's so, that's so too!

(While they are singing chorus, scene closes in to—)

SCENE III.—*Shylock's House—Three "Golden Balls" hanging in front—*JESSICA *discovered in the doorway. Music—"Naughty, Naughty Men."*

JESSICA   *(sings)*.

Your pantaloons are gorgeous, your coat it fits, oh,
    Lord, yes,
Your vest is brilliant moleskin, oh, you naughty,
    naughty man!
Your boots with blacking glimmer, than you no one is
    slimmer,
Your hat is Knox's patent, oh, you natty, natty man!
But ah, when we're united, my fond hopes may be
    blighted,
Your hair is all you care now, oh, you natty, natty man!
You'll beat your wife and curse her, or else you'll
    treat her worser,
Your clothes are all you think of, oh, you natty,
    natty, stupid blockhead man!
(musing) Oh, dear Lorenzo, why are you not here?

(Enter LORENZO.*)*

LORENZO. I'm out of *breath*, my *breth*ren want me dear,
           But I escaped them, and you see I'm here.
JESSICA.   Your *ear*, Lorenzo—
LORENZO.   Well, I said I was.
JESSICA.   Oh. bosh! don't bandy words, because
           My father's out, *let's seize* the day, and go!
LORENZO. *Let's see*, my dear, have we now a good show?
           'Twere cruelty to animals to fail, you know.
JESSICA.   Oh, bother cruelty, you surely quite forget,
           That the humane society has met!

This Grotesque Essence

Wherever *Harvy* or *Van-am-Burgh*[7] go,
We poor beasts surely have *the best of show*!

LORENZO. Then, come, your father's ducats we must thieve,
My *ducat diamonds!* let's make haste and leave,
I've got a few five-twenties in my pocket—
Come, close the door, put up your *chain and locket.*

JESSICA. Suppose we should be caught, my dear Lorenzy?
I've *caught his eye* a gleaming in a frenzy!

LORENZO. Come on, I say, you *cauterised* my heart.

(As they are going—Enter SHYLOCK.*)*

SHYLOCK *(shaking fist).*
Tief! murder! robbery! my daughter and my mart!

LORENZO. Will you shut up your head? we wasn't going,
We were merely stepping out to hear the rooster crowing.

(Music—"Gipsy's Warning.")

SHYLOCK *(sings).*
Trust him not, oh gentle lady, for he *owes* me many stamps;
　　Heed him not, he will ill-treat you, like the
　　　　other Christian scamps.
Of your money he will beat you, better men can sure be got;
　　Come back to my house and seat you, gentle lady,
　　　　trust him not.

JESSICA. You're a stupid, you were *trusting* to a reed with rotten core;
As he swindled you I love him better, far, than e'er before!

LORENZO. Yes, I'll be a *little mother.*

JESSICA. You dry up! or I shall wish
That you were a *little father.*

SHYLOCK. Give me back my dear monish.

(Exeunt JESSICA *and* LORENZO. SHYLOCK *dances off frantically.)*

SCENE IV.—*Trial of* ANTONIO—*The Dook discovered at a table, with a pint pot and a stack of clay pipes before him—*SHYLOCK

---

7 Menageries. Vanamburgh's menageries were exhibited in New York in 1865 and again in 1867, when it was the star attraction at Barnum's Museum.

Shylock

L., *with large knife*—ANTONIO *with the mumps*—PRINCE OF ARAGON[8] *in full armor.*

ANTONIO *(musing).*
    I'm quite *down-hearted*, if I ain't I'm *dashed*,
    My money's gone, and all my hopes are smashed;
    Of Winslow's Soothing Syrup I will take,
    And see what changed condition that will make.

SHYLOCK. What means this talk? Be certain that
    No *Syrup-titious* grumbling you be at,
    And if again I hear you hoot,
    I'll fix your case with a little *boot*.

P. OF ARAGON.
    Now by my halidome, whatever that may be
    This crafty Jew is full of *Jeux d'esprit!*

THE DOOK. Right, right, good Prince, but come, let's get to work,
    I think poor Tony finds the *Jew a Turk*.
    (to SHYLOCK*)* What is your plaint, come, spit it out at once,
    This Christian owes you two-pun-ten? The dunce
    To borrow from a Jew—

SHYLOCK. What! revile my claim,
    Oh, mighty *Khan*, oh, sweet *a merry Khan*,
    Don't bubble over in your righteous wrath,
    A *Khan*, you know, should hold some else than *froth*.

THE DOOK. Well, what say you, Jew, will you consent
    To take it from his hide? the cash you lent
    Is clearly lost, so do what you think better,
    To rid yourself of an insolvent debtor.
    *(*SHYLOCK *advances flourishing knife.)*

    (Enter PORTIA *and attendants.)*

PORTIA. Hold you willain! I'm not *willin* yet
    Antonio's buzzum shall be upset;
    But, now wade in! like a duck in the mud,
    But remember, you *draw not one drop of blood*!

---

8 Omitted from the list of characters in the acting edition.

This Grotesque Essence

SHYLOCK   *(shrinking back).*
      The game is up, I cannot solve this riddle,
      I'm trembling like a cat-gut on a fiddle;
      I've lost my *flesh*, my *monish*, and my *daughter*,
      Now I'll sneak out like a lamb to the slaughter.

OMNES.   No you don't.

They all rush after him, bring him back, crying out, "Toss him in a blanket." They get large canvas and toss him in the air until

CURTAIN.

Jack's the Lad

This piece was intended as a burlesque of a melodrama of the same name which served primarily as a finale on variety programs or as an innocuous star vehicle for the big name talents of the day. What this burlesque lacks, and what was characteristic of many of the better afterpieces written by Griffin, is a sense of cohesion among the comic elements. The sparse plot episodes, character sketches, slapstick antics, and verbal humor fail to combine for an overall cumulative effect. This may be a result of the fact that the piece was written without the influence of Christy's directorial sense of how a burlesque should build upon itself. The Christy and Griffin collaboration was apparently a turbulent one from its beginning in the early 1850s to Christy's death in 1868. In the fall of 1859 their troupe, then known as Christy's Minstrels, began an extended run at Niblo's Saloon in New York. By January of 1860 the tension among the performers was so high that Griffin, R. M. Hooley, and S. C. Campbell left Christy to form their own troupe, taking with them most of the better talent from the original group. *Jack's the Lad* was written during this rift, probably in September or October of 1860. The following text is reprinted from the acting edition published by Samuel French.

JACK'S THE LAD:

An Ethiopian Drama,
As Performed By
Hooley, Campbell & Griffin's Minstrels,
At Niblo's Saloon, Broadway, New York.
By G. W. H. GRIFFIN, *Esq.*

CAST OF CHARACTERS

WILLIAM	E. J. Melville
AUGUSTUS NICETY	J. B. Donniker
CAPT. CUTLETT	S. C. Campbell
BUMBLEBEE	G. W. H. Griffin
BARNEY O'HAY	James Unsworth
SAM	Ben Cotton
BOY	Boot-black
ADELIA	Master Eugene
MRS. PARRISH	J. Hilliard

SCENE I.—*Kitchen in 2*—MRS. PARRISH *discovered knitting and rocking baby*—ADELIA *sewing frock*—*each sitting at table set for breakfast*—SAMMY *playing round the room with ball, etc.,—child cries in cradle.*

MRS. PARRISH.   Dar, dar! hush your little rosy-posy mouth! De poor little Carolina potato! Why, she cries as if her little heart would broke! What *can* be de matter wid de picaninny? Why, if your fader should hear dem ere sympathetic tones, why, de poor man would go crazy! *(takes baby out of cradle, and finds cat hid away under the clothes—throws cat on the floor, exclaiming):* Oh! it's *you*, is it? you confounded beefsteak thief! You ain't satisfied wid stealing all de meat off de table dis morning, but you must sneak into de cradle and try to eat up de dear little picaninny! Let me cotch you in dar again, and I'll pull your whiskers! *(puts baby back in cradle)* Dar, dar! Now hush your mouf, and go back in de arms of murphys, as de white folks say. *(looks up and sees* ADELIA *weeping)* Why, bress your heart, Adelia! why don't you cheer up? Does you let your spirits drop down in your shoes because your husband is three or four days longer from home than you expected? Take my word for it, gal, de ship is all safe and sound, and she'll arrive here before soon if noffin happens.

ADELIA.   But, mother, only think! William has been gone almost two years, and the officers at the Navy Yard say she should have arrived here a week ago. Oh dear! if anything should happen to William, what should I do? And our dear child, too! I should never survive his loss!

MRS. P.   Dat's right! I like to see you show your confection for your husband, and child, it shows you have de blood of your mudder in your veins. I recollect poor Mr. Parrish, your father, when he was about the age of your William. Ah! didn't I love him, though! Yes, Adelia, I loved him better dan locusts and honey; but de poor man was very unlucky; he nebber went out of the house wid a shilling in his pocket but he was sure to drop it in de street, and lose it! And one night de poor man lost his breff, and soon after dat he died! It was a sad loss to me, for he always paid de rent, and went fishing Sundays.

(SAM, *during this speech, has been stealing sugar and cakes from the cupboard—he sees large pan upon top shelf, and climbs upon back of chair to reach it—chair tips, he falls, bringing down pan of flour— Business.*)

ADELIA.   Now, you young scamp, there goes my nice batch of bread that was already to mix for supper! I'll pay you for that!

(MRS. P. *gets broom,* ADELIA *gets shovel—they chase him around stage— he falls into cradle—cradle breaks—baby cries—he gets out of cradle, and gets under table—upsets table—*ADELIA *smashes tray over his head— tableau of horror.*)

SCENE II.—*Street in* 1. *Enter* AUGUSTUS NICETY, R.)

AUGUSTUS.   I really believe them saucy boys put a chalk mark on my back, but I am afraid to take my coat off to look for fear of catching cold! I took my gloves off in the street the other day and caught a severe cold in my hands.

(*Enter* STRANGER, R.)

STRANGER.   Ah! can you inform me where the City Hall Park is?

AUG.   Yes, sir, with pleasure. You see that large building?

This Grotesque Essence

STRANGER.   Yes.

AUG.   Well, that's Niblo's;[1] about half a mile above that is Union Square; and some distance beyond you will find a place they call Harlem, and just beyond that is the City Hall Park.

STRANGER.   I had no idea it was so far, but I'm much obliged to you for your honest kindness. *(exit, L.)*

AUG.   I think I am even now for the tricks they have played on me to-day.[2] *(going)*

(Enter SAM, R.*)*

SAM.   Hello! I think you are the very man I am looking for.

AUG.   Indeed!

SAM.   Yes. Is your name—now let me see—

AUG.   Nicety; Augustus Nicety.

SAM.   Yes; that's the very name. Well, I have been sent after you: you have got a wife?

AUG.   No, nothing but a mother and sister at home.

SAM.   I mean a mother. What did I say? a wife! What a fool! I mean your mother. She was up on top of the chimney, brushing off the cobwebs, and she lost her balance and fell down the chimney ka-swash! Your sister was boiling potatoes, and the old woman fell into the potato pot, upsetting the boiling water all over your sister, and scalded the hide all off of de kitten. *(During this speech he has chalked him all over.)*

AUG.   Gracious! what a chapter of accidents! I'll hurry home immediately. *(exit,* L. *running)*

SAM.   Ha! ha! ha! I guess I made a fool of him! I never saw him before in all my life! *(takes out pocket-book, with string attached—throws it down on the ground)* I guess someone will bite at this; here comes a mick.

(Enter BARNEY, R.*)*

BARNEY.   Bad luck to the likes of me. They told me when I come to America, that I could pick up dollars in the street, but divil a dollar have I seen but a half I see a feller drop, and I wouldn't stoop

1   Niblo's Gardens, of which Niblo's Saloon was a small part, was a resplendent New York entertainment "temple" on Broadway in what is now lower Manhattan.
2   City Hall Park is actually in the Bowery a mile and a half south of Niblo's. Augustus sends the stranger ten miles or so in the wrong direction.

to pick up a half, and divil a whole dollar or a half have I seen since, and I'm here some two months. I havn't had even a roast potaty for the last forty-eight hours! They drive me out of the free lunch houses because they say I always eat more than six men, and never buy a drink! Bad luck to them! I havn't had a six-pence to buy a drink with for two months! *(sees pocket-book)* Oh! shade of my great grand-ancestors! And is it there ye are, looking me right up in the face? Ah, but ye look nice and fat! What poor divil had the misfortune to drop ye? Come to my arms! *(Goes to pick it up—*SAM *pulls string—*BARNEY *follows up 'till he comes close to* SAM, *and looks him in the face.)* Ah! bad luck to you! It's you playing a trick on me, is it? Away with you, you thaving nigger! *(beats him off,* L.*)*

SCENE III.—*Whole Stage—large man-of-war ship discovered in the distance—everybody enter, looking for the ship—*MRS. P. *and* ADELIA *appear very anxious—all anxious to get a view of the expected ship—* SAMMY *gets upon a bale of cotton, and* BARNEY *knocks him off into the water—cry of "Boy overboard"—bring him in on a board—get pump, and pump the water out of him a la Ravel,*[3] *then all exeunt—ship then moves slowly across the stage, during which Quartette sings "Home Again." Close in.*

SCENE IV.—*Kitchen in 2. (Enter* ADELIA *and* MRS. P., L.—*take off bonnets and shawls, and begin to put the room in order.)*

MRS. P.   Oh dear! I never was so tired in all my life! I feel as if every minute would be my next, and that great big fool, Sammy, must go and fall in the river, to make things worse. Poor feller! I thought he would choke to deff with the salt water he swallowed, but I give him a strong dose of Spaulding's Glue, *hot,* and I think he'll feel better soon.

ADELIA.   Oh mother! I am *so* glad William has returned, I hardly know what to do! But we must get some refreshments ready, for he will be awful tired and hungry, I know, and I shouldn't wonder if he was most froze to death. Oh dear! won't he be surprised to see the little rosy-posy baby?

3   The Ravel family. See the preface to "Scampini."

107

MRS. P.   Yes; and won't he be surprised to see the rosy-posy baby's face all cut up, like a plate of hashed meat!

ADELIA.   That was all on account of that rascally boy. I wish de sharks had got him when he fell overboard, for he never does anything but mischief!

MRS. P.   Ha, ha! de sharks won't never touch *him*! He's too strong—he's cooked too brown! *(baby cries)* Oh, dar's de little picaninny crying again! I'll go take de little lamb out of the cradle, and have him dressed up nice before his father comes. *(exit, R.2. heavy knocks, L. 1E.)*

BUMBLEBEE *(outside)*.   Kitchen ahoy-a!

ADELIA.   That must be William. Oh, how glad I am that he has come! Come in: 'tis I, your own Adelia! *(Embraces* BUMBLEBEE, *thinking it is* WILLIAM—CUTLESS *and* BUMBLEBEE *enter together.)*

BUMBLEBEE.   My name's Jack Bumblebee. *(She breaks from him.)*

CUTLETT.   Yes, he was christened John—John Bumblebee. He was christened on board of the Hornet, on her cruise in the West Indies for a load of honey. But hear him! he might have been christened anything, with such a mind as he's got!

BUMB.   Whereby—why not—if so—what's the odds? Can any man say otherwise?

CUT.   In course not.

BUMB.   Well then, so it is—and so let it be.

CUT.   There's head—there's sense—there's argument! Bring me a man as can come near that!

ADELIA.   Oh, my dear sailor-friend! tell me, tell me true, before this palpitating heart, now beating with anticipated joy and hope of a reunion with my dear, dear husband, shall burst the chains of suspense, and lay me prostrate at your feet! Tell me, I say, and I will bless you! Is William—*my* William among your crew?

CUT *(sings)*.   "Does my sweet William sail among your crew?" Now then, Jack, overhaul your hintellec wigerous, and tell the young lady if her William has arrived safe or no. Now give us an opinion as *is* an opinion. *(*ADELIA *puts chairs at table—*BUMBLEBEE *and* CUTLETT *sit opposite each other,* ADELIA *at back. Business eating, &c.* BUMBLEBEE *pours wine from bottle.)* There's wisdom!

BUMB.   This is the pint.

(Enter SAMMY, *with box.)*

SAM.   Golly, that's near a quart!

ADELIA.   Goody me! what a time the sea-creature is!

CUT.   Hush! he's working it out.

ADELIA.   For heaven's sake, sir, speak, and relieve this terrible anxiety!

CUT.   Hush! his mind is in deep water; 'twill come up to the surface directly.

BUMB.   My name's Jack Bumblebee.

CUT.   Now it's coming—stand by.

BUMB.   Skipper!

CUT.   Give him sea-room.

BUMB.   I says what I says, and what I says I sticks to; you want to know as how—as if your William has returned safe in our ship?

ADELIA.   Yes, yes!

BUMB.   Well, my opinions and my observations goes to two pints.

CUT.   Listen to the sense! There's mind! See it looming out! Go on, ship-mate—two pints—that's just one quart.

BUMB.   Either your William has returned with us, or he has not returned with us, d'ye see? Now if so be he is, why so—if so be he is not, why so also. That's my opinion, and I don't care who knows it! so keep a bright outlook, and recollect, in particular, that my name's Jack Bumblebee.

CUT.   There! didn't I tell you he'd give you an opinion worth having?

ADELIA.   But what does he mean?

CUT.   Nobody knows but himself! His wisdom is all his own.
(knocks outside, L. 1E.)

(Enter WILLIAM.)

WILL.   Adelia!

ADELIA.   William! *(They embrace affectionately.)* Oh William! I had begun to fear the worst, for it is now more than a year since I received a single line from you! I almost believed you had perished at sea.

WILL.   No, Adelia, your image has been my good star, and when surrounded by danger, either in my silent watch on deck, or in slumber below, these words always cheered my heart, and I knew that I was safe:
   "There's a sweet little cherub that sits up aloft,
      Keeps watch o'er the life of poor Jack."
Now tell me, love, how you've been, and everything that's happened since my departure.

ADELIA.   Oh William! our child! You have not seen the little dear yet!

WILL.   Child! Why, have we got a child? Let me see the little dolphin!

MRS. PARRISH *(running in with child).*   Has you got a child! Just look at that little lump of California gold! *(Baby's face is all patched up.)*

WILL. *(taking child).*   Why, the poor little fellow looks as if he'd been in a heavy engagement! Here, mother, you'd better lay this little craft up for repairs. *(gives baby—she takes it, and exits)* Now, then, I'll show you what I've brought for you from foreign lands. *(distributes trinkets from small casket)* Now then, what do you suppose I've got in that box?

ADELIA.   I don't know; what is it?

WILL.   No, it ain't a "What is it," but it's for the man that owns the "What is it." It's an anaconda for Barnum. I brought it from Africa for his Museum. It's perfectly tame, and would not harm a mouse—the reason is, it's asleep, and don't wake up but twice a year. This is New Year's day, and I'm going to present it to Barnum as a New Year's present.

(During the preceding speech SAMMY *has business with the snake, putting his finger in box.)*

ADELIA.   Now then, William, we have made up a party to celebrate the beginning of the new year by a skating frolic on the Central Park; so you and your ship-mates must join us, and we'll have a jolly time!

WILL.   All right, lovey!

BUMB.   My name's Jack Bumblebee. I can skate or ride a sperm whale with any barnacle that sails the hocean.

WILL.   Now then, let's all away to the skating ground; but first of all, I must look after my anaconda. Here, Sammy, shoulder this box and take it down to the Museum, with this letter, and I'll give you a half dollar when you return.

SAM.   I'll do it, and then come up to the skating ground and have some fun. *(*SAMMY *shoulders box, and all exeunt.)*

SCENE V.—*Street in 1. (Enter* SAMMY, *with box—sets it down in one corner of the stage, near first wing, to give chance for someone to hook on the snake to Sammy's trousers.)*

SAM.   Golly! dat box grows heavy! Dat 'conda must have been eating

110

roast beef lately! I wish I had a pair of skates, I'd leave this 'conda in the store 'till I get back, then go up to the Park. Hello! here comes a feller with a bully pair! I'll see if I can't get him to lend 'em to me. *(Enter* BOY, *with skates.)* Say, boy! what'll you take for them skates?

BOY.   Don't want to sell 'em.

(SAMMY *takes skates, examines them, and then gets* BOY *to look into the box—*SAMMY *then shouts snake! and frightens* BOY *so that he runs away —*SAMMY *takes skates, and begins to strap them on his feet—while he is doing so, someone off the stage hooks snake on to the seat of his trousers— he keeps talking all the time of what a good time he will have, and how nicely he frightened the boy out of the skates—finally feels the snake bite him—at last he jumps up, dragging the snake out of the box, and runs off stage.)*

SCENE VI.—*Snow scene. Draw off and exhibit the whole stage—snow falling—trap covered over with paper, for* SAMMY *to fall though—some sliding, and others skating—after awhile* BUMBLEBEE *and* CUTLETT *appear, on skates—*BUMBLEBEE *falls down—*CUTLETT *tries to save him, and falls also—next come the* LADIES, *skating—after awhile* SAMMY *appears, with snake still attached to him—runs around, upsetting everybody, and finally falls through trap. Tableau.*

THE END

Rose Dale

The following afterpiece compares favorably with *Jack's the Lad* if for no other reason than that the play on which it is based is available for comparison with the minstrel version. Adapted from Edward B. Hamley's novel *Lady Lee's Widowhood*, Lester Walleck's *Rosedale; or, The Rifle Ball* was one of the most popular plays in the history of American theater. It was first performed on September 30, 1863, and in the next fifty years went through innumerable revivals to fulfill audience demand for its successful blend of comedy and melodrama. The Griffin and Christy version is not an exact parody of the original by any means. Ragley and Waxend are minstrel creations; and in the original Rosedale is the name of an English country estate. But the burlesque does contain a surprising number of thinly veiled allusions to the original play, so that a comparison between the two reveals which incidents were considered most sensational and therefore which conventions most clearly defined melodrama's popular appeal.

Performance information about the following piece is sketchy. All that can be ascertained is that it was offered sometime after March 18, 1867, when Robert Hughes joined the Griffin and Christy troupe, and before the close of their run on June 29 of the same year.

ROSE DALE;

an

Ethiopian Burlesque

on

LESTER WALLACK'S "ROSEDALE,"

As Performed By

GRIFFIN & CHRISTY'S MINSTRELS,

at the

"Fifth Avenue Opera House," New York.

CAST OF CHARACTERS

AUNT ROSE DALE	Geo. Christy
RAGLEY	G. W. H. Griffin
WAXEND	Otto Burbank
ARTHUR	R. Hughes
POLICEMAN	W. Palmer

SCENE.—*Street or wood—at curtain rise* AUNT ROSE *discovered counting clothes in different piles; to herself, counts*

One, two, three, four, five, six. Six pieces, this week, for old Skinflint, the miser! Why, how clean he is getting! It's only four weeks ago since he had his last washing! Six pieces of clothes in four weeks! That is very extravagant! Let me see: twelve pieces for Mrs. Pumpkins—fourteen for Mrs. Jewsharp; and here is a very fine handkerchief that Uncle Simpson will lend me fifty cents on. I think I only put two shirts to spout last week, so I can go the handkerchief this week. Mr. Brown came down to raise a muss about them are shirts; but of course I didn't know noffin about 'em; so he said the servant at his boardin' house must have stole 'em; an' that's all I heerd about 'em. Ya! ya! noffin' like havin' cheek in this world. (ARTHUR *heard crying in the distance*) There! there is my dear little boy crying agin: some big rascal has been hurtin' the poor child. (*Enter* ARTHUR, *crying.*) There, there! hush, my dear little darling, an' tell your mammy what ails you.

ARTHUR (*bellowing*). Well, I was comin' out of Mr. Smith's cellar with the clothes, and a great big boy, eight years old, insulted me, so he did.

113

This Grotesque Essence

AUNT R.   Insulted you! poor child! He ought to have been ashamed of himself to insult a defenseless little boy like you!

ARTHUR.   An' I wasn't sayin' a thing to him, either, so I wasn't.

AUNT R.   The big, overgrown, cowardly rascal! But what did he say to you, my dearest?

ARTHUR.   Why, he hollered out to a lot of boys: "There goes one of Horace Greeley's chillun." [1]

AUNT R.   The insultin' villain! But never mind, my rosebud; dry your eyes, like a good little boy, and don't mind when people abuse you in that way.

(Enter RAGLEY.)

AUNT R. *(to RAGLEY, solemnly).*   Ragley, art come again to annoy me?

RAGLEY.   Aunt Rosy, I art come agin.

AUNT R.   Why dost haunt this magnifluous aboding domiciliary?

RAG.   I want my clean clothes, forthwithously!

AUNT R.   Ragley, hast gold?

RAG.   I hast none—not even greenbacks.

AUNT R.   Greenbacks! *Chased* greenbacks! [2] I want none of such things as they! I have had enough of your *promises to pay* already! [3]

RAG.   Madame, my clothes.

AUNT R.   You can't have 'em.

RAG.   I will!

AUNT R.   You shan't!

RAG.   I will, I say! *(starts toward her, threateningly)*

AUNT R.   Ha, monstrociousness! will you insult a defenseless female?

AUTHUR   How dare you insult my dear mammy?

RAG.   Ho, youngster, we'll fix you! *(steps one side, and gets a small tree; comes in chopping off the branches)*

AUNT R.   Ragley, What art goin' to do with that largely hemlock?

RAG.   I'm goin' to teach that young infant of yours not to insult me!

AUNT R.   If you do, it must be over my alabaster brow.

1   Because of his strong abolitionist sentiments, Horace Greeley—at that time editor of the New York *Tribune*—was credited in popular jokelore with having fathered the Negro race.
2   Salmon P. Chase, Secretary of the Treasury during the Lincoln administration, was responsible for establishing greenback paper currency as a means of financing the Civil War.
3   Greenbacks were widely unpopular in the years following the war because of the government's inability to keep its promise of redeeming greenbacks with gold.

Rose Dale

(They parry; AUNT ROSE *hits* RAGLEY, *and knocks him down; enter attendants to carry him off. To attendants.)* Take away that piece of injured black walnut. There! I've done a tremenjously brave thing! *(To* ARTHUR*)* Come, my little pet. After that job I feel as though I wanted a lunch! *(exit, leading* ARTHUR*)*

SCENE II.—*Aunt Rose's kitchen—fire in fireplace—enter* AUNT ROSE *and* WAXEND.

WAXEND. Well, darling, now that we have settled about our marriage, I feel much easier, don't you, my petness?

AUNT R. Yes, Waxey, muchly more such, except that my fisticuff sorely hurteth me. I tell you, Waxey, I guv him a kerwollopper under the peeper!

WAX. Ha! ha! you raised him, did you?

AUNT R. Yes sir-ee, hoss! I raised a mouse under his sky-light soonly, if not more quicker.

WAX. Served him right! served him right! and now I must see to your delicate palm: that hand that you gave to me forever—that hand that is to—

AUNT R. Wash your shirts, sugarness, when thouest and Iest is spliced.

WAX. Prezactly, prezactly, my petness. You're a poet, hid under a cloud of steam from the wash tub. *(brings from side a tub, a demijohn, a sheet, and a bed-cord)* Here, my loveness, the doctor, who is a nephew to the step-son of my aunt's grandfather, sends this tonic for your wounded fist. You are to wet this small piece of cloth with the ablution contained in this small phial every thirty-six hours, so as to keep the cloth moist! You are then to tie the cloth on with this piece of thread; then put your hand to bed, and let it sleep until it wakes. Let me bind it up at once, myself. *(Pours out water, and wets sheet—they both wring it out.)* There, my snow-bird! now hold out thy delicate palm!

AUNT R. Be greatly careful, for my palm is a delicate palm, and muchly requireth a gentle handling.

WAX. Careful, my sweet! how else could I be but careful *(winds it round)* of what is my own?

AUNT R. Oh, you are a dear soul! but *(screams)* oh my sakes and soapsuds! how it did hurt! But just try it again.

WAX. I will, and will try to do better this time.

AUNT R. Be cautiously; something hurts.

WAX. Does it hurt?

AUNT R. Hold on; yes, I think so. You'd better take it off again. Waxey, do you know I'd like to have you do this all night?

WAX. Would you, my love?

AUNT R. Yes, my sugarness.

WAX. And why, sunflower?

AUNT R. So you could be near me.

WAX. And dost love me suchly as those?

AUNT R. Love ye, love ye! *(Holds open her arms; they embrace—she with the sheet over his head.)*

WAX. *(catching his breath).* My! I am nearly conflummuxed! You guv me a bear-hug, that time!

AUNT R. You are as pale as a ghost. Did I squeeze the love all out of you?

WAX. No, my tulip! I am resusticated now; so let me try my hand agin.

AUNT R. Try *my* hand, you mean.

WAX. Yes, I meaneth so. *(binds on cloth)* Is it too tight, my sweet?

AUNT R. I think not, my loveness.

WAX. There, now for the thread! There you are, splendidly bound in cloth! Now, then, I must depart me and leave thee. Remember! to-morrow night I shall come and expect to see you ready for the ball. So good-night, Mrs. Dale.

AUNT R. Ajew! Mr. Waxend.

WAX. *(returning).* Pardon me, but my mammy always called me by my given name, Alphonso Philander Adolphus!

AUNT R. Oh! good-night, then, Alphonso Philander Adolphus! Ex-squeeze me, too, but my landlord always calls me Rose.

WAX. Oh! good-night, then, Rose. *(exit)*

AUNT R. What a dear man he is, and how I love him! Dear me, what a thing this love is! I'm so full of it that I'm afraid I shall either boil over or bust! Well, well, I'll sit me adown and try my meerschaum. *(sits down in chair by fire, and sticks her feet on the grate)*

(Enter RAGLEY by door—stage brilliantly lighted.)

RAG. *(groping his way).* Ha! I am here at last! I found the secret entrance, entered it, passed through it, and now I am in the old kitchen. Little do they think that I know every knot-hole and rat-hole in this palace. My grandfather had a shirt washed here two thousand years ago, and therefore he knew every corner of the building. He gave the information to my paternal forerunner, who, in turn, willed said knowledge to me, and now I'm goin' to make use of the education. But how dazzlingly dark it is. I must fire a dip, and make some bright moonlight. *(gropes his way to table and lights candle—draws out a large sheet of paper)* Now for my dispatches. *(reads)* Lift the latch, and the door will open into the sumptuous apartment. Go two thousand feet to the right, and you will find a table, if there is one there. On said table you will find a two-cent candle provided the Dutchman at the corner will trust her for one! Four hundred feet in some direction or other, you will discover a cupboard. On exploring said cupboard, you may behold a wash-basin of soft-soap, a paper of blueing, a soap-dish without a bottom, and a gin-bottle; but be careful not to upset the jars of preserves or catch your foot in a rat trap. About eight hundred feet in a northsouthwardly direction, you may diskiver, in the dim distance, a fireplace, with all the modern improvements, near which may be found the clothes washable. *(folds up paper)* Ha, I have it! Now, then, for a *tower* of exploration. *(opens cupboard—discovers the soap, gin-bottle, &c.)* The sight of those things makes me hungry; I feel very much like takin' a lunch. And now for my under-wearables. *(Goes toward fireplace—startled at seeing* AUNT ROSE—*she awakes.)*

AUNT R. Ha! Ragley, artest it thouest again?

RAG. It art.

AUNT R. Why here, Ragley?

RAG. Hist, madam! you are in my power.

AUNT R. In your power! Nothin' of the sort! I'm in my own parlor.

RAG. Hold your clatter, I tell you; I am armed. You are not, and therefore I don't fear you. If you utter a loud scream, I will send you to—

AUNT R. To whencesoever?

RAG. To Wendell Phillips.[4]

AUNT R. Oh Lord!

4 A cultural lecturer who, in the company of such Brahmin luminaries as Ralph Waldo Emerson and Oliver Wendell Holmes, was in great demand from the late 1850s to the mid 1870s. Phillips was best known as one of the most outspoken abolitionists in America.

This Grotesque Essence

RAG. Rose, do you consern a gash under my peeper?

AUNT R. There is a large one under your nose!

RAG. What does it resemble mostly?

AUNT R. Your mouth.

RAG. Bah! There is a gash under my eye, which you can discover by looking through a stereoscope. It is two feet long, by three feet deep. 'Twas the work of thy battering-ram!

AUNT R. Well?

RAG. Well! it is not well; nor won't be in two months.

AUNT R. I mean you are doin' well. Purceed with your nonsense, my child.

RAG. Nonsense! Why, really, you're the most coolest individuality upon this undine hemispherical globular!

AUNT R. No French, Ragley; no French; or the President will want you to go on a mission to Paris.

RAG. No aspirations on my character, madam! I am a reliable contraband.

AUNT R. You'm like a good many of dem contrabands, Ragley. You'm reliable because you lie, an' den you re-lie, good many times. How are you, Kilpatrick's guide![5]

RAG. Hist, madam! you make a deal of noise, and should there be a policeman widin sixteen blocks (although that is not probable), he might hear you, an—

AUNT R. An' what, Ragley?

RAG. An' run away; so hush thyself quietly, and list. This Vesuvius crater-like gash under my eye shall never go unaveangedreveanged. See! *(draws a gridiron from the fire)* I am goin' to make my mark.

AUNT R. Would'st make a Free mason of me, Ragley?

RAG. Nay.

AUNT R. Would'st map out the city of New York on me, Ragley?

---

5 Hugh Judson Kilpatrick (1836–1881) was a major general in the Union army. The term "Kilpatrick's guide" alludes to an incident in 1864 when Kilpatrick, directing the Union assault on Richmond, deployed part of his troops under the command of Colonel Ulrich Dahlgren to perform a flanking movement as part of the attack. Kilpatrick assigned a local black to serve as a guide for Dahlgren. Under this poor fellow's directions Dahlgren's forces wound up hopelessly lost in the Virginia countryside and were captured by Confederate forces. The incident was primarily responsible for Kilpatrick's failure to capture Richmond.

RAG.   How, Rose?

AUNT R.   By leaving the *tracks* of the *gridiron* all over me.

RAG.   Nay! but I will put a scar on thy frontispiece that will last until the sawdust of life be run-ed out-ed. *(goes to stamp her)*

AUNT R.   Hold, Ragley! I am a young widow, and still in the market. If you spare my lily-white alabaster brow, I will reward ye.

RAG.   Reward me?

AUNT R.   Aye, if you will give me your word not to harm me. Art agreed?

RAG.   I art.

AUNT R.   Then unloose this thread, that I may have the use of these scrubbers, an' I will give you a check. *(RAGLEY unlooses her.)*

AUNT R. *(going to window).*   What do you see down there?

RAG.   A nigger on a cellar door, skinning eels.

AUNT R.   See! I project to him this. *(throws something out of window)*

RAG.   What is it, Rose?

AUNT R.   A dumplicate of this. *(hands him a card)*

RAG.   What is this?

AUNT R.   The check I promised you.

RAG.   This a check!

AUNT R.   Yes, one of Meschutt's checks for coffee and cakes.

RAG.   Ha! you have broken faith with me.

AUNT R.   Nothing of the sort. I promised you a check, and you have it. *(with animation)* But hark! The check I threw out of the window is a counterfeit one. In twenty-four hours that man will go to Meschutt's for his coffee and cakes. They will discover the counterfeit; the man will tell who gave him the check. In about two days the police will be around here to arrest me, so that if you stay here three days the house will be swarming with somebody, and I shall have you tooken up.

RAG.   Woman, you have deceived me!

AUNT R.   I havn't. I promised you a check; you have it. I have keepen my word.

RAG.   And I have kept mine.

AUNT R.   You have not.

RAG.   Whyfore?

AUNT R.   Didn't you give me your word not to harm me?

RAG.   I didst.

This Grotesque Essence

AUNT R.   Then how could you keep your word if you gave it to me? Ha, ha, ha!

RAG.   Bah! *(rushes through window, running against* AUNT ROSE, *and knocking her down—sound of broken window glass)*

(Enter WAXEND.*)*

WAX.   Well, my sunflower, you are most ready for the ball?

AUNT R.   Ah, my sugarness! but sorrowfully do I feel. This day, one hundred years ago, was the memorial morning when that little flower was stolen from its parent stem. Poor little Arthur! He was drowned, and his body never was found; but his little Panama leghorn beaver hat was found by a policeman, floating in the mudgutter. Boo, hoo, a hoo-hoo! *(cries)*

WAX.   Yes, poor child! It is supposed that the rascal, Ragley, made away with him to secure his immense fortune—a five-cent postage currency that was in one of his pockets. But cheer up, petness, for I have good intidings to impart.

AUNT R.   Oh, tell me! is it about my Arthur?

WAX.   Can you stand it all if I tell you?

AUNT R.   Yea, if not I will sit! So tell me forthwithiously.

WAX.   Then listen. I have found Arthur! He is here!

AUNT R.   Oh, show me my babe! *(Enter* ARTHUR, *bawling.)* My child, my dear little infant!

WAX.   Ha! I knew that would cheer you up. But now that you have got him, you'd better look to his morals; for I found him, after fourteen years search, in bad company.

AUNT R.   In bad company! Oh tell me, where stayed he?

WAX.   Why, I saw so much nigger in the Tribune, that I thought I would go down to that office to ask 'bout him, and sure nuff, there he was, along with Horace Greeley!

AUNT R.   Oh, goodness preserve us! The child is ruined!

(Enter RAGLEY *and* POLICEMAN.*)*

WAX. *(to* ROSE*)*.   Ah, there goes Ragley, at last! *(to* POLICEMAN*)* What are you going to do with that blackbird?

POLICEMAN.   Take him to a stone cage, sir.

WAX.   For why such conduct as those?

POLICEMAN.   Well, you see, he jumped out of a window, and went through a barrel of whiskey, and he is arrested because he wouldn't pay for what he drank while sailing through.

AUNT R.   Ah! poor fellow! He is about to expatiate his crime on the island, and in order to encourage him in his exile we'll all have a dance, and make him pay the fiddler. *(All join in Walk-around Dance.)*

THE END

The Black Crook
Burlesque

On September 12, 1866, a production of Charles M. Barras' *The Black Crook* opened at Niblo's Gardens in New York. Before the close of its fourth revival in 1872, some 774 performances later, theatrical history had been made. *The Black Crook* could not be classified as opera bouffe, burlesque, ballet, or drama, although theatrical historians have generally credited it with being the grandfather of American musical comedy. Rather it was a spectacular hodge-podge of almost every theatrical form to be found on the nineteenth-century popular stage. Such extravaganzas, as they were called, had been imported from Europe in the late fifties and early sixties; but never before had American audiences been exposed to fantasy on such a grand scale. The opening performance of *The Black Crook* ran six hours and five minutes during which time hundreds of actors, singers, and titillatingly clad dancers romped through scenery of unprecedented lavishness in a dreamlike riot of sensuality that has moved theater historians to hyperbole ever since.

Kelly and Leon's Minstrels was apparently the first of several New York troupes to burlesque *The Black Crook*. By January 14, 1867, they had added to their bill several sketches that played on Barras' piece. On February 25 of that year Griffin and Christy introduced the following version and drove off all competition.

The claim that this piece ran for ninety nights is questionable. After April 6 Griffin and Christy stopped advertising it but may very well have continued it on their bill. In any case *The Black Crook Burlesque* was noteworthy in a time when ten or fifteen consecutive performances of an afterpiece constituted a hit.

Because *The Black Crook* was the epitome of theatrical excess, it was particularly well suited as an object of minstrel burlesque. Like the Griffin and Christy version, the original had a Faustian plot for its frame; but its major appeal depended on the visual display in the scenery and ballet. Similarly, the comedy in the Griffin and Christy version relies primarily on the sequence of exaggerated visual images and represents the grotesque essence of minstrel humor in its most immediate and most fundamental form. The following text is reprinted from the acting edition published by Samuel French.

THE BLACK CROOK
BURLESQUE
written and arranged by

G. W. H. GRIFFIN

and performed by

GRIFFIN & CHRISTY'S MINSTRELS

*for a succession of ninety nights, at
the Fifth Avenue Opera House.*

CAST OF CHARACTERS

WOLFGANG HEDGEHOG (Black Crook) . . . . . G. W. H. Griffin
LUCIFER . . . . C. F. Shattuck
MOLLY BONFANTI[1] . . . . Christina

1 Alludes to Marie Bonfanti, one of the principle danseuses in the original Niblo's production of *The Black Crook*.

This Grotesque Essence

BETSY REGALIA[2] . . . . Husietta
LUCALICO . . . . Burbankiana
DUCKLEGS . . . . Hodgkiniana
RITALANDA SOMEGALLUS[3] . . . . Lesliana
MISERY . . . . Boycetta
GOSSIPER . . . . Nobodiana

SCENE I.—*A wood—den of the* BLACK CROOK. *At rise of curtain, wild music, allegro.*

(*Enter* BLACK CROOK, R. 3E. *He is dressed in black tights—black blouse reaching to the knee—black belt—black shoes with buckles—black wig with hair standing in all directions. If done in black face the forehead should be washed clean with a sponge, leaving it perfectly white; rub a little of the black off from under the eyes, so as to give the face a wild expression. If done in white, the forehead must be painted green. He carries a cane to lean upon—it should be an old fashioned one with a cross piece for handle. He is nearly bent double as he enters leaning upon cane. He walks around two or three times, then stops in* C. *of stage. Music stops.*)

B. C. Now to conjure up the spell
That shall do my bidding well!
More of riches I must have,
More of pleasure still I crave.
But should the spell impotent prove,
While the sprites of earth I move,
Then my power on earth is done!
Then I'll invoke the Evil One!

(*Music repeats.* BLACK CROOK *takes cane and draws circle on stage, then uses cane in flourishes, as if invoking evil spirits. Music ceases.* CROOK *walks down* L. *in despair, then putting his hand to his forehead, speaks:*)

B. C. Alas! I fear I have no power
to aid me in this trying hour.
What shall I do? My brain grows wild.
And through the air on fire I ride!
I'll call to aid the Evil One,
He's just come on from Washington.

2 Alludes to Betty Rigl, a principle danseuse of the Niblo's production.
3 Alludes to Rita Sangalli, a principle danseuse of the Niblo's production.

124

He'll aid me in my dire distress,
Then send me on to con-ge-ress!

(Wild chord by the orchestra. LUCIFER *appears, either through trap, or from* R. 3E. *Flash of lightning and sound of gong. He is dressed in red tights, with red hood on his head, and two horns. In his right hand he holds a scroll with which he points at* CROOK, *who shrinks from him in fear.)*

LUC.   Well, here I am! all right, you see,
Now what is it you want of me?

B. C.   *(creeps up to him).*
I want a dozen magic lamps,
To aid through life in picking up stamps.

LUC.   Thou hast thy wish, fool, even now,
The stamp of Cain is on thy brow.
Come, tell me what thou dost desire—
I'm getting cold without a fire.

B. C.   Well, then, I s'pose I must tell all,
The best of men will sometimes fall.
The people call me the "Black Crook,"
Because I read the "Magic Book."
They've robbed me of my magic spell,
And now myself to you I'll sell.

LUC.   Out with it, knave! name the condition
On which you'll join me in perdition.
You are the kind I wish to see,
For such as you resemble me.

B. C.   Then, first, I want the privilege
To be the first on "Broadway Bridge,"
Then I'd be pointed out to all,
As the young man, graceful and tall,
Who was the first to cross the street
Without wading through mud twelve inches deep.

LUC.   The first I grant! Now name the other,
Come, hurry up! I've no time to bother!

B. C.   Then first I'd know, as you're a resident,
About what time they'll impeach the President?[4]

LUC.   Bosh!

4 The impeachment of Andrew Johnson occurred on February 24, 1868.

This Grotesque Essence

B. C.   Another thing I wish you'd tell,
As you are bound to go to quell
Disturbance in this land of ours,
Who, at the next election, will hold the bowers?

LUC.   You shall know all, avaricious fool,
If you'll bring to me each year a soul;
Each year, when the clock strikes the hour of night,
A soul from you shall be my right.

B. C.   Enough! each year a "sole" I'll steal,
And with it bring you a toe and heel,
And, if your majesty it suits,
Next year I'll bring you a pair of "boots."

LUC.   'Tis well, now I must be a going,
Methinks, I hear some "rooster" crowing;[5]
Now don't forget, on land or sea,
That crooked trunk belongs to me.

(LUCIFER *vanishes* R. *through flames of red fire.* CROOK *hobbles off,* L. 3E.)

SCENE II.—*A garden.*

"GRAND ENSEMBLE DE BALLET."

In this scene can be introduced as many Ballet Girls as you please; however, six or eight is the usual number. They are all dressed in burlesque style, excepting one, who is to be a good dancer in order to show a contrast between herself and the others. The ladies who compose the Grand Ballet are dressed in white gauze dresses, reaching nearly to the knee; without hoops. The waists are red or blue satin, abundantly stuffed to form immense bosoms—large heavy shoes—white stockings stuffed, to form "big limbs"—fashionable lady's wig, with tremendous waterfall—green wreaths upon the head.

At change of scene they come from all the entrances upon their toes, with hands elevated; moving to "slow music." Move around awkwardly for about thirty-two bars, then change to

SECOND MOVEMENT.—WALTZ BY BALLET.

---

5 Before the cartoons of Thomas Nast saddled the Democratic party with the image of a donkey, the party was associated with the figure of a rooster. Thus, the crowing of a rooster often meant the oratory of a Democrat.

126

THIRD MOVEMENT.

The leading dancer comes from R. 3E., *dressed in beautiful style, and executes* LA ARIEL. *Moving over to each corner alternately, and tending gracefully back, each Ballet Girl, as she approaches, strikes comical attitude. At end of dance she retires back.*

FOURTH MOVEMENT.

LA SYLPHIDE *is burlesqued by one of the comedians, after which someone from the gallery throws a large cabbage, with large envelope stuck in it. Dancer takes it, kisses envelope, looks up at gallery, and puts envelope in his bosom.*

FIFTH MOVEMENT.—VILLAGE HORNPIPE—*Burlesque.*

SIXTH MOVEMENT.—LA BAYADEN—*Burlesque.*

SEVENTH MOVEMENT.—MAY POLE DANCE

MAN *brings on May Pole and holds it on stage—it has six strings of different colored muslin hanging from the top. Each Ballet Girl takes one, and they all dance* MAY POLE DANCE. *They finally get entangled in the muslin, winding up the man's head, &c., and all run off with May pole. Then immediately re-enter and form for the last scene.*

PALACE OF DEW DROPS.

With real water streaming from EMERALD FOUNTAINS. *Members of the "Corps de Ballet" form on each side of the stage in comical attitudes. Fancy Dancer is placed upon a soap box, C. Two little demons, dressed in red, rush out from either side with pans of red fire, and form each side of Fancy Dancer; forming Tableaux on their knees, in front of stage. At each corner is placed two Irish women upon boxes, pouring water from green watering-pots into a tub. A string of stuffed legs, boots, strings of onions, little dolls, cabbages, old clothes, bottles, &c. is let down from above by means of a rope held by some one in 3d entrance, and kept moving slowly up and down.* LUCIFER *and* BLACK CROOK *swing off, holding onto ropes suspended from beams above. They swing back and forth. Music appropriate.*

THE END

Feast

This final piece from the Griffin and Christy troupe represents another category of afterpieces—the burlesque Italian opera. From the 1830s to Reconstruction the popularity of Italian opera, though not overwhelming, was great enough that the genre held a dominant position in the formal theater in America. Stars of the form, such as Clara Louise Kellog and Parepa-Rosa, were in their day as familiar to New York audiences as Forrest, Booth, or Walleck; and several of New York's more resplendent theaters thrived on repertoires of the works of Rossini, Bellini, Donizetti, and Verdi.

Feast is a burlesque of the conventions of Italian opera rather than of a specific work, although the character of Armenia may very well have been intended as an allusion to Amina, the heroine of Vincenzo Bellini's popular *La Somnambula*. As in *Shylock* the humor in *Feast* centers upon the sustained use of a single verbal device, in this case the comic Italian inflections in the recitative. And, as in *Shylock*, the effect of the device is primarily cumulative. The cast list of *Feast* suggests the piece was offered at the Fifth Avenue Opera House in May or June of 1866. The following text is reprinted from the acting edition published by Samuel French.

FEAST,

an

Ethiopian Burlesque Opera,
performed with great success, by

GRIFFIN & CHRISTY'S MINSTRELS.

arranged by

G. W. H. GRIFFIN.

CAST OF CHARACTERS

DUKE DE HARDTACK	Mr. G. W. H. Griffin
COUNT SMASHER	Mr. George Christy
ANGEL OF LIGHT	Mr. J. T. Boyce
ARMENIA	Mr. Fred Abbott
PRINCE FULLHAND	Mr. F. G. Harding
BARON NEVERPLAY	Mr. C. F. Shattuck

Citizens, Soldiers, Retainers, Populace, &c.

SCENE.—*A Wood in 3 and 4.*—*"Omnes," Discovered in groups walking about stage; they appear as if conversing and plotting a conspiracy; they have on Black Dominoes, and there are masks upon their faces; at rise of curtain the Orchestra play the introduction to the* "CHORUS FROM ERNANI,"—*they all rush to the front in time to commence singing.*

ERNANI CHORUS.
> Hurrah! come on, be gay,
> We'll hie to the woods before we stray;
> Delay not! be off, quick, fly!
> We heed not the wind that's whistling by.
> Then follow! then follow! o'er hill and o'er hollow
> Our horns shall resound;
> The screech-owl loud may yell,
> To fright us darkies off our path,
> Yes, off our path.
> We heed no lightning's flash,
> Nor yet the thunder's wrath;

(solo) The old coon he did stray,
> We'll hunt him night and day,
> We'll hunt him all around;
> The old coon he did stray,

129

We'll hunt him night and day,
We'll hunt him all around.

O'er hill and dale's the possum's nest,
We'll seek him out before we rest;
(repeat)
    Upon some bank perhaps he's laid,
    (1st time) To rest in the shade,
    (2nd time) To rest himself beneath the shade;
    So let's away, so let's away.

(All go off at different entrances, singing the end of chorus. COUNT SMASHER *remains on the stage, and watches them suspiciously as they move off.* MUSIC, "THE LAST ROSE OF SUMMER.")

COUNT *(sings).*
    "I'll si gretto barnyard a foozlem,
    I'm undone! I'm undone! I'm undone!
    Sacramento a la Bamboozlem,
    I must run! I must run! I must run!" *(music,* CHORD*)*

(Enter "ANGEL OF LIGHT," *R. 1E. with large wings, and bearing huge letter in his hand. Sits down on one knee to the* COUNT, *and sings in recitative.)*

ANGEL *(sings).*   A leterio!
COUNT.   You don't say so. *(speaking)* From-a-whom-a? *(singing)*
ANGEL *(sings).*   From your lovi–e–ri–o.
COUNT.   Em–m—Em–m!
ANGEL *(sings).*   She desires to meet you in the back garden–er–ii–o.
    (COUNT *takes letter and looks at the superscription, then kisses it and turns to* ANGEL.)
COUNT.   Enough! thou art a faithful servant, take this—*(giving him a kick behind)* for thy reward.
ANGEL *(sings).*   I fly—erio. *(flies off stage, R. 1E. while* COUNT *is reading letter)*

Music:—*"As I view now this scene so charming." ("Somnambula.")*

COUNT *(sings).*
    "As I view now these lines so charming,
    With fond remembrance my heart is warming,
    Of day's long vanished—of days long vanished;

Oh this trunk! oh this chest is filled with pain!
Finding darkies that still remain."

(repeat)

"While those days and those night,
And that must ne'er come again."

(DUKE DE HARDTACK, *who has been watching the* COUNT *from the back part of the stage, comes stealthily forward, and as the* COUNT *makes the last note of the "Cadenza," the* DUKE *snatches the letter from his hand at the same time. Music, "Chord"—The* DUKE *has an umbrella in his hand, and the* COUNT *a small rattan; the* DUKE *seizes his umbrella, and the* COUNT *his stick, as if they were swords, and they were about to draw them and attack each other; they are close together, and eye each other fiercely; they finally shove the stick and umbrella back under their arms, and walk slowly away at opposite sides; the* DUKE *goes to* L. *corner and opens letter.)*

DUKE *(sings).*   A letterio, *(chord)* from my daughterio! *(chord)* You black-hearted scoundrelerio.

COUNT *(sings).*   I loverio, you daughterio, and I shall marry-ri-o your daughterio, and that's what's the matter–e–ri–o.

DUKE.   If you do, I'll be blow'd–e–ri–o. *(Music. They walk back of stage, then forward in a passion.)*

DUKE *(sings).*

Draw! draw! villain draw,
'Less by my soul I'll run you through;

COUNT.

War! war! bloody war! now 'twixt me and you.

DUKE.

Draw! draw! villain draw,
'Less by my soul I'll run you through;

COUNT.

War! war! bloody war! now 'twixt me and you.

DUKE *(speaking).*   This shall decide it. *(music, hurry)*

(They draw each his weapon, and make comic business on approaching each other; they finally come to quarrel, and commence combat; make this as funny as possible; finally the DUKE *runs his umbrella under the arm of the* COUNT, *puts his foot against his body and draws it out; the* COUNT *holds on with both hands as if he was wounded;* DUKE *sings "Victoria," and exits* L. 2E. *Music.)*

131

This Grotesque Essence

COUNT *(coming down, sings)*.
> "I'm stuck, but with an umbrella,
> And I s'pose that I must die;
> Farewell, my dear Amenia,
> Your love was all in my eye." *(music, minor, doleful)*

(COUNT goes up stage, looks about him to see if any one is looking, then feels about on floor to find a "soft board;" finds one, then goes to entrance, gets a few spears of straw, puts them down for a bed, lies down, takes his hat and puts it under his back, gives a groan, and dies.)
> Music.—"Travatore."

(Enter ARMENIA R. 1E. in long white robe, tremendous large wig, with flaxen hair reaching nearly to the stage; she has loose flowers in her hands.)

ARMENIA *(sings)*.
> "Oh dear, oh jeminee,
> Where can my smasher be,
> May-be he's in the sea,
> Skedaddled from me;
> I wish that he was here,
> With his Ar–me–ni–ri;
> But I have cause to fear,
> He has gone dead."

(She turns, and discovers the COUNT as he lays on the stage; she goes to him, and seizes his hand, kisses it, and acts very extravagantly, then walks around, and scatters the flowers on his body; every time she hits him in the face with one he sneezes, ARMENIA screams, and everybody rushes in; they discover the COUNT and are much excited.)
> Music.—"Fra Diavola."

The music plays until the DUKE *(who enters* L. 3E.*) gets to left hand corner; they all look at him in astonishment.*

DUKE *(sings)*.
> "'Twas I that killed that lobster,
> That titled loafer lying there.

(They all draw their swords and make a motion towards him.)

> In his hand a letter I found,
> From my daughter fair; *(They all draw back.)*

'Twas I that killed that lobster,
That titled loafer lying there. *(Same business.)*
In his hand a letter I found,
From my daughter fair;
(OMNES.)
Armenia! oh Armenia,
Oh what a dreadful fate is his,   *(repeat)*
Oh Ar–me–ni–a."
PRINCE FULLHAND *(sing in recitative).*
"Prepar–e–ri–o
To carry out the dead–e–ri–o."
DUKE *(raises his head and sings).*
"The dead–e–ri–o is ready to be carried out–e–ri–o."
Music.—*"John Anderson my Joe."*

(They approach the COUNT, *two take him by the arms, and the other two by the legs.* ARMENIA *forms behind the rest.* DUKE *raises his umbrella and forms at the head of the procession.)*
Music.—*"Soldier's Chorus."—Faust.*

(Procession starts, march around stage, crossing and re-crossing until back to 3d *entrance, then all march off* 3E., *singing as they march.)*

THE END

Africanus Blue Beard

As professional minstrelsy declined in the last quarter of the nineteenth century the typical minstrel performer changed in character. A few early figures had sidelines (Dan Bryant, for example, was renowed as an Irish comic, Griffin had moderate success in vaudeville after the death of Christy, and S. C. Campbell was an exceptional performer in grand opera), but most were thoroughly identified with burnt cork. Later performers were more accurately represented by a man like Frank Dumont. Perfomer, composer, author, technician, and general factotum, Dumont gained his fame from the quantity and variety rather than the quality of his creations. In addition to hundreds of minstrel afterpieces and songs, he wrote melodrama, comedy, and farce for the legitimate stage as well as songs, jokes, and sketches for vaudeville.

Africanus Blue Beard is only one of numerous forms the Blue Beard legend took during the nineteenth century. Originally a seventeenth-century French tale by Charles Perault, the legend was before the American public in some form throughout the 1800s. Burlesque versions became highly popular in the 1840s and 1850s and culminated with the American premier of *Barbe Bleue*, Offenbach's opera bouffe, on June 20, 1868. The following version of the legend attests less to the comic talents of Dumont than to the spectacular appeal of the legend itself.

What is significant about this piece is the form in which it was printed. Then as now, printing scores was much more expensive than printing texts. Since minstrel afterpieces were published as ephemeral, mass-market items, costs had to be kept at a minimum. Most publishers printed afterpieces that used popular songs or well-known operatic melodies for their music, thus eliminating the need for a score. In cases where scores were necessary for amateur productions, most publishers sold the music under separate cover. Rarely was the score published with the text as in the following piece.

The cast list of *Africanus Blue Beard* is for the premier performance by Duprez and Benedict's Minstrels on September 11, 1874 in Gloucester, Massachusetts. The following text is reprinted from the acting edition published by Robert M. De Witt in 1876.

AFRICANUS
BLUE BEARD.
A Musical Ethiopian Burlesque
By FRANK DUMONT.
Music arranged for the Pianoforte by
ALFRED B. SEDGWICK.

CAST OF CHARACTERS
BLUE BEARD (a model husband) . . . . J. T. Gulick
GRIPSACK (his attendant) . . . . Lew Benedict
BEPPO ⎱ Fatima's brothers ⎰ . . . . Frank Dumont
GREPPO ⎰ ⎱ . . . . Thos. B. Dixon
FATIMA (Blue-Beard's "latest") . . . . Frank Kent
MAFAIRY (a mother-in-law eternally in the way) . . . D. H. Smith
THE ROYAL PAGE . . . . Master H. Lino
CHIEF LUNCHIST . . . . W. Dunn
Guests, Huntsmen, &c.

135

This Grotesque Essence

COSTUMES

BLUE BEARD.—Blue whiskers, gaudy turban, Turkish trousers and big shoes. Blue coat, gorgeously trimmed—long coat and sash. Scimitar, large wooden key, and bunch of iron keys.

GRIPSACK.—Yellow slashed trunks, striped stockings, large shoes—velvet jacket—colored shirt—cap, with feathers.

BEPPO and GREPPO.—Velvet trunks and jackets—caps, with feathers—top-boots, or colored stockings.

HUNTSMEN and LUNCH-FIENDS.—Comic negro costumes.

FATIMA.—Gorgeous wench of the period.

MAFAIRY.—Black dress, blonde wig—large pair of spectacles, etc.

SCENE.—*Palace arches—backed by Palace.*

136

Africanus Blue Beard

(Enter GRIPSACK, *with combat sword, followed by Fatima's brothers. Huntsmen and Lunch-fiends—some with crackers, others with ham-bones, &c. Music until all the party is on stage.)*

GRIP.   Ain't we having a bully time! I tell you, every time Blue Beard gets a new wife it makes him awful generous to the boys.

LUNCH-FIENDS.   So it does—so it does!

GRIPSACK *sings.*

137

This Grotesque Essence

longs to Bar-be Blue! When he gets a new wife! Oh yes, up-on my life! He sets up the beer for the boys.

GRIP. Ah! here comes the wedding party. Stand aside, lunch-grabbers, and let the high-toned darkies pass.

MUSIC. *Repeat No. 1.*

(Enter BLUE BEARD, *arm-in-arm with* FATIMA: *followed by his mother-in-law,* MAFAIRY. *All bow as they enter.)*

BLUE B. The wedding ceremony is now over, and I've got a new wife to put in the Blue Chamber, when I get tired of paying her board.

FATIMA. Welcome, kind friends, to this Castle Hall. Tell me, mother, how do I look in these robes of gorgeous hue?

MAFAIRY. Immense! beautiful! You look too good for that homely nigger, with the blue whiskers.

FATI. Hush, ma! don't let him hear you. Excuse her, my lord, my mother is from the country.

BLUE B. I'll get rid of this mother-in-law's gab. I'll take her out some day and get rid of her in a cheap way.

SONG.—BLUE BEARD.

No. 3.

Allegretto.

Kind friends, let me now in-tro-

138

Africanus Blue Beard

duce you Mistress Blue Beard! My wife Number Two!

Be mer-ry and gay at our wed-ding! There's

cake and e-nough to drink, too! To-

mor-row off hunt-ing I'm going; Not long from the

house will I stop! Be jo-vial and gay in my

This Grotesque Essence

BLUE B. I shall start on my hunting trip at once. Don't let my absence mar your pleasure.

MAFAIRY. You don't mean to tell me you are going alone! Why don't you take your wife?

BLUE B. Have the kindness to keep your jaw to yourself.

SONG.—FATIMA.

140

This Grotesque Essence

way, No hard work will be done! Sleeping in the sun, Or loaf-ing at the door! You may believe we'll nev-er grieve If he re-turn no more.

Repeat Chorus ƒ *Quicker for symph.*

BLUE B. So you want these keys. (*produces several large iron keys from girdle*) Here they are. Look in every room; but in the one this key opens (*shows large wooden key*) you must not look.

GRIP. Oh! that must be his watch-key.

FATI. No; it's his whis-"key."

BLUE B. You are wrong; this is "key-no." (*holds up the key*)

GRIP. What row?

BLUE B. Top row!

GRIP. Give me another card; I've lost.

BLUE B. This key, remember, must not be used. Don't look in the Blue Chamber.

FATI. I will not look into that room, if you don't wish me to.

GRIP. No; she won't look into it: only give her a chance, that's all.

MAFAIRY (*coming to Gripsack*). No, she won't. My daughter is not curious like some women.

GRIP *(shrinking from her).*   Phew! go 'way. You've been eating onions.

MAFAIRY.   My daughter does not want to see the Blue Chamber—do you, dear?

FATI.   No, ma. *(aside)* But when we get a chance, we'll take one peep.

MAFAIRY *(aside).*   You bet we will!

BLUE BEARD sings 1st verse.

Here's the key of the cellar full of beer! Here's the
key of a room o-ver here! And here's the key that
looks so queer. So in that room don't peep, my dear!
Oh, no! Oh, no!

This Grotesque Essence

2d verse, FATIMA.

Yes, my love, these keys I'll keep:
In that room I will not sleep;
Not even in it would I peep—
No, not even a single peep.
(Orchestra.) Oh! no! Oh! no!

3d verse, GRIPSACK.

Oh, she don't care for at all to see,
Or unravel this mysteree.
Was there ever a woman that would not be
Full—yes, full of cu–ri–os–ity.
(Orches.) Oh, no! Oh, no!

BLUE B.   Now I will leave you. I'd like to catch the old woman while I am out shooting. I'd let go the double-barreled gun at her. Well, good-bye. My return will be announced by the sounding of the horn. Good-bye.

GRIP.   Ta, ta! bye-bye!

Repeat first 8 bars of No. 1, *until* BLUE BEARD *exits.*

(BLUE B. *embraces* FATIMA. MAFAIRY *comes forward to embrace him also. He turns from her, and exits* R. 2dE., *followed by Lunch-fiends and Huntsmen.* FATIMA *retires to back of stage.* MAFAIRY *turns to* GRIPSACK, *and extends her arms.*)

GRIP.   The old lady is going to make love to me. Come to my arms, sweet sparrowgrass. *(dodges under her arms)* Go West, old woman, and get shaved. *(exits* R. 2dE.)

FATI.   Now, ma, we are all alone, let's look into that Blue Chamber.

MAFAIRY.   Lead the way; I'll follow you. *(They exit at back* L.)

(Enter GRIPSACK, R. 2dE.)

GRIP.   Oh! what a nice game old Blue Beard is playing on us—pretending to go out hunting for a few days; and as I live he's returning.

(Loud screams are heard. MAFAIRY *runs in through arches, followed by* FATIMA. MAFAIRY *staggers over to* GRIPSACK.)

MAFAIRY.   Oh! that old villain! that old Mormon! He's got forty wifes hung up in that Blue Chamber.

GRIP.   He's got a "full hand," hasn't he?

MAFAIRY.   Catch me, I'm going to faint! *(staggers over to* FATIMA, *who holds her up)*

FATI.   Brace up, ma! you're awful heavy.

MAFAIRY.   I'm going to faint. Go out and get me some gin and sugar.

GRIP.   Gin and sugar? Well, I'll faint with you.

MAFAIRY.   That old Mormon! what shall we do with him? *(Horn sounds outside.)*

FATI.   O dear me, there's the horn that announces Blue Beard's return. Look at that fatal key! See, there is a stain of blood upon it.

GRIP.   Blood! no, it's tobacco juice.

FATI *(burlesque tragedy)*.   What shall we do? Wretched woman! We are lost! we are lost!

GRIP.   He'll put a head on you when he comes back.

Repeat 1st 8 bars of No. 1.

(BLUE BEARD, BEPPO, GREPPO, *and Huntsmen return.* FATIMA *comes forward to greet* BLUE BEARD.)

FATI.   What! Blue Beard! returned so soon?

BLUE B.   Yes: I've postponed my hunting excursion. You'll have the kindness to return those keys!

FATI *(confused)*.   The—keys?

BLUE B.   Yes; the keys. Give them to me.

GRIP.   Now you're going to get it!

FATI *(to* MAFAIRY*)*.   What shall I do, mother?

MAFAIRY.   Give him these. *(gives iron keys to Fatima)*

FATI.   Here they are! *(gives them to Blue Beard)*

BLUE B. *(examining keys)*.   They are not all here!

MAFAIRY.   I say they are!

BLUE B.   Silence, you old viper.

145

This Grotesque Essence

SONG.—BLUE BEARD.

Africanus Blue Beard

presence; Your lit-tle game I see! I want that key, this

D. S.

in-stant! So, give it back to me!

(MAFAIRY *passes the key to* FATIMA.)

FATIMA *sings verse 3d.*

Oh, here's the key you seek, my lord;
Upon it there's a stain. (*orches.*)
I'll go at once to try
To rub away the stain.

(BLUE BEARD *takes the key away from her and examines it.* BLUE BEARD *sings.*)

What's this I see upon this key?
'Tis blood! you've told a lie. (*orches.*)
You've peeped into that room;
You must prepare to die. (FATIMA *screams.*)

GRIP.   Take her to the slaughter house.

BLUE B.   You've disobeyed me, and your life pays the penalty. (*Draws wooden scimitar.* FATIMA *screams, and kneels imploringly to* BLUE BEARD. *Mock tragedy business.*)

FATI.   Spare me, Blue Beard! spare me! I am but a che-ild, and did not know any better. Spare me!

BLUE B.   No: prepare to die.

GRIP.   Here, take this sword; it is sharper than yours. (*Gives combat sword to* BLUE BEARD. BLUE BEARD *rushes forward to dispatch* FATIMA,

147

This Grotesque Essence

when BEPPO *and* GREPPO *with combat swords attack* BLUE BEARD. *Music hurry until* BLUE BEARD *falls.)*

No. 7. Hurry kept up till the end.

Hurry. Allegro.

(Kept up till Blue Beard falls.)

(Short combat of three, between BLUE BEARD, BEPPO *and* GREPPO. *They disarm and stab* BLUE BEARD, *who falls. They shout and exit* R. 2dE. *followed by* MAFAIRY.)*

FATI.   Thus perishes the tyrant! Die! die! die! *(tragic and burlesque exit, L. 2dE.)*

*(*GRIPSACK *runs in* R. 2dE. *with Bellows, to which two fish-horns are attached, and blows a blast in Blue Beard's ear. He starts up; another blast, and* BLUE BEARD *jumps up.* GRIPSACK *chases him out, blowing blasts upon the bellows as he follows after* BLUE BEARD.)*

CLOSE IN, OR CURTAIN

Helen's Funny Babies

In 1876 John Habberton, a minor American humorist, published *Helen's Babies*, a novel about the mischief perpetrated on adults by a pair of precocious children named Budge and Toddie. The novel was a raging success, the most popular work in its day from the "bad boy" school of humor which produced such classics as Mark Twain's *The Adventures of Tom Sawyer* (1876), the bad-boy stories of George Wilbur Peck, and America's first daily comic strip—Rudolph Dirks's *The Katzenjammer Kids* (1897). Then as now, successful entertainment had a way of quickly spreading through a variety of artistic forms. Within a year after its publication Habberton's novel was on stage in New York in several versions. As early as the spring of 1877 burlesque sketches of it were being offered on variety bills; the fall of that year saw numerous minstrel versions (including the following one by Dumont); and in February of 1878 a full dramatic adaptation opened at the Broadway Theatre.

It was common in minstrelsy for different troupes to offer different burlesque versions of the same material at roughly the same time, particularly when the familiarity of a spectacular public event ensured huge audiences; and frequently a popular minstrel afterpiece "made the rounds" if given enough time and audience response. But simultaneous production was unheard of, particularly during minstrelsy's heyday. The fact that *Helen's Funny Babies* received such production suggests both that Habberton's original story had more impact on American audiences than historians of American humor assume and that minstrelsy, like most other popular entertainment during the Gilded Age, was moving in the direction of assembly-line production.

HELEN'S
FUNNY
BABIES.

An Ethiopian Burlesque,
in one scene.

BY FRANK DUMONT.

CAST OF CHARACTERS

BUDDLE	. . . . Mr. E. F. Dixey[1]	. . .	Charley Backus[2]
TODDLE	. . . . Mr. Matt Wheeler	. . .	Billy Birch
UNCLE HARRY	. . Mr. Geo. Frothingham	. .	Bob Hart
DOCTOR OUNCE	. . Mr. E. A. Weslyn	. . .	H. W. Frillman
SNIFFLE	. . . . Mr. Jas. Griffin	. . . .	George Powers
PERKINS	. . . . Mr. J. Rice	. . . . .	Chas. Gibbons
BUDDLE	. . . . Dave Reed[3]	. . . . .	Mr. John Harris[4]
TODDLE	. . . . Hughey Dougherty	. . .	Mr. Archie White
UNCLE HARRY	. . F. B. Wilson	. . . . .	Mr. J. T. Gulick
DOCTOR OUNCE	. . Billy Bryant	. . . . .	Mr. Frank Dumont
SNIFFLE	. . . . C. R. Clinton	. . . . .	Mr. Reese
PERKINS	. . . . J. Pelham	. . . . . .	Mr. Murphy

1 Carncross and Dixey's Minstrels, September 17, 1877.
2 The San Francisco Minstrels, October 15, 1877.
3 Bryant's Minstrels, October 15, 1877.
4 Duprez and Benedict's Minstrels, September 17, 1877.

Helen's Funny Babies

COSTUMES

BUDDLE.—Waist, trousers, cap, etc.

TODDLE.—Make-up as a fat boy.

HARRY.—Vest, pants, dressing-gown, and cap.

DOCTOR OUNCE.—Business suit and spectacles.

SNIFFLE.—Genteel dress.

PERKINS.—Genteel dress.

SCENE.—*Plain chamber. Table with tablecloth. Small bell.* HARRY *discovered seated at table. Wears dressing gown and cap.*

HARRY. Confound those imps. Everything is destroyed, and the house is fast becoming a wreck. I've been sick just one week, and during that time they have ruined everything of value. Helen sent the babies here to wait on me, and I have to wait on myself at all times. *(rings bell)* Buddle! Toddle! where are you? Buddle! Toddle!

(Enter BUDDLE, R. 1E., *holding behind him a stuffed rat in one hand, and its tail in the other. He is weeping and bawling.)*

HARRY. Stop that infernal noise! Do you hear me? *(*BUDDLE *weeps louder.)* Stop! stop! You'll drive me mad! Where have you been?

BUDDLE *(crying)*. I was down in the barn playing Jonah and the whale, and an accident happened to Jonah. Oh! oh! oh!

HARRY. Down in the barn playing Jonah and the whale, eh? Where's Jonah?

BUDDLE. There he is! *(shows the rat, and bawls very loud)*

HARRY. Stop your noise. What accident happened to Jonah?

BUDDLE. I was playing with Jonah, and I pulled poor Jonah's tail off. *(shows tail of rat)*

HARRY. Throw it out; it's a nasty rat.

BUDDLE *(sobs)*. 'Taint a rat, Uncle Harry; it's Jonah.

HARRY. Throw it out, I tell you!

BUDDLE. The whale might come along and swallow him.

HARRY *(raises cane)*. Throw that rat out or I'll break your back. *(*BUDDLE *cries, and throws out rat and tail,* R. 1E.) Now, sir, how long have I got to ring this bell?

BUDDLE. It's your bell. You can ring it just as long as you like.

HARRY. Did you hear this bell ring?

BUDDLE. Yes, sir. I thought dinner was ready, and I run all the way.

151

This Grotesque Essence

HARRY. You thought dinner was ready? Where have you been all the morning?

BUDDLE. You ought to see the goat me and Toddle's got. Oh! he's a bully goat. We've got him fighting with your chickens, and the goat killed seventeen of 'em. Ha! ha! ha!

HARRY. Killed seventeen of my spring chickens?

BUDDLE *(joyfully)*. Yes, sir. Knocked 'em all to pieces.

HARRY. You villain! you rascal! You let that goat kill my chickens, did you? *(raises cane)* I'll warm your jacket, you villain!

BUDDLE. 'Twasn't me, Uncle Harry. The goat done it. I couldn't help it. *(cries)*

HARRY. Wait until I get stronger. I'll pay you for this.

BUDDLE *(crying)*. I know something about Toddle.

HARRY. What do you know about Toddle?

BUDDLE. You know that nice gold watch of yours?

HARRY. Yes. What about my gold watch?

BUDDLE. Toddle took a hammer and mashed it all up.

HARRY. Mashed my gold watch? What for?

BUDDLE *(laughs)*. He wanted to see the wheels go round.

HARRY. I'll let him see the wheels go round when I catch him.

BUDDLE. Oh, he's a bad boy, aint he?

HARRY. I'll fix you both! Wait until I grow stronger. Killed my chickens—smashed my watch! What next? Where's Toddle?

BUDDLE. He was down in the river swimming, and I took his clothes and hid 'em. He can't find 'em, so he can't come home. Ha! ha! ha!

HARRY. You hid his clothes, did you? now go and get his clothes for him. Gather up my dead chickens——

BUDDLE. There aint nothing left of 'em but a few feathers!

HARRY. Go and do as I tell you! Send that goat away instantly—and should any of the neighbors call with jellies, cakes or other delicacies, send them away, I don't want them; for they expect me to repay these favors. If the doctor calls say I feel better. I'm going to my room. *(removes gown and cap)* As soon as I am well I will attend to you with this cane. *(Going towards* L. 1E., *he turns and catches* BUDDLE *laughing.* BUDDLE *pretends to cry, but laughs as soon as* HARRY *turns his back. Business ad lib.* HARRY *exits* L. 1E.*)*

BUDDLE. I ain't going to tell the neighbors to take away the pies, jellies

and delicacies—no, sir. I'll put on Uncle Harry's dressing gown
and cap, and get all them nice things myself. (*Puts on gown and cap.*
TODDLE *heard crying,* R. 1E. BUDDLE *rings the bell.*)

(TODDLE *enters,* R. 1E.)

TODDLE.   Uncle Harry! boo! boo!

BUDDLE (*in gruff voice*).   Where have you been?

TODDLE.   I was down in swimming, and Buddle hid my clothes so I
couldn't get home, and you'd scold me.

BUDDLE.   That Buddle is a bad boy. Go and get me a glass of ale! (TOD-
DLE *exits and returns with glass of ale.* BUDDLE *drinks it.*) Go and get
me another glass. (*As* TODDLE *exits he turns and discovers it is* BUD-
DLE. *He enters with glass of ale*—BUDDLE *reaches for it.*)

TODDLE.   Here's my regards. (*drinks*)

BUDDLE.   What do you mean, sir? Drinking my ale?

TODDLE.   You think you're smart, don't you? I'm going to tell Uncle
Harry that you've got his clothes on. (*starts* R.)

BUDDLE (*catches him*).   Hold up! Don't tell Uncle Harry!

TODDLE.   Yes, I will. You can't fool me.

BUDDLE.   Look here! the neighbors bring in lots of delicacies for Uncle
Harry, and he's sick and can't eat 'em; now I'll sit here and pre-
tend I'm uncle and we'll get all the good things, and I'll give you
half!

TODDLE.   All right. Mind, I get half.

BUDDLE.   Yes. (*Sits at table,* TODDLE *fans him. Knock at door.*)

(*Enter* SNIFFLE, R. 1E.)

SNIFF.   How is your Uncle Harry this morning?

TODDLE.   He's very feverish. He imagines every one is bringing him
something nice to eat. (BUDDLE *groans.*)

SNIFF.   I brought a nice orange for him; here it is.

(BUDDLE *grabs for it, but* TODDLE *secures it and commences to peel it.*)

TODDLE (*to* BUDDLE).   Be quiet—you're sick!

BUDDLE.   Give me that orange. (*makes attempts to get it without allowing*
SNIFFLE *to discover him*)

TODDLE (*to* SNIFFLE).   He's got fever! and the best thing for fever is an
orange—not the inside of an orange. It's only the peeling that's
good for fever. (*gives peel to* BUDDLE, *who makes a wry face and eats*

peel, while TODDLE *devours the orange.* BUDDLE *tries hard to get at*
TODDLE.)

SNIFF.   I also brought some of my imported port wine. *(shows flask.*
BUDDLE *attempts to get it, but* TODDLE *grabs it, and, turning his back to*
SNIFFLE *he drinks the contents of flask.)*

TODDLE.   Port wine is bully for fever.

SNIFF.   I'll bid you good morning and call again to-night. *(exits R. 1E.)*

BUDDLE *(jumps up—catches* TODDLE*)*.   Say, how is this? I do the groan-
ing, and get sick with the fever, and what do I get?

TODDLE.   Didn't I give you the peel? Now, the next comes in is yours!

BUDDLE.   All right. *(sits at table)*

TODDLE.   Be sick! be sick! *(Knock at door. Enter* PERKINS, *with piece of pie*
on a plate.)

PERKINS.   How is your uncle this morning?

TODDLE.   He's away out of his head. He thinks there's been nice things
for him to eat, and he imagines that he sees oranges.

PERKINS.   Perhaps this pie would not be good for him. *(going)*

TODDLE.   Yes, it would. He can eat pie. *(* BUDDLE *makes an effort to get the*
pie, but TODDLE *gets the pie, leaving the plate in Buddle's hands.* TOD-
DLE, *with his back turned to* PERKINS, *devours the pie, while* BUDDLE
frantically endeavors to get some of it.)

BUDDLE *(aside to* TODDLE*)*.   Give me some of that pie, you hog!

TODDLE.   Shut up—you're sick! *(to* PERKINS*)* What kind of pie is this?

PERKINS.   Prune pie.

TODDLE.   Well, a prune wouldn't hurt him. *(gives small piece of pie to*
BUDDLE*)*

BUDDLE.   I don't want to eat the pits. I want some of the pie.

PERKINS.   I'll call in by-and-by, and bring in some nice custard. *(exits,*
R. 1E.)

BUDDLE *(leaps up and grasps* TODDLE*)*.   Here! this is played out. I had to
do all the sick business, and you've been eating.

TODDLE *(mouth full of pie)*.   Sick people oughtn't to eat; but the next
comes in is yours.

BUDDLE.   You bet I'll get the next comes in. *(Sits at table as* DOCTOR
OUNCE, *with medicine-case, enters,* R. 1E. BUDDLE *groans very loud.)*

DOCTOR.   So my patient is worse, is he? What seems to be the matter
with him?

TODDLE.   He's got cramps.

DOCTOR.   Then I'll have to prescribe camphor; but, should the cramps grow more violent, we'll give him a big glassful of whiskey. (BUD-DLE *begins to groan and shout, "I'm worse," etc.; rolls and kicks in his chair.* PERKINS *and* SNIFFLE *enter,* R. 1E.)

DOCTOR.   Whiskey will do him no good. I must give him some cholera mixture. (*opens case, selects a bottle*)

BUDDLE.   I don't want any. I'm better!

SNIFF. *and* PERKINS.   Take the medicine. (DOCTOR *forces bottle to Buddle's lips and comes to C.; opens case, starts; calls* TODDLE, SNIFFLE *and* PERKINS *to him.*)

DOCTOR.   Don't say a word. I've made a terrible mistake. Instead of giving him cholera mixture I've given him a deadly poison called oil of catnip, and enough to kill twenty men. For Heaven's sake, fly for an antidote! (DOCTOR, TODDLE, SNIFFLE *and* PERKINS *rush off,* R. 1E.)

BUDDLE.   They're going after the whiskey. (HARRY *heard calling* "TOD-DLE!" "BUDDLE!" *and heard coming,* L. 1E.)

BUDDLE.   I don't want Uncle Harry to catch me with his clothes on. (*takes off gown and cap, and hides under table as* HARRY *enters,* L. 1E.)

HARRY (*puts on gown and cap*).   What's all this scampering all over the house mean? (TODDLE *rushes on,* R, *with glass of water.*)

TODDLE.   I couldn't get the nanny-goat; but here's some boiling hot water. (*dashes glass of water over Harry's face.* SNIFFLE *rushes on with bottle, forces it to Harry's mouth.* PERKINS *rushes on with spoonful of flour—dashes it into Harry's face.* DOCTOR *rushes on with large tin pump.*)

HARRY (*starts up*).   What do you mean, you lunatics?

DOCTOR.   I've given you oil of catnip instead of cholera mixture. You're a dead man! (BUDDLE *rolls out from under table.*) You're poisoned.

BUDDLE.   'Twas me took the oil of catnip.

DOCTOR.   Quick! Use the pump! (BUDDLE *lies upon his back.* DOCTOR, *placing end of pump to his mouth, pumps away, all the rest shouting, etc.* DOCTOR *opens lid of pump, and empties several cats or kittens out of the hollow pump.*)

CURTAIN

De Maid ob
de Hunkpuncas

Americans have always been fascinated by the Indian but never more so than in the nineteenth century when the nation still had a wilderness frontier. Americans tended to see in the figure a paradoxical blend of demonic brutality and savage nobility, a concise and spectacular embodiment of the danger and beauty of the wilderness as a whole. The extremes of behavior which could fancifully be attributed to savagery made a natural vehicle for the dramatic expression of America's conflicting attitudes toward the frontier. As a result, the Indian story became one of, if not *the* most significant entertainment motif in the nineteenth century. In captivity narratives (both real and fictional), in live museum exhibits, in the dime novels of frontier adventure, and in a flood of stage melodramas and exotic romances, the figure of the Indian was presented in a grotesquely exaggerated form that held captive the American popular imagination. More reasonable minds, though, recognized the lack of realism which distinguished most of this entertainment. By the 1840s the spirit of ridicule had turned on the subject and resulted in three of America's recognized burlesque masterpieces—John Brougham's *Metamora; or, The Last of the Pollywogs* (1847), his *Po-Ka-Hon-Tas; or, The Gentle Savage* (1855), and Charles Walcut's *Hiawatha; Ardent Spirits and Laughing Water* (1856). Of these, *Po-Ka-Hon-Tas*

156

was the most successful and went through numerous revivals in the thirty years following its first performance.

De Maid ob de Hunkpuncas is representative of the numerous minstrel contributions to the Indian burlesque tradition, its main objective being the comic exposure of the excesses of Indian plays. It is tempting to conclude that this anonymous piece dates from before the Civil War because of its structural resemblance to the olio sketches of minstrelsy's early decades. But, the character of the manager was probably intended to remind audiences of A. M. Palmer, who entered theatrical circles when he was appointed manager of New York's prestigious Union Square Theatre in 1872; and Dan Boozikaw is an obvious caricature of Dion Boucicault, the Irish born actor and playwright who was a reigning influence in American theater throughout the second half of the nineteenth century. The presence of these apparent references suggests that *De Maid* was inspired by the one recorded collaboration between Palmer and Boucicault in the fall of 1873 when Palmer produced *Led Astray*, Boucicault's adaptation of Octave Feuillet's *La Tentation*. The following text is reprinted from the acting edition published by the Happy Hours Company in 1874.

DE MAID
OB DE
HUNKPUNCAS.
An Ethiopian Interlude
In One Scene.

CHARACTERS
MR. PALMER (a manager)
DAN BOOZIKAW (an author)

This Grotesque Essence

COSTUMES

MR. PALMER.—Genteel business suit.

DAN BOOZIKAW.—Shabby evening dress, much too short for him, coat buttoned up to the neck, battered white hat, with crape band; large figured handkerchief sticking out from coat-tail pocket.

SCENE.—*A Room in 3d G. Table and two chairs, C.*

(MR. PALMER *rushes on wildly, followed by* DAN BOOZIKAW *with a cleaver.* MR. P. *takes refuge in a corner with both hands up, Dan standing over him with cleaver, brandishing a MS.*)

MR. P.   There, there—don't strike; I'll strike instead.

DAN.   You'll strike? What wid? *(looking round)*

MR. P.   Strike my colors, of course—give in—surrender. And if all my company don't "strike" when they hear you, I'm in luck. Let's bury the hatchet.

DAN.   Well, dere den. *(throws away cleaver)* Let's do t'ings comfortable. *(Both take chairs. Dan tilts back his chair, and puts feet on table, and proceeds to unroll his MS. After sundry coughings and spittings.)* De play dis time am de highfalutin' drammer ob

DE MAID OB DE HUNKPUNCAS.

MR. P.   Is that an "emotional drama?"

DAN.   No, it's *com*-motional, 'cause dere am a great deal ob commotion in it.

(reads) Scene Fust.—De 'riginal wilderness. Party ob hunters diskibbered, eatin' and smokin' round de camp fire.

CHORUS.

In de wild Injun's track
At de brokin' ob morn,
Lef us take a horn, lef us take a horn;
Den we'll follow de buck
At a pace nip-and-tuck—
Tra–la–la–a, tra–la–la!

MR. P.   O, come! You can't impose upon *me*; that's the Chamois Song in "Amilie."[1]

1 An American opera; music by W. Rooke, libretto by J. Haines; first performed in 1846 and quite popular during the middle of the nineteenth century.

De Maid ob de Hunkpuncas

DAN. It aint a sham song, neider. Well; dey all up and take a drink, and jus' den dere's de deblishest combobolation in de bushes. "Ow–ow–ow!" and a passel o' Injuns rushes in wid a lot o' warpaint and heaves it all ober de hunters, to quick music and yaller fire.

MR. P. Stop, stop, my dear fellow! the war-paint is what the sons of the forest paint their faces with when they're going on the warpath.

DAN. Say, look hyah! who's a'doin' ob this? eh! You jist keep quiet, or you'll git *me* on de warpath. Don't de 'spatches always say "dey come off wid *flyin' colors?*" Well, when dey hear dat, de head feller jumps and says: "It am de war whoop ob de Scalliwangas; git for your lives!" And when de Injuns comes on a trundlin' deir hoops before um, de fellers breaks fo' de wings—

MR. P. Mr. Boozikaw, I am surprised you don't know better than that. A war whoop is a yell—such as *you* make when a feller gets your head in Chancery in a fight.

DAN. I'm safe dere. Got took prisoner by de Injuns myself once; chief come at me wid his club and smasht it to splinters ober my head, and I butted him to def in a hurry! Well, den, on comes de Ripsnorter. Says he:

"How sultry am de air ob dis hot wedder! Methought I heard a warcry, but perhaps 'twas but the murmuring of the vexed coyote. *N'importe*, I'll rest awhile and think of her I love. Ah, Oneota!"

He trows down his cane and umbrell' and takes off his white kids and wipes his face off de presperation wid em—

MR. P. Why, the Rip-snorters of the prairie don't talk in that way, and they don't carry canes and umbrellas and wear white kids. Somebody's been fooling you.

DAN *(with great dignity).* Sir, dere libs not de man dat kin do dat same! I scorns de insinavation, but to de p'int. Mine isn't a common Ripsnorter—didn't you tell me 'riginality was de t'ing? Den says de Blood-red one, says he:

"Now to de buffalo licks, and arter dat, hey for a flask of champagne and Oneota!"

MR. P. Champagne in the wilderness?—pooh, pooh! it's more likely your Blood-red one was thinking of his redeye.

DAN. 'Twasn't red, nudder—it was black—got it in a scrimmidge. All to once dere am a wild skreek heard in de bushes, and Oneota

159

rushes out, cryin'—"Save me, sa-ave me!" and frows herself onto his neck.

"What!" says de Rip-snorter, "de darter ob de Hunkpuncas, and in distress? Come forth, my trusty ally!"

And wid dat he draws his howitzer from his pocket——

MR. P.   Tut, tut! how could he carry a howitzer in his pocket!

DAN.   It was a small one, you know, wid a stopper in it, and was labeled "Old Rye!" and he stuck de howitzer into her mouf and she took a pull, and it discharges itself down her t'roat, an' he follows suit.

MR. P.   Of course he *follows soot*, if she's as dark as you are.

DAN.   Dat's personal. Well, h'ya!—while dey is billin' and cooin', old Scalliwamgus, he comes on, and says he:

"White man, de snows ob de mountain come down to meet de lilies ob de valley, but de clouds ob de tempus cannot mingle wid de drippin's ob de daisy. Unhold dat gal!"

MR. P.   Why, sir, your original Indian talks like one of the poets in a sentimental magazine. Next you will have *him* wearing kid gloves, too.

DAN.   Well, dey hab a scruffle and de hero he gits him down and Oneoty she pounds dem bofe wid de howitzer, and den you hear de blast ob de bugles in de distance, and de ole hunts dey comes tumblin' in, followed by de Injuns, and after de hunts is all scalpt, some sojers rushes on and takes de Injuns pris'ners; and den de Rip-snorter ob de Red-eye he gits onto his feet and hugs de gal up close, and says he: *(rising from chair and striking an attitude)*

"We are sabed, my Oneoty!"

(MR. P. goes to wing, L., and procures stuffed club, which he keeps concealed behind his back, and walks over to DAN.)

"Who'm you'm?" axes de cappin' ob de sojers.

"I's Giner'l Spandango, de head ob dis diwision, and your chief."

Den dey all goes down on deir knees wid deir heads off and deir hats in deir hands—I mean deir hats off and deir heads in deir hands—*(Pantomime business)*—no, I mean—quit puttin' a feller out, will yer? And de cappin' axes:

"What shill we do wid de captives?"

"Gib um a service ob silber plate and send um to Washin'ton free."

Den dere am a dance and a choris, and dat wind up de 'formance.

MR. P. *(sarcastically)*. O, that's *your* wind up, eh? Well now I'll show you how *I* would wind it up. *(Gives Dan a terrific whack with club, which doubles him up. As the club is about to descend again,* DAN *makes a break for the wings,* L., *but falls and is clubbed off by* MR. P. *Quick close, or—)*

CURTAIN

Julius the Snoozer

Occasionally individual productions of a play gain fame totally separate from the reputation of the play itself. Such was the case when on December 27, 1875, a production of *Julius Caesar* was offered at Booth's Theatre in New York. That production boasted one of the finest casts and some of the most expensive scenery ever assembled in America. The trio of Lawrence Barret as Cassius, E. L. Davenport as Brutus, and Frank C. Bangs as Antony provided imcomparable star appeal that has since moved George C. D. Odell to refer to the production as "one of the glories of the mellow 70's and of our stage histories as a whole" (*Annals of the New York Stage*, X, 10). Booth's production ran until April 1, 1876, over one hundred performances. During that interval no less than four separate burlesques of the play sprang up in New York, including a variety sketch with G. W. H. Griffin in the title role, and the following afterpiece offered by New York's San Francisco Minstrels in February of 1876.

As suggested by Robert C.Toll in *Blacking Up: The Minstrel Show in Nineteenth-Century America* (Oxford University Press, N.Y., 1974), the afterpiece did not develop as an effective weapon for conscious social and political satire until after the Civil War. Topical barbs were common elements in the earlier pieces; but above all things the antebellum burlesque was a broad comic fantasy. Life in the northeastern urban centers changed radically after the war, however, and fantasy often gave way to cynical and sometimes strident attacks on the social and political problems of the Gilded Age. Shocked by the scope of the scandals in the Grant administration, significant numbers of both major political parties broke with their organizations in 1872 to support reform candidates for national office. In New York City, the exposure of how William Marcey "Boss" Tweed and his ring had plundered the city coffers to the tune of some $200 million provided material for almost daily news accounts throughout the first half of the decade. In 1874 Tweed was finally tried and convicted. He served one year in prison and upon his release was returned to debtor's prison from which he escaped on December 4, 1875. In the months which followed, the city papers were filled with stories tracing the rumors of Tweed's whereabouts. He was in fact traveling incognito and trying desperately to reach Spain, where he could avoid extradition. It was in this highly charged atmosphere of public outrage that *Julius the Snoozer* was performed. The production at Booth's proved well timed for the minstrel satirist. The tradition of burlesquing current stage hits gave Addison Ryman a particularly appropriate plot structure on which to hang enough topical allusions to create a fanciful account of Tweed's demise. The following text is reprinted from the acting edition published by Robert M. De Witt in 1876.

JULIUS
THE SNOOZER;

or,

The Conspirators of Thompson Street.
An Ethiopian Burlesque in Three Scenes,
By ADD RYMAN.
Arranged
By CHARLES WHITE.

CAST OF CHARACTERS

JULIUS THE SNOOZER (an ambitious politician) . .   Mr. Billy Birch
MARC ANTONY (with every attitude a picture, and every picture
      perfect) . . . . Mr. Charley Backus
BRUTUS (the working man's friend) . . . . .   Mr. Billy Carter
CASSIUS (the skeleton lobbyist) . . . .   Mr. Add Ryman
DECIUS (one of the gang) . . . .   Mr. Geo. Powers
PINCHBACK (an outsider imported expressly for this piece) . . .
                        Mr. Jas. Johnson
CAMPHORINA (the Snoozer's wife, after Goddess of Liberty) . . .
                        Mr. F. M. Ricardo
Senators, Chicken Thieves, Keno Sharps and Tramps, by 1,000
Auxiliaries, weighing 280 lbs., and standing 8 feet in height.

COSTUMES

JULIUS THE SNOOZER.—Black Tights; Roman Toga; large Nigger Shoes;
Vegetable Crown and Baton.

MARC ANTONY.—Black Tights; Roman Toga; large Nigger Shoes.

BRUTUS.—Black Tights; Roman Toga; funny Shoes.

CASSIUS.
DECIUS.   } Similar to the above; all on the Roman style,
PINCHBACK.   but very extravagant; funny Wigs, etc.

CAMPHORINA.—1st, any Calico long Dress; at finish, Goddess of Liberty.

AUXILIARIES.—All sorts of funny styles, soldiers, etc.

164

Julius the Snoozer

SYNOPSIS

SCENE 1ST.—STREET BELOW BLEECKER.[1] Triumphal return of the Snoozer from a Jersey clam bake. The conspirators. Bloody blood must flow. How the public money is spent to carry on the elections. Beer and trouble brewing. SCENE 2D.—CHAMBER IN THE ROYAL PALACE. The wife's dream. Business about to be delayed. The dream interpreted. A hazardous investment. SCENE 3D.—THE SENATE. The Ides of March. The will of the people trampled under foot. Lively scene in the Senate Chamber. The conspiracy thickens. The Snoozer grows defiant. Great excitement. It thickens. It gets thick. The signal. Awful death of the Snoozer. Brutus in the chair. Marc Antony's grief and graceful posturing over the dead body of Julius. Flight of the Senators. Grand ovation to Brutus, and burning of the Snoozer's body.

And as the smoke to the sky ascends,
The curtain on the play de——drops.

> SCENE I.—*Street in 1st Grooves; Shouts outside; Enter Procession L. 1E., marching; They cross and exit R. 1E.; Enter* PINCHBACK, DECIUS, JULIUS, MARC ANTONY, BRUTUS *and* CASSIUS L. 1E.; BRUTUS *and* CASSIUS *occupy* C. *of Stage;* JULIUS *and* MARC ANTONY L.C.; PINCHBACK *and* DECIUS R.C.

MARC ANTONY *(to JULIUS).*
Brutus and Cassius, friends you admire.

JULIUS.
When I call Cassius friend, call Julius liar;
His look is cadaverous and lean.
He's not as fat as hamfatters I've seen,
He stalks into my presence like a Western ghost
That has been caught napping on an Indian post;
But come to the Senate; a proclamation I will make:
(reading) Let no guilt-edged man escape.

(Exit R. 1E., followed by MARC ANTONY, DECIUS *and* PINCHBACK.*)*

---

1   The setting of this piece is an area of lower Manhattan just south of Washington Square, roughly corresponding to what is now the eastern half of Greenwich Village. During the 1870s the area was primarily a haven for Irish immigrants under the control of Boss Tweed's political machine.

This Grotesque Essence

BRUTUS.   My noble Cassius! thy love I too well know,
             But, why urge me on to strike this deadly blow?
CASSIUS.   O Brutus! Your love for Julius will ruin the colored *race*,
             This moke must die while you do take his place.
BRUTUS.   But, noble Cassius, should we fail, what then?
CASSIUS.   Follow the example of some other men.
             For instance, the one left by Oakey Hall——[2]
             The very best and latest of them all.
             For, when in the "Crucible" he found a flaw,
             To restore his reputation he went to law.[3]
BRUTUS.   Cassius, I'll do this act with the excuse all politicians
                 make—
             That 'tis not for office, but for my country's sake.
CASSIUS.   Would it not be policy to expose your platform?
             We live, you know, in the age of reform.
BRUTUS.   Say I favor Hard Money, the School Question, Whiskey
                 Rings,
             Canal Frauds and Inflation,
             Or any other little snap to enrich the nation.[4]
             Take this dollar and lay it out for beer,
             And, as they drink, let them for Brutus cheer.
             Away! Be quick! the time has almost come
             When bloody blood through Thompson street must run.
                         (shouts outside)
CASSIUS.   Friend!
BRUTUS.   Brother!

(They clasp hands and exit, R. and L. Enter JULIUS *and* CAM-
PHORINA, *R. 1E. Shouts outside.)*

---

2   A. Oakey Hall, a fashionplate, notorious playboy, and member of the Tweed ring,
served as mayor of New York from 1869 to 1872.
3   Hall was one of the first of the Tweed ring to be indicted in 1871. Though tried and
acquitted, he failed in his reelection bid for the mayoralty and turned to the theater
where he tried to make a career as an actor and playwright. In 1875 he wrote and
starred in "The Crucible," a play about a man unjustly accused, tried, convicted, sen-
tenced, and imprisoned, but ultimately found innocent and released. The play was a re-
sounding flop.
4   Brutus offers a catalog of the major political scandals attacked by the reform movement in the early 1870s.

Julius the Snoozer

CAMP.	To me these terrible shouts a fearful warning seem;
	Besides, last night I'd a most distressing dream.
	There, be a good boy, and for once your darling please.
JULIUS.	I knew you'd dream last night when you ate that
	Limburger cheese.
CAMP.	My lord, if not for me, then for your country's sake,
	I pray you a timely warning take;
	For in my dreams I saw go past your door,
	With faces masked, full twenty men or more,
	In three different squads—first four, then eleven,
	then forty-four.
	Each plunged a knife in your kingly breast, and
	Washed their hands in your royal gore.
JULIUS	(trembling).
	Indeed your mysterious dream has a suspicious tone.
CAMP.	Why, what's the matter, my lord?
JULIUS.	I want to go home.[5]

(Enter DECIUS, running, R. 1E.)

DECIUS.	My most noble lord, shall I bid the Senate meet?
	The Senators are waiting and anxious to take seat.
JULIUS.	Ah! Decius, my wife in a dream did see
	Twenty knives stuck into me,
	While twenty coons, or even more,
	Washed their hands in my royal gore.
	After this warning the best place for me is home;
	If they ask my reason, say I would not come.
DECIUS.	Noble Snoozer, some excuse, if only to tickle their vanity.
JULIUS.	I have no excuse.
DECIUS.	There are many; let me suggest one—feign insanity.
JULIUS.	Shall Julius the Snoozer lie to please this noble scum?
	The cause is in my will; say "I will not come."
DECIUS.	This dream or vision you do misconstrue,
	As in no way does it appertain to you;
	Four, eleven, and forty-four
	Is political policy—nothing more.

5 Tweed was often satirized in the New York press for being superstitious.

This Grotesque Essence

Knives in your royal body stuck
Signifies the people reviving blood do suck;
While great men at the Senate meet
To crown you king of Thompson street.

JULIUS.   That settles it. *(to* CAMP.*)* Here's five cents; play 4 first;
Here's ten cents more;
Put a saddle and gig on 4, 11, and 44.[6] *(Exit* CAMP.,
running.)
You stand in with it if I make a hit;
But, come, let us to the Senate git. *(exit* L. 1E.*)*

SCENE II.—*Senate Chamber; Throne and Chair,* R. 2E.;
Platform, R. *of* C.; *Shouts inside; Music and Procession enters*
R. 2E., *and march down to footlights, then up to platform; En-*
ter PINCHBACK *and* BRUTUS; *Cheers and Drum roll; Enter*
CASSIUS *and* DECIUS; *Cheers and Drum roll; Enter* JULIUS;
Cheers and Drum roll.

BRUTUS   *(aside to* PINCHBACK*).*
Should this monster refuse to sign our petitions wise,
At a signal from Cassius the Snoozer dies.
Don't strike him openly, that would be rash;
Slip up behind, and carve him like a dish of hash.

*(*JULIUS *stands on platform in front of chair.)*

JULIUS.   Most noble Senators, the Ides of March are come.
CASSIUS.   You'd saved your hide had you stayed at home.
JULIUS.   Are we all ready for the business of the day?
SENATORS.   We am.
JULIUS.   Then squat-a-vous-la *(all sit).* *(*DECIUS *kneels.)*
What have you to say?
DECIUS.   Most gracious Snoozer, I would repeat
That Pinchback be allowed to take his seat.

---

6   In policy rackets a gig is a bet on any number combination. "Saddle and gig" is a
variation in which, by increasing the wager, a player can collect if only two of his three
numbers turn up winners.

Julius the Snoozer

	He's tried in Washington year after year,
	But failing there, he wants to ring in here;[7]
	Will your majesty grant this great request?
JULIUS.	No! Let him take a fast mail train and travel West;
	Give his head a soak, and pull down his vest.
	(BRUTUS *kneels.*) Well, what's the matter with you?
BRUTUS.	On bended knee I present this petition new:
	The law annexing South Fifth avenue with Murray Hill
	Is much against the colored people's will.[8]
	They hope through me your clemency will yield,
	And have at once the law repealed.
JULIUS.	Give me the paper (*tears it in pieces and throws it in* Brutus'
	face). Take a back seat. I'll see you later.
PINCHBACK	(*kneeling*).
	Most noble Snoozer, grant me, I pray, a seat;
	I'm tired all but to death standing on my feet.
JULIUS.	You're Pinchback?
PINCHBACK.	Yes.
JULIUS.	What's the matter with your legs?
PINCHBACK.	My feet I said.
JULIUS.	Well, if your feet are played out, stand on your head.
CASSIUS	(*aside*).
	They all have failed, yet I must chance it.
	(*kneeling*) My plans, most noble sir, for Rapid Transit.
	From the Battery to Harlem Flats, in less than a minute.[9]

7   The character of Pinchback alludes to Pinckney Benton Stewart Pinchback (1837–1921). The mulatto son of a Mississippi plantation owner, Pinchback was raised as a free black in Ohio. He fought for the Union during the Civil War and was an active force in Louisiana politics during Reconstruction. In 1873 he was elected to the United States Senate by the Louisiana legislature. The election was contested by the Democrats, however; and upon his arrival in Washington Pinchback was refused permission to take his seat in Congress. The controversy was a heated one and remained unresolved until 1877 when the Senate finally voted to nullify Pinchback's election.
8   In the 1870s South Fifth Avenue and Murray Hill were the sites of opulent residences of New York's 400—the families that made up the cream of the social elite.
9   The 1870s were an age of phenomenal growth in New York. With increases in space, the need for rapid transit was acute. Various plans were proposed, perhaps the most adventuresome of which was the Beach Pneumatic Tunnel, a plan whereby carloads of passengers would be propelled all the way from the Battery to the Harlem River by a single, massive blast of air from a huge blowing machine.

This Grotesque Essence

JULIUS	*(looking at paper).*
	A noble plan *(pats* CASSIUS *on head).* I'll bet there's millions in it.
CASSIUS	*(holding up another paper).*
	This is for the education of "Our Boys."
JULIUS.	Hold! Like Lester Wallack, you're oversighted;
	Augustine Daly has "Our Boys" copyrighted.[10]
	Of all his plays he boldly claims this one,
	As no one knows the "Novel" he took it from.
CASSIUS.	Our dirty streets want cleaning; to this you've no objection?
JULIUS.	We'll have them cleaned just before our next election.
BRUTUS.	Our tenement houses, crowded pens of slaughter.
DECIUS.	I'd call your attention to our filthy water.
CASSIUS.	Your royal highness, a request I'd make
	To stop fox hunting in Jersey State.
BRUTUS.	A police reform is asked for everywhere,
	And a street car law, "No seat no fare."[11]
DECIUS.	To the Canal frauds I'd call your attention.
CASSIUS.	I call for a vote on the Third Term question.
BRUTUS.	A thousand other evils could be named,
	But what's the use when there's nothing to be gained.
DECIUS.	A deaf ear you turn to all our good intents,
	Waiting to be bought for ten or fifteen cents.

(Senators applaud and shout.)

JULIUS.	Silence! The first man that speaks, his brains I'll scatter.
CASSIUS.	Oh! that's too thin.
JULIUS.	Would you were fatter;
	I like not lean men, and that's what's the matter.
PINCHBACK.	For the last time, I demand a seat.

10   "Our Boys," a play by H. J. Byron, was produced in New York by Augustine Daly in 1875. Daly was taken to court by Lester Walleck, who disputed Daly's legal rights to the play. Walleck lost the suit.

11   The omnibuses which served New York's major thoroughfares in the 1870s were so overcrowded that they inspired critical commentary even in the European press. "No seat no fare" was the popular slogan reflecting the sentiment that if a person were forced to stand on public transit, he should not have to pay.

Julius the Snoozer

JULIUS.   Pinchbackaronia,
           Can't you see we've standing room only;
PINCHBACK. I'll have a seat, if I have to unseat you.
JULIUS.   Not if the Court knows herself, and I think she do.
BRUTUS.   Is my petition to be recognized?
CASSIUS.   Are the wishes of the people to be sacrificed?
DECIUS.   Beware, Old Snoozer, you'll find the people stronger.
JULIUS.   One at a time, and you'll last the longer.
BRUTUS.   I will be heard.
CASSIUS.   I've got the floor.
PINCHBACK. I want a seat.
BRUTUS.   Guards, close the door.
JULIUS.   Ye hounds! Dost think to scare me with this idle clatter?
           I'll tear ye limb from limb, and as I scatter
           Your worthless bones upon our mother earth,
           You'll curse the hour that gave you birth.
           You accuse me of being brutal, which is a lie—
           I close this Senate, "*sine die*."
PINCHBACK. In vain I sought to gain my seat,
           Kneeling at your royal feet;
           You spurned, you scoffed, you hurled insult
           Until you caused this wild tumult.
           Now, like a dog, roll in the dust,
           Despised, and by your country cussed. *(business)*
BRUTUS.   You brute! You monster! Your time has come—
           Your sands of life have nearly run—
           Your seat at length to me you'll yield,
           And seek a site in Potter's field.
           No tears over your lonely grave we'll shed,
           But plant a clapboard at your head. *(business)*
CASSIUS.   Ambitious wretch! thy wicked life is done;
           You die to-day, and by your countrymen;
           We've tried in every way we can
           To make you an honest, solid man.
           'Twould be a pity to let you longer live,
           So now I'll thus the signal give—
           (rushes upon platform and shouts) Speak, hired
                 hands, for me.

171

This Grotesque Essence

(PINCHBACK *shoots* JULIUS *with cannon.* JULIUS *rushes down. They all strike him with boxing gloves. He rushes over to* BRUTUS, *who hits him in face with flour.*)

JULIUS   *(staggering back).*
And the red-headed brute, too!

(*Falls and dies.* BRUTUS *snatches crown off Julius' head, and mounts throne chair.*)

BRUTUS.   Freedom! Liberty! and Civil Rights!

(*Senators shout and rush off* R. *and* L. *The scene draws off to shadow curtain, when those assigned keep a constant jumping over light until curtain falls.* CASSIUS *places lighted candle on Julius' breast. Martial music and quartette come on playing and singing "Star Spangled Banner." Goddess of Liberty on chair in* C. *of stage, waving American flag. Fire crackers in barrel* R. 2E. *and* L. 2E.[12] ANTONY *rushes on as soon as candle is placed on Julius' breast, and shouts and strikes attitudes until curtain falls. Red fire lit at signal.*)

END

---

12   This patriotic display is an example of the numerous centennial celebrations incorporated into public entertainments in 1876.

'Meriky; or,
The Old Time Religion

During minstrelsy's best years professional troupes were well ac-
customed to reworking standard afterpieces in order to get as
much mileage out of them as possible. But in the 1870s as a direct response to the increasing amateur demand for materials, a
new form of afterpiece began to appear. These were adaptations
of non-minstrel material. Comic sketches from magazines as well
as whiteface farces from the variety stage were "niggered up" (in
the terminology of the trade) and printed to fulfill the rising demand for amateur fare. These adaptations constituted a separate
category of afterpieces; for, unlike the traditional minstrel burlesques, they did not rely on the audience's ability to recognize
the original. The majority of these adaptations have no record of
professional production; and the authors responsible for them
were invariably obscure figures who cannot be traced in the history of professional minstrelsy.

   The following piece by Henry R. Evans is a revision of a short
dialect sketch entitled "The Old Time Religion" by Julia Picker-
ing, which appeared in the October, 1876, issue of *Scribner's
Magazine*. There is very little difference between the two versions.
Evans did change the piece from a narrative to a dramatic form,
but otherwise the adaptation is identical to the original in terms

173

of plot, character, and dialogue. The following text is reprinted from the acting edition published by A. T. B. De Witt in 1883.

'MERIKY;
OR,
THE OLD TIME RELIGION.

An Ethiopian Farce, In One Scene,

By HENRY R. EVANS.

CHARACTERS

BROTHER HORACE *(a gentleman of the old school)*
BROTHER SIMON *(another)*
G. WASHINGTON JOHNSON *(a rustic swell)*
'MERIKY *(a colored fashion-plate, slightly cracked)*

COSTUMES

BROTHER HORACE.—Black pants, tight; low-cut vest; huge standing collar; spectacles; white wig; long linen duster.

BROTHER SIMON.—Black pants; fancy vest; standing collar; exaggerated necktie; spectacles; white wig; bald; an old style dress coat, tails very long; cane.

G. WASHINGTON JOHNSON.—Light pants, and gaiters; short-cut coat.

'MERIKY.—Extravagant burlesque on city fashions.

SCENE.—*Country Kitchen. Door at C. Window, L. A table, R. Chairs, &c. At the rising of the Curtain,* BROTHER HORACE *and* BROTHER SIMON *discovered seated at table, smoking, and in earnest consultation.*

BROTHER SIMON.   I say, brudder Horace, I hearn your darter 'Meriky has come home; got tired, I spose of livin' in sarvice in Richmun town?

BROTHER HORACE.   Wall, no, not 'zactly tired, brudder Simon, but I spose she wanted to see the old uns agin. Course we is all glad to

174

see our darter, but you b'l'eve dat girl aint turned stark bodily naked fool? Yes, sah; she aint no mo' like de 'Meriky dat went away jes' a few monts ago, dan chalk's like cheese.

SIM.   What ails de gal, brudder Horace?

HOR.   You see, I'se allers been a plain, straight-sided nigger, an' haint never had no use for new fandangles, let it be what it mout, 'ligion, politix, bisness—don't keer what; Ole Horace say: de old way am de bes' way, an' you niggers, dat's all runnin' teetotleum crazy 'bout ebery new gim-crack dat's started, better jes' stay whar you is: an' let dem things alone. But dey wont do it, no 'mount ob preachin' wont sarve um.—An' dat is jes' at dis purtickler pint 'Meriky's mind dont seem to segashiate 'cordin' to doxology.

SIM.   Lor', brudder Horace, you don't mean it!

HOR.   Yes, sah; de bar' footed facs ob de case am dese: when 'Meriky kom home las' Saturday a week ago, she walked in dis back kitchin' wid her close pinned tight enuff to hinder her from squattin', an' her hair a-danglin' right in her eyes, jes' for all de worl' like a ram a-lookin' fru' a brush pile, an' dat nigger actilly done forgot how to talk de way she was brung up. She jes' rolled up her eyes ebery oder word, an' fanned, and talked like she 'spected to die de nex' breff. She toss dat mush-head ob her'n, an' talk proper as two dixunarys. 'Sted ob she callin' ob me "Daddy," an' her mudder, "Mammy," she say, "Par an' Mar, how can you bear to lib in sich a one-hoss town as dis? Oh! I think I should die;" an' right about dar she hab all de actions ob an ole drake in a thunder storm.

SIM.   Wall, I 'members my ole woman sayin', she thought 'Meriky was a-lookin' oncommon peart. She passed our house dis berry evenin' in kump'ny wid a young buck, an' her head was flung up as proud as de Queen Vict'ry. She was a-goin' down to de Baptis' Meetin' house, so I spose she's all right on 'ligion.

HOR.   Dat's whar mos' ob de crazyness cums in, brudder Simon—she's clean done forgot she's a Baptis'; calls herse'f a 'Piscopelian. Las' Sunday mornin', she went to meetin' in sich a rig, an' a-puttin' on sich airs, she couldn't keep a straight track. When she kum hum she brung kump'ny wid her. I jes' kep' my ears open, an' ef dat gal didn't disqualify me dat day, you kin hab my hat.

SIM.   What did she do, brudder Horace?

HOR.   Jes' listen; bime-by de kump'ny all git talkin' 'bout 'ligion, an' de chu'ches, an' 'Meriky went on gyratin' 'bout de preacher whar she cum from, a-cumin' out in a white shirt, an' den runnin' back an' gettin' on a black un, an' de people a-jumpin' up an' jawin' ob de preacher outen a book, an' a bowin' ob dar heads, an' sayin' ob a long rigmarole ob stuff, till my head fairly buzzed, an' I was dat mad at de gal I jus' couldn't see nuffin in dat room.

SIM.   Brudder Horace, your 'Meriky is cert'nly in a bad way. I allers was aginst dose hifalutin' city doins. How are you gwine to bring de stray lamb back into de fold?

HOR.   Brudder Simon, you knows yourse'f I never has no dejection to 'splainifyin' how I rules my folks at home an 'stablishes order dar when it is *pintedly* needed; un 'fore gracious! I lebe you to say dis time, ef it aint needed, an' dat pow'ful bad. I've jes' made up my mine to gib dat gal de terriblest beatin' dat ebber nigger had. I'm gwine to convart her dis bery evenin'; an' I'm purwided wid de materials for her convarshun. *(goes to wall and takes down bunch of hickory switches)* Whin I gits fru, I boun' she won't stick her nose in dem new fandangle chu'ches no mo'. I'll lay a ten-pence she'll be singin' all de good ole hyms, an' lookin' as peart as a sunflower by tomorrow mornin'.

SIM.   Yes, dat she will, I be boun'; ef I does say it, brudder Horace, you beats any man on chu'ch guberment an' family displanment ob any body I eber has seen.

HOR.   Brudder, I does my bes'. You mus' pray fur me, so dat my han's may be strengthened. *(glancing out of window)* Hist! here cums 'Meriky in de front gate dis very instep alongside ob sum young buck; we'll jes' sit here in de corner, an' keep an eye on de carryins on. *(They withdraw to one corner of the room.)*

(Enter 'MERIKY *and* G. W. JOHNSON.*)*

'MERIKY.   Walk in, Mr. Johnson, do!

JOHNSON.   Thanky, Miss 'Meriky; but only fur a minute.

'MERIKY *(introducing)*.   Par, dis is Mr. Johnson; uncle Simon, let me make you 'quainted wid dis gemman here. (JOHNSON *bows* a la *society;* OLD MEN *nod.*)

'MERIKY *(with manner)*.   Jes' take one of dem recepshun chairs, Mr. Johnson, an' make yourself at home. *(pointing to kitchen chair)*

'Meriky; or, The Old Time Religion

JOHN.   Thanky! *(seated; short silence)* You've been havin' a gay winter in de city so I hearn, Miss 'Meriky.

'MERIKY.   Oh! Mr. Johnson, it has jes' bin like one long delicious nightmare, jes' one everlastin' roun' of concerts, church fairs, recepshuns, an' cake-walks. Sumthin' agoin' on ebery blessed ebenin'. I declar', Mr. Johnson, I am quite spiled fur de country.

JOHN.   Wall, I hearn tell dat Richmun' society was de bes' in de worl'. By de way, Miss 'Meriky, what did you think ob de revival meetin' dis ebenin'?

'MERIKY *(disdainfully)*.   I can soon settle de hash ob dat question, Mr. Johnson; I takes no intelligence in sich matters; dey is all too common for *me*. Baptisses is a foot or two below my grade. I 'tends de 'Piscopelian whar I resides, an' 'spect to jine dat one on de nex' anniversary ob de Bishop. Oh! dey does ebery thing so lobely, an' in so much style. I declar' nobody but common folks in de city goes to de Baptis' church. It made me sick at my stummick to see so much shoutin' an' groanin' dis ebenin', 'tis so ungenteel wid us to make so much circumlocutions in meetin'.

(BROTHER HORACE *steps up suddenly and confronts* JOHNSON.*)*

HOR.   I say, young man, you needn't let what 'Meriky tol' you 'bout dat chu'ch, put no change inter you. She's sorter out ob her right mine now; but de nex' time you comes, she'll be all right on dat an' on seberal oder subjec's.

JOHNSON *(rising slowly; embarrassed)*.   Wall—wall—good evenin', Miss 'Meriky, I'll drap in on some more suspicious 'casion, an' get your furder 'pinion 'bout 'Piscopelians an' 'ligion in de city. Good ebenin', brudder Horace; ebenin', brudder Simon. *(backs out)*

'MERIKY *(pertly)*.   Bong-swore, Monseer; olive oil.

HOR *(after pause)*.   Darter, what chu'ch is dat you say you gwine to jine?

'MERIKY *(promptly)*.   De 'Piscopelian, par!

HOR.   I'se mightily concerned 'bout you, kase I know your min' aint right, an' I'll jes' hab to bring you roun' de shortest way possible. *(exhibiting bunch of hickories)*

'MERIKY *(jumping up)*.   What makes you think I loss my senses?

HOR.   Bekase, darter, you done forgot how to walk, an' to talk, an' dem is sure signs. *(beats her)*

177

(All through the beating, 'MERIKY continues screaming and springing up and down.)

'MERIKY. Oh! Lordy! daddy! my good ole daddy, don't gib me no more.

SIM. *(intensely delighted)*. Bress de Lor'.

HOR. You're improvin', dat's a fac';—done got your nateral voice back. What chu'ch does you b'long to, 'Meriky?

'MERIKY *(sobbing)*. I don't 'long to none, par.

HOR. *(resuming beating)*. What chu'ch does you 'long to, darter?

'MERIKY *(choked with sobs)*. I don't 'long to none!

HOR. *(still beating)*. What chu'ch you 'longs to *now*, 'Meriky?

'MERIKY *(shouting)*. Baptis', Baptis', I'se a deep-water Baptis'!

SIM. Bress de Lor'! Amen! Amen!

HOR. Berry good. You don't spec' to hab your name tuck offen dem chu'ch books, eh, darter!

'MERIKY. No, daddy; I allers did despise dem stuck up 'Piscopelians— dey aint got no 'ligion no how.

HOR. Lem me see den, ef you can jine in wid me an' dis good brudder here, in dat good ole hym you usened to be so fond ob. You knows, brudder Simon, how de words run—

All Sing and Dance.
"Baptis'! Baptis' is my name,
My name's written on high;
'Specs to lib an' die de same.
My name's written on high."

(Disposition of characters at fall of curtain.)

BROTHER HORACE.   'MERIKY.   BROTHER SIMON.

CURTAIN

The Black Chap
from Whitechapel

On April 17, 1860, the American boxer John C. Heenan (a miner's son from Benicia, California) met the British champion Tom Sayers in a world title bout in Barnboro, England. The public interest in the event was intense. Most American fans insisted on interpreting it as a definitive struggle between two mutually exclusive political systems. Patriotic feelings ran so high that the New York *Times*, in an editorial on March 24, 1860, was moved to remind its readers that should Heenan lose it would not necessarily mean that a monarchy "is more conducive to the physical vigor of the body politic" than is a republic. One of the products of the public interest in the fight (which, incidentally, ended in a draw after forty-two rounds) was the variety farce *B.B.; or, The Benicia Boy in England*. There is no public record of the piece other than its performance during the first week of May, 1860, at the Bowery Theatre in New York. That such an obscure piece should show up later in a form directed toward an amateur minstrel audience attests to the increasing pressure that mass-market demands were placing on the art form.

There is no way to determine how much of the original was retained in Williams' adaptation. Certainly the situation of a visiting sports figure echoes with a slight twist the real-life situation that inspired the original; and the comic use made of boxing slang would not have been out of place in *B.B.* But to assert any other similarities would be sheer speculation. The obscurity of the source of *Black Chap* does, however, help to make evident a certain truth about minstrel adaptations. Unlike burlesques, they had to succeed as self-contained comic structures. Thus, more often than any of the burlesques, the adaptations came closest to being full-fledged one act comedies. *Black Chap* is a clear illustration of this. It exhibits a self-sustained and unified plot centered on the comic device of mistaken identity. On this structure is hung a textbook display of minstrelsy's visual and verbal comic techniques. The following text is reprinted from the acting edition published by Robert M. De Witt in 1871.

THE BLACK CHAP
FROM
WHITECHAPEL.
An Eccentric Negro Piece.
Adapted from
Messrs. Barnard and Williams' "B.B."
By HENRY L. WILLIAMS, JR.

CHARACTERS

SAMPSON CARD (advance agent of Pickleson's Romanticon, a travelling show)

CLAUDO BLOWER (keeper of the Clamtown Hotel—ex-pugilist)

POMPILIOUS (chief engineer of the hotel)

CHARLEY DASH (a village dandy)

The Black Chap from Whitechapel

COSTUMES

CARD.—White hat with black band, dark suit, long drab overcoat, short crop wig.

BLOWER.—Short crop wig, made up stout.

POMP.—Curly wig, white vest, apron.

DASH.—Very showy fast man's dress, check vest, striped trousers, fancy wig, shiny hat, gloves, fancy scarf and large diamond pin.

SCENE.—*Interior in 2d grooves.*

(POMP *enters with his pockets full of newspapers, and with chairs, one in each hand, to C. Puts the chairs down, sits on one with feet up on the other.*)

POMP. Heyah's a comfortable situateoyourshin at lass. Gy! I rader *conk*lude I knows whar to lay my head. *(sits very much at his ease)* I'se a fortnight chile for to get into dis place. Me clerk, an' what dem Frenchees calls a *chef* cook, dough why dey should call me a Jeff cook when my name am Pomp, I can't comprehend. Me clerk an' cook in a big hotel, a place of trust; and de way dat de mare-jarity of our talkative bar-room militia don't pay does make 'em a place of berry much trust! I say, once more agin, for dis 'casion only, dat I am clerk an' cook here in Mr. Blower's tavern, when I was actually druv out of Cooney Holler on a accusation ob petty larceny, when—if I took anything—it wasn't lard but a box of axle grease. But den it's pooty hard to tell de difference betwix' dem two articles dese yere days. *(rises)* Yer see, I was rader out ob pocket in de Holler, an' I kind o' sa'ntered into de bank, whar de quill-driver looked at me, an' says he: "What yer want, yer coun-terfit nig?" To dis rude execration I answered dignificantly, "Sah! I take no note ob your lager beer talk!" Wharupon dat crumpled-headed specimen said: "You don't take no notes out ob dis ginu-wine bank." Dat took my breff away, but I hurled de charge back in his teef, and said: "Look heyah! whar's yer superior officer? I'll jess tell him how to keep de money secure wid you for de cashier! Yes, sah! he'll find de currency all right if he'll lock you up wid it in de safe obernight!" De lass I seed o' him, he looked to be getting ober dat counter to'ards me, probably to faint at my feet. But I was leaving at dat time, and I neber like to turn round when fokes behind me am calling out: "Come back, you sable scoundrel!" It makes it look as if one knowed it was him. Yas, *(walks about)* dey may say now dat I can't run a hotel! I kin—ha, ha! I kin walk 'em dough! and I'se good at decanters, too! So I'se de representative ob Mr. Blower—nuffin to do when he's off to de railroad depot to get boarders, but to loaf, an' water de whiskey an' read de papers. *(sits down)* I'se berry fond ob reading de papers—dat is, de right kin' o' papers, and de right kin' o' papers to me is de fight kin' o' papers. *(takes out* Clipper[1] *and unfolds it)* What a *(holds it up at arm's length)* high kind o' paper de Clyper is! "News ob the Millers." Flour has gone down? Oh, no—it's a blow to de oder grinders: "Nat Langham's Black and de Spider." I'm fly to dis sort o' ting. "His dexter mawley countered heabily on de back ob de Spider's left molar!" Dat's what dey call suffering immolation! Dat was— where was I? Oh! "Round de two-two—oh! round de double two'th!" "De Whitechapel Nig went with great gusto to toe." *(slowly repeats)* "with gusto—to—to—to"—oh, I see! "to toe the scratch, making no pause to lay his paws on de claret-cup ob de web weaving insect." Oh, dat's fine! Do away wid pugilism indeed! what would de wo'ld wid nary milling for de men fokes, and no millingnary for the women folks? "First color for de cullud gem-man." Dar's description for ye! Talk ob Shavespoke's Jumblet arter dat! He couldn't call up Wilkes' Spirit[2] from the vasty deep, could he? How would his talk hang in the Sporting Noose? O course not, o' course, nohow! dat's what I say. *(turns paper)* Oh, here's some more ob de grace hoop, de old original charmed cir-cle. "In consequence ob de unraisinable pearseedings agin' prize-fighters in England, numbers ob de Fives Courtlers seek fresh fields and pastures new. Among dem who arrove in de Monro-vian, am de celemabrated shining light ob de heaby weights, Squasher Cuff, alias de Sockdologer!" Eh? Hooray! De Black Chap ob Whitechapel come to dis country! Oh, happy land! "He will go forthwith into training for his approaching turn-up wid

1 The New York *Clipper*, a nineteenth-century newspaper which emphasized cover-age of sports and the arts.
2 George Wilkes (1819–1885) founded the *Spirit of the Times*, a New York journal of recreation and the arts, in 1859. Wilkes' *Spirit* was modeled on the original and more famous *Spirit of the Times* founded in 1831 by William T. Porter, from whom Wilkes re-ceived his newspaper training.

Micky M'Anaw, if he cannot get on with Carrotty Rourke."
(scratches head) Oh! dese fellers fight wid dem dey *kin* "get on" wid!
jess de opposite from de gineral lot ob people. "He will plant his
colors at de hostlery ob our well-known Boniface Claudo Blower."
(rises) Blower! Claudo Blower! Why, dat's my massa! our hostlery
—why it am our hostler dat am given to rye. Hyah! De Ethiopiano
playing in our roof! under our werry house! Oh, dis am *(strikes the
chair)* rap-ture! Dis am *(walking about, flourishing unfolded papers)*
equal to de fourf ob July! *(to* R.*)*

(Enter, R., BLOWER.*)*

BLOWER.   "You lie—you lie!" What do you mean, sir? Dar, dar—hole
your sassy tongue! I'se gwine down to de depot.

POMP.   I know. *(flourishes the paper)*

BLOW.   You knows? Am dat any reason you should give me a *Clipper*
on de nose?

POMP.   I'se jess read all about it. De Sockdologer am acoming here for
his training-ground.

BLOW.   Dat am so. He'll come here, and dar'll be *piles* of people *drive*
ober from de city to see him! Dey'll run extra trains to see de
Sockdologer.

POMP.   Won't yer sock dollars, old man? *(whistle off)* Dat's de train.

BLOW.   P'raps he's aboard. Now, look a-hyah! until I'se made all de
pepperations to gib him a hot deception; don't let's hab any rum-
bustification hyah, or dar'll be some *(shakes fist under nose of* POMP,
who trembles) rum-bust-if-I-catch you at anything ob dat nature.
Hab a first-chop dinner ready, too, to warm him—or I'll warm
yer! *(exit,* L.*)*

POMP.   Anybody could see to oncet dat he was a fighter in his day. Well,
I'll go an' see if I can't buy some hankercher for de colors ob de
Sockdologer. Dey am *(refers to newspaper)* a red, blue and orange
ground, striped wid purple and black, and dotted wid sprigs ob
white and violet. I tink I shall match dat—easy. *(exit,* R.*)*

(Enter SAMPSON CARD, L., *with bag and bundle of brushes and poles.)*

CARD.   House, house! No answer. *(puts bag on one chair and bundle on the
other, looks around for something to sit upon)* Kind o' comic retreat
dey've recommended to me. A good resting-place? whar's de
place to rest? *(lays bundle from chair to chair and sits upon it, falls and*

183

gets wedged in between chairs) Help, help! I'm left to flounder about by myself—not a soul in de place. "To what *bass* uses may we come at last." *(rises, holds up poles)* Dese am extending-rods dat I hab used to pos' up a mammoth ten-sheeter on de highest house on our route—I call dem my high-story-cal poles. I wouldn't lose dem for lub or money—less dan I can get for dem. An' I want to sit down bad—or good, I should say, arter de tough-an'-rumble joggling dat I hab had. Only tink ob a railroad truly wuss dan de Jarsey ones; twelve miles in two hundred and forty hours! including stoppages for de conductor to turn over a new leaf in his account book, rig up his tickets, and drink wid de signal men. One spot we gets bothered by de bullgine refusing to go on ahead. Dat compelled us to on afoot. Fac', we had to get out and walk. So dar's my trunk, full of de extree showbills, posters and placards, leff in dat fast train. Fast train! stuck fast train. Let's in-west-I-get. *(feels in vest pocket for papers and produces them)* I'se sent as advance agent for Pickleson's Romanticon, or Solidified Milky Way of Circus Celebrities, to do de billing ob dis town, cover up all de posters ob de rival combinations, gib de mayor his season tickets, hire a hall—and make my haul out ob de greenies who likes to stand treat to de horsemanship fellah. Dat's Othello's ockerpation in dis hotel-oh! It's as easy to me as kiss my hand. And Othello—whar's my hankercher? *(feels in pockets)* Dar's de money—all I got ob cash-oh! Whar's my hand—oh! I recollect now—I put it in dis pocket. *(puts hand in tail pockets of coat)* Yah I neber forget anyting —dat's my pecooliarity. *(while searching in pockets his hat falls off, showing handkerchief in it)* Oh, dat's jess whar I leff it. Hullo! dis ain't my hat; dis ain't my hankercher! *(laughs)* Ha, ha! Here's letters worked in de corner, "S.C.P.R." Why dat's me—"Sampson Card, Pickleson's Romanticon." I wonder wheder de fellah dat's got my beaver is dat berry benevolent chap dat wouldn't frow his pipe out ob de winder at my perlite request. "Frow my penny clay out ob de winder," said he; "I'd be delighted to hab de frowing ob you out arter it!" Such a funny speaking rhinoceros, too! Kep' talkin' about wind-up and de fancy! I didn't see no fans, nor no watch to wind up. He mus hab been a berry strong man, dough; he said he and a friend ob his, could raise a thousand pounds a-side—I s'pose in each hand—as-ton-ishing. But, whar's all de inhabitants? *(calls)* Ho-yoi! *(dances, upsets a chair, puts his poles, R., pounds with his poles on stage, and then places them against wing, R.)* Dat ought to wake up some one or two. *(tightens the cord on the bundle of poles)* I hope I habn't damaged dem.

(Enter, L., POMP, *with carpet-bag and trunk.)*

POMP. Whew! *(fatigued)* Hyah I is, wid de whale-lease and de Saratoga. *(sits on trunk)* Hyah's de famous names! *(reads letters, holding up carpet bag)* "S.C.P.R." "S.C.," dat's de card.

CARD. Eh? *(turns)* "S.C."—de Card! Allow me to remark, juvenile, dat your greasy han's is a-dis-greasing my bag.

POMP. You' baggage, sah! *(rises, drops bag, trunk falls)* Oh, pardon!

CARD. Oh, pardon! Den don't hop 'ard on my goods dat style.

POMP *(kneels to him)*. Don't hit me! Spare my life!

CARD *(aside)*. Drunk as an owl!

POMP *(goes up and looks at Card's hat)*. Dat is him! "S.C.P.R."—Squasher Cuff, ob de Prize Ring. How near he come to squashing me wid a cuff. Lucky ting as eber was dat I got his colors. *(draws out handkerchief, comes down)* Sah, sah! may I be flavored wid de honor ob de submission to gib you free cheers.

CARD. Thank'ee for one.

POMP. An' a tiger?

CARD *(aside)*. He knows dat I'm in de menagerie line! Offers me a tiger!

POMP. Den, *(waves handkerchief)* huzzah! huzzah!

CARD *(aside)*. What under salvation am he guilty ob! P'raps it's a Clamtown custom.

POMP *(laughing, joyfully)*. Huzzah!

CARD. Upon my word, I don't know who is R.?

POMP *(gets up on chair)*. Huzzah!

CARD. I ax you, who *is* R.? I'm a stranger here, I is.

POMP *(falls off chair)*. Hooroar!

CARD. Who roar? My amiable but wide-moufed frien', I should say, *you roar*!

POMP *(sitting on stage where he had fallen)*. Tigar–r–r–r!

CARD. No, sah! I don't want any tigers—we is full supplied wid dat animile, and den de fokes ob dis village am too lazy to look at any-

185

thing livelier dan sloths. (POMP *rises and dusts himself with the handkerchief*) And now, den, am you de landlord?

POMP. No, sah. (*receding in fear from* CARD'S *offered hand*) I is de chief clerk.

CARD. Den begin by stopping you many ac's ob maniacal proceedings.

POMP (*chuckles*). Want it kep' squiet, sah? I perceive.

CARD. I want you to keep squiet, sah!

POMP. Oh, it's de usual way here when de *pugs* come to town.

CARD (*aside*). A pug! call me a pug? (*feels his nose*) When Matilda Jane always taught him a Grecian bend.[3]

POMP (*tries to feel* CARD'S *arm*). Hyah's shape! Oh, what a libely house we will hab! I railly mus' gib him anoder cheer. (*close to* CARD'S *ear*) Hoo——

CARD. Now don't ax me again who Ray is, because I'se a stranger here. (POMP *opens mouth to cry out, when* CARD *shoves the handkerchief* POMP *holds, up into it*) Don't make that din here! you'd much better see about my din-ner!

POMP. Dinner, sah! nuffin worth your eatin' ready yet!

CARD. Then a luncheon——

POMP (*jumps*). Don't, sah, on me!

CARD. Don't what, sah, on you?

POMP. De punch, on me——

CARD. I say, luncheon! (*aside*) Dis dandy waiter seems pretty cibil—I tink I'd much de better take him into my confidence. Look hyah, Mister—Mister——

POMP. Pomp, sah.

CARD. Pomp? (*aside*) Name ob good augury jess as I'se gwine to pump him. (*aloud*) My deah frien' Pomp, you mus' know dat de objeck ob my trabel into Clamstown am——

POMP. Oh! we know all about it, sah! we suspected you all de day.

CARD (*slaps his left hand with right fist, making* POMP *jump*). Dat opposition agent has been warning 'um agin' me!

POMP. Yes, sah, an' my fuss fear was dat dar wouldn't be a bed long enough for you!

CARD. All engaged? couldn't keep one long enough for me, eh?

3 In the nineteenth century a Grecian bend was a stylish affectation in walking with the body thrown slightly forward. Women exaggerated the affectation by wearing large bustles, also called Grecian bends.

POMP. Don't be mad at what I'm gwine to say——

CARD. Friend Pomp, in my business, nobody can draw in a good net profit widout he is a *seine* man!

POMP. So I tought—but, sah—*(edging away from* CARD*)* don't be offended at it——

CARD. I never do get offended—I always go end-on.

POMP. Den I'se squite disappointed at your personal appearance——

CARD. Ha, ha! *(to* C., *puzzled)* What does he mean? my purse-onal appearance! De opposition agents *hab* been setting dem agin me all along de road. *(aloud)* My purse-onal appearance, young man? Learn, sir, *(slapping his pockets)* dat I is always de lead in de ring business.

POMP *(aside)*. Dat's de way to talk. Oh, what a libely house we will hab! *(aloud)* I mean about your size, sah.

CARD *(puzzled)*. "I'm in about your size?" What's dat? Does he refer to putty is as putty does? *(gives* POMP *money)* Dah, sah; is dat con-glue-sive?

POMP. Thank'ee, sah! De talk made me tink——

CARD. Oh, I see; somebody's been talking about me. Don't you be afraid; when it comes to *blows*, I can hurricane ober Windship himself.

POMP. But de lunch, sah? what do you say to a bit ob nice brown roas' guinea-fowl——

CARD. Fotch de feadered biped hyah an' you'll see some fowl play. Dat's de mos' pea-benevolent observation I'se heerd in dis hotel yet.

POMP *(goes* R., *waves handkerchief mysteriously, and exits,* R., *shouting)*. Hooray for de Squasher!

CARD. No! I don't want any squashes—neber mind. *(goes* R.*)* De wedge-at-tables—I can find an opening for de chicken widout dat. *(to* C.*)* Dis is de fust floor, I beliebe, but it's berry lune-attic. Let's see, dat fancy-headed dark, arter inquiring for my knowledge of R, which I only know as a respectable letter residing between Q and S. He axes me not kill him. De opposition agents mus' hab been on a healthy tear here, to hab filled de population wid such a terror. *(suddenly)* Oh, dey don't like de show-folks! dey's going to pay it back on de next comer! I'se de nex' comer! "What's my size?" Dey see I'se a meejium size and dey's going to try de spirit hand on me.

This Grotesque Essence

I see it all. I won't stop for no guinea-pig—guinea-hen—I'll scoot while dar's a chance. *(runs about with his things in his hands)* I really forgot which am de way to git out! *(exiting, R.)* Hyah's my life saved!

(Enter, L., BLOWER, wiping his forehead.)

BLOWER.   I jess missed de champion at de depot. Lucky I got his fixin's all right, an' sent 'em on here by Pompey. Whar kin he be? Stop! he's in de *prime* ob life, and would hab trabelled at de charge step. O' course! Den he's hyah! I bet. What honor to my sporting *drum* —I've only had *beats* in it before! dis will make it an object ob remark—regularly *tattoo* it! Here I am, Claudo Blower, formerly the well known prize-fighter, known as the Guinea Nigger, *the* Guinea Nigger, *spar neckcellence*, as de French say, when I put on "de hug," now de entertainer of de great *Sock*-dologer—how he will put de *stock in* my house! I'm in such a state ob flusteration dat I—I—whar's dat boy, Pomp? *(goes R.)*

(Enter R., frightened, passing BLOWER, without seeing him, things under arm, CARD.)

CARD *(aside).*   A bull-dog, in de back yard! You'd better believe I made a back'ard movement, fust ting. I'll try de oder way. *(He runs against BLOWER, drops all the things, both stooping to pick them up, strike heads and fall back on stage, they sit.)*

BLOW. *(aside, feeling his head).*   What an un-conce-iably hard head he has got, to be sure.

CARD *(aside, feeling his head).*   I railly t'ought de lightning had struck de house. I beg your pardon, sah; don't do dat agin, or you'll git hurt. *(rising)*

BLOW. *(afraid of him).*   Don't get offended!

CARD.   Not git off-end-ed! Tink I'd stop seated all day? *(rises)* Git up, ole man.

BLOW. *(afraid of CARD's offered hand).*   Don't let your angry passions rise.

CARD.   Neber mind my passions; you rise. It don't look venerable for an ole man to lie dar when you'se able to git up. *(BLOWER rises and takes the fallen things from CARD.)*

BLOW.   My dear boy, don't tire yourself wid dese tings——

CARD.   But dese is my clothes in here—I *do* 'tire myself wid dese tings!

188

BLOW. I insist——

CARD *(lets go bag,* BLOWER *nearly falls, aside).* He insists, I'd better humor him. De ole cove don't look deep, but it has de 'pearance ob baggage smashing. (BLOWER *puts things up* C., *then goes about listening mysteriously at* L. *and* R., *watched by* CARD.) He's wusser dan de oder fellah!

BLOW. *(comes down, makes* CARD *sit in chair,* C., *sits in chair, facing him, brings his chair up close, slaps his thigh with his fist).* Ahem!

CARD. Eh? Ahem! no, sah! *no porko cure-ante* for me, as our Iatlian rider says.

BLOW. When fust I set eyes on you, I neber expected to fine you what you are—but I'm not surprised to find you what you are now that I know that you are what you are!

CARD. You couldn't fine breff to do that ober again, could you?

BLOW. I mean dat I was disappointed in your size—you ain't got de quarter ob what I sposed yer.

CARD *(aside).* He's arter my money. *(blusteringly)* Who ain't got no quarters? I kin size your pile by haff—

BLOW. Fistiany[4] gave you out as taller.

CARD. Fisty Anna did? Oh, did she? I'm berry much indebted to her—

BLOW. Not de only one.

CARD *(rises).* Sah! (BLOWER *pulls him down.*)

BLOW. For Boxiana said de same—

CARD *(aside).* All de gals ob Clamtown are tattling about me now. Oh, so I ain't tall enough for dis town! got to put de bills up high, eh? de boys is on de tear! oho!

BLOW. Well, de boys can handle deir pickers and stealers. *(flourishing his hands)*

CARD *(fends off* BLOWER's *hands).* Oh, I've brought my rods, I'd only be too glad to see any rushin's under my poles.

BLOW. I noticed dem! Oh, dar's plenty ob space—dar's my garden— you kin stake out your ring dar to practice on—

CARD *(aside).* Now he's coming to business. Den you'se de owner here?

BLOW. I'se de landlord.

CARD. Oh! dis looks safer.

BLOW. Dar's lots ob money in town—we shall rope 'em in.

---

4 *Fistiana*, a nineteenth-century publication which set down the principles, history, and training techniques of boxing.

This Grotesque Essence

CARD *(laughing).* Make de Clamtonians shell out—see? Clamshell.

BLOW. *(laughs).* Ha, ha! we shell. *(then seriously)* Sorry you ain't loftier.

CARD *(aside).* At it again. *(aloud)* So am I! I tried to grow—but I couldn't do de feat—I may say, de six feet.

BLOW. Neber mine. I hab de greatest confidence in you since you knocked me down—

CARD. I wonder if I do it again, if it will increase his trust.

BLOW. Your noggin is hard as stone.

CARD. Hardly, arter your knock-in it about. *(feels his head)*

BLOW. How's your arm?

CARD. Pretty well, thank'ee. How's yourn?

BLOW. *(pinches CARD's arm).* Some on de muscle.

CARD. Don't, I shall be black and blue. *(rises)* I wish you'd hurry up my lunch. If de fowl ain't ready all, let's have one of the wings or legs devilled.

BLOW. Sa'tanly! *(rises)*

CARD. That's a hint.

BLOW. *(puts chairs back).* Of course you must have your peck—

CARD. I make a pint ob dat.

BLOW. But I forgot to introduce myself—you neber saw me before— not before you in de ring! *(laughs)*

CARD. Ha, ha! I neber did. *(aside)* What's de joke?

BLOW. You'd hab been for gitting me under your hand.

CARD. I'd be for forgitting you altogether.

BLOW. You are well acquainted wid all my chums—my ole second for one—

CARD. Your ole second? I neber seed his fust! *(aloud)* Pshaw!

BLOW. Yas, Shaw, Jem Shaw. Do you remember his peculiar drive in de left lug? *(spars and taps CARD under left ear)*

CARD. Oh! I say, don't! *(puts up his hands)* Dat's all ugly work.

BLOW. *(holds CARD's hands in the position he lifted them).* Stop a bit, till I see de defence. Dat's novel.

CARD. Your acts are romantic! Keep on, an' I shall go off in *historics.* *(drops his hands)*

BLOW. Is dat how you bested "the Gas-man?"

CARD. Bedstead de Gas-man? I don't sleep wid our gas man! What a blower he is!

BLOW. Blower! I knew you knew my name.

CARD. Oh den you are——

BLOW. I'm de *(attitude)* Guinean Nigger.

CARD. Oh! you are de guinea-hen nigger? *(laughs)* ha, ha! I see, you are *cool an' dark*, but I t'ought it would be a *nice an' brown* one! and it looks more like you are roasting me! *(goes up)*

BLOW. Ho, ho, ho! fust-class! tip-top! *(tumbles over bundle of poles, going up)*

CARD. You've tipped up my things agin!

BLOW. Beg pardon! dat's quite one ob my old knocks.

CARD. "Old Knox," are you? Cool for a Southern darkey.

BLOW. Charley Dash is awful eager to be your backer, and I don't mind tellin' you he will stand heabily on you——

CARD. Stand heabily on me! Not if I let him.

BLOW. He's good for a couple of C's.

CARD. He must have oceans of money. *(aside)* Some influential youth ob dis crazy village.

BLOW. I'se making a book on you myself——

CARD. I'se gitting celebrity thrust on me. Go it.

BLOW. I'se put my whole pile on you——

CARD. Then the sooner you take it off, de better.

BLOW. Pooh, pooh! it's healthy as de bank.

CARD. Healthy as de bank? Cholera Banks! But why tax me with your yarns! I'm savage as a meat ax for my *dish-yarn-es*, as de French say.

(Enter R., POMP *with table on which is luncheon laid, places table* C., *and arranges chairs to it.* CARD *sits eagerly* L. *side of it,* BLOWER R. *of it.* POMP *bustles about.)*

POMP. Sorry to keep you so long, sah; but Massa Dash detained me down 'tairs.

CARD *(impatiently)*. Detained you—yas, I heerd about his *C's*!

POMP. What is your flavorite liquor, sah?

BLOW. *(mysteriously)*. Be careful!

CARD. Beak harf full? who's beak's harf full? I haven't had a taste yet for my bill. *(aside)* I suppose his mystery means de lager is stale. *(aloud)* Let's hab a tumbler ob "chain lightning."

POMP. Yes, sah. *(going* R.*)*

BLOW. *(in horror)*. I'm thunderstruck! Not for de world!

CARD. No, it ain't for de world; it's for myself. What's it your biz?

BLOW. I'se your frien'. No mixed drinks; either one glass ob good ale——

POMP. Which we habn't got.

CARD. You needn't bring it, den.

BLOW. Or barley water.

POMP. Barley water; yes, massa. *(to R.)* Isn't he a picture to bet money on. *(waves napkin)* Hoorah! (CARD *carving fowl)*

BLOW. *(waves handkerchief)*. Hooraw! *(Exit, R.)*

CARD. Raw? well, it ain't particularly well done. Oh, I'm *mint hencely (shoves bowl out of his way)* hungry.

(Enter BLOWER, R., *with bowl and spoon.)*

CARD. Barley water, indeed. Then bar-ley-water would soon settle my 'ash; I'll engage. *(eating)*

BLOW. *(puts bowl on table)*. Don't.

CARD. Don't what?

BLOW. It's poison to you.

CARD *(drops knife and fork)*. Massysnakes!

BLOW. Pomp must have been mad to gib it to you.

CARD. Some one is mad under dis roof; I'm secure.

BLOW. *(pulls things from* CARD's *end of table)*. I know what you want, a raw porter-house steak, jess shown to de fire; anything else would hab riled you.

CARD. I'll brile you before I'll eat raw meat!

BLOW. *(flourishes carving knife)*. I must insist——

CARD *(aside)*. A knife in de loon's paws. *(aloud soothingly)* All right, den.

BLOW. I won't trust de sarvints. *(takes up dishes)*

CARD. Don't; only trust your boarders.

BLOW. I'll be back im-me-gently.

CARD. Don't hurry yourself. *(rises)* Tings are getting to a nice pass—puts me in a passion. I'll go—hullo! a step! Some one approaches! Should dat hefty crazy man, who fancies himself a guinea hen come back, he'll force me to eat a raw steak, and—how-rye-ble thought! make me swallow the barley water! He shan't do dat—for—*(takes up bowl and goes L.)* I'll soon bowl dat out. *(throws bowl off L., scream heard)* Dat'll stump him. Oh! I've drowned a man. *(to C., behind table, agitated)*

(Enter L., DASH, *wiping his face with handkerchief.)*

The Black Chap from Whitechapel

DASH *(fast man style).*   What de debbil you doin'? You've spiled my coat! Dar'll be a large-size muss in about free seconds! I've a big mine to put you eyes in mourning! *(chases* CARD *around table)*

CARD.   Keep off! it's dangerous!

(Enter R., BLOWER, *who seizes* DASH. CARD *gets behind table.)*

BLOWER.   My dear Dash, you don't know what you are about——

DASH.   About to dash at him!

(Races CARD *twice round the table, followed by* BLOWER, *who seizes his coattails, the third time* DASH *turns, and running the other way, meets* CARD, *who thereby knocks him down.* BLOWER *falls over* DASH. CARD *stands L. front, holding a chair before him, breathless.)*

BLOW. *(sitting on* DASH, *whispers).*   I told you not. It's the—*(whispers inaudibly to* DASH, *they rise)*

CARD.   Now, what Fawksey conspiracy am dat guinea hen hatching? *(puts down chair)*

DASH *(runs to* CARD, *and brings him to* C.*)*   My dear fellah, I humbly beg your pardin. I did not know you till—till you knocked me down.

CARD *(aside).*   They're like tan-pins; they've got to be knocked over before dey see de winning force ob de ball.

DASH.   Let me introduce myself—I am Charley Dash; de friend ob de manly art!

CARD.   You wouldn't expect me to have a womanly heart, would you?

BLOW.   Your backer it is. *(goes up)*

CARD.   No, I should think it was his back hurt, hit is.

DASH.   Yas, ye see I laid heabily——

CARD.   I *saw* you laying heabily.

DASH.   You'll excuse my not twigging you at fust, but de fack am—now take it kindly—I was rader vexed about your size.

CARD.   Anoder glue dealer! dey'se all in de hoof-biling trade hyah!

DASH.   But, all over, you'se in capital condition.

CARD.   I'll be in slap-ital condish, if you don't dry up pinching me.

DASH.   You've been on de train lately——

CARD.   Jess came off.

DASH.   I thought so; you'be got no flesh to spare. I've no bones to pick wid you on dat.

CARD.   No flesh to spare, no bones to pick! dey'se a couple of cannon-balls.

DASH.   Yas, sah! *(goes* R., *to whisper with* BLOWER, *they go* L., *pretending to lock the doors, dodged by* CARD*)*

CARD (C., *aside*).   Locked in wid a pair ob mad men! I ought to hab been more on de *key vive. (aloud)* I say, boss, I should like——

BLOW.   We thought you should like it. All's square.

DASH.   All's square. *(Exit* BLOWER, R.*)*

CARD.   All's square! dey'se coming round on me.

DASH *(to* CARD*)*.   It must be kept close, or we shall hab all de town swarming into de house. I'm your friend. I guess you'll oblige me by having a turn-up wid de Guinean?

CARD.   A turn-up! I'be already expressed my disgust for vegetables——

DASH.   Yes, I know. Only five minutes.

CARD.   Demolish de guinea hen in five minutes—only five? Why, I could put daylight through an ox in dat time.

DASH.   Good! Eager for de fray, eh? You see, I've got de poultices.

CARD.   De poultryesses? I don't understand——

DASH *(produces boxing-gloves)*.   All serene for a quiet set-to wid de Guinean. I want to see your new guard. He'll go in somehow, dis yer way—*(puts on gloves)* one, two—at you *(spars at* CARD.*)*

CARD.   Oh, drap dat! *(lifts up his shoe and puts* DASH's *hands down)* Will he? Not while I sail in dese skiffs.

DASH.   But, in fine, o' course, yer mustn't hit back.

CARD.   No; I shall hit front.

DASH.   I'll just step down an' see if he am ready. You kin prepare yourself in de meantime——

CARD.   A mean time it is.

DASH *(at* R.*)*.   Pompey!

(POMP *appears,* R.*)*

POMP.   Yes, massa.

DASH.   Don't let anybody in or out ob dis room.

POMP.   No, sah. *(waves end of handkerchief familiarly to* CARD*)*

DASH *(to* CARD*)*.   I'll fetch de Guinean back, and we'll have a round or two——

CARD.   Ob toast wid de fowl?

DASH.   All gay an' pleasant. *(waves handkerchief)* Hoorah! *(exit,* R.*)*

POMP.   Oh' won't we hab a libely house! *(waves handkerchief)* Hooraw! *(exit,* R.*)*

CARD (*alone*). A set-to! gay and pleasant! Dat gallus ruffian is a gwine to fetch back de Guinean, an' he's gwine to go into me, one, two— (*upsets a chair*) It's a plot ob de Clams-towners! dey'se been set agin our circus by de rival combinations. It's berry cl'ar dat I muss pull up stakes! git up and git! But how? de doors am fast, an' dat fancy waiter am hard an' fast by it! de brack guard! I do beliebe he's saying "hooray" to himself on de door-mat. Is dar no escape? I'll make effort, an' den—(*takes up his bundle of poles, and hammers at* L. *wing with them*) The door gives—it gives—two minutes more——

(*Enter,* R., DASH *and* BLOWER, *ready for fight.*)

DASH. Hullo! whar is he?

BLOW. Dar he is; a-working up his muscle afore he pitches into me. Squire, hadn't you best put de gloves on, and let me be de judge? (*shows fright of* CARD *from this out*)

DASH (*to* L.). Sah, sah! (CARD *turns and nearly strikes* DASH *with the bundle.*)

CARD. Ha! discovered! (*shoulders the bundle, going backwards to* C., *followed by* DASH, *and not seeing* BLOWER, *hits him with bundle.*)

BLOW. Oh! (CARD *drops bundle in turning round, and it rolls upon* DASH's *foot,* DASH *kicks it, and it gets under the feet of all three. Business.* DASH *finally kicks it up* C.)

CARD. What do you kick dat for? (DASH *recedes from him.*)

BLOW. Dat's it—gib it to him! (DASH *closes in upon* CARD, *and gets him to put on gloves.*)

DASH. Dat's a good fellah! put us up to de latest wrinkles.

CARD. You're old enough to hab dem youself.

BLOW. De newest strikes. (*squares off*)

CARD. De last place I come from dar was only de tailor's strike.

DASH. How's de best way to meet a punch in de mouf?

CARD (*keeps off* BLOWER). I neber meat it. I *drink* de punch in de mouf.

BLOW. How to purvent a dribe in de——(*he and* CARD *strike out together.* BLOWER *doubles up, panting.*) Wind, wind! (*drops left glove.*)

CARD. Air, air! (DASH *picks up dropped glove. He and* BLOWER *box with* CARD, *they using each one gloved hand, he both, between them.*) Water, water! fire, fire! (*comic fight*)

(*Enter,* R., POMP.)

POMP. Oh, ain't dis a likely house!

195

CARD *(up C.).* Help, help! *(breaks through between* DASH *and* BLOWER, *who strike each other and fall.* CARD *comes down,* C. *To* POMP*)* If you are a brack man, protect me from dese slaughterers.

POMP. Protect yer? What yer mean?

DASH. }
BLOW. } *(coming down).* What yer mean?

CARD. Mean? I'm not gwine to stand still and be knocked into de middle ob next week. I'll hab de law ob you, as sure as my name's Sampson Card!

ALL. Card!

DASH. What! den you ain't de Whitechapel pet?

CARD. I'be shaken carpets for white chaps, offen.

BLOW. Not de Sockdologer?

CARD. Neber heerd ob sich a name afore.

POMP. Den you'se not going to fight Micky M'Knaw?

CARD. Don't know de Grecian.

DASH. What am your appleation?

POMP. It ap-*pears* to be on your trunk.

CARD. You'se drunk, all ob you. "S.C.P.R."—Sampson Card, Pickleson's Romanticon; *(quickly)* de only show on de face ob de universe dat combines construction wid confusement, thirty cents admission, editors, children under ten months, and ginuine widows half price, sogers paid to come in.

BLOW. Sampson Card! dat ain't Squasher Cuff.

CARD. No; I'se advance agent, I tell yer! a gent as you need make no more advances upon. *(throws gloves off)* Our circus is coming to town——

BLOW. Den dat's de ring you figure in?

CARD. Yas, de sur-prise ring. You shall hab tickets for it—arter I've had my grub; you've *(to* BLOWER*)* deprived me ob dat! *(to* POMP*)* Grub, grub! oh, won't I be so ill-bred dis time as to make de butter fly!

BLOW. I'se berry sorry!

DASH. We're all berry sorry. S'pose we all dine togeder for once in de way? I'll stand treat.

CARD. For once in de way! You won't be in de way den. *(embraces* DASH*)* Come to my arms!

BLOW. We'll hab all de village in and hab a grand bit ob fun.

196

POMP. Oh, won't dis be a libely house! *(dances a step or two.)*

CARD *(shakes hands with all)*. I accept de dinner as a ham-end honorable. Don't limit it to once but as offen as you like. But none ob your "One, two," and de only rounds to be dose ob applause.

BLOW. Yes, if de gen'rous public dat has so often encouraged my efforts, will smile on us now——

POMP. Dar will be——

ALL. A libely house.

CURTAIN

A Brief
Annotated Bibliography

Browne, Ray B. "Shakespeare in American Vaudeville and Negro Minstrelsy."
   American Quarterly, XII (Fall, 1960), 374–91. Browne offers a discussion
   of structural principles in afterpieces and explores minstrelsy's use of
   verbal devices for burlesque effect.

Green, Alan W. C. "'Jim Crow,' 'Zip Coon': The Northern Origins of Negro
   Minstrelsy." *Massachusetts Review* (1970), 385–97.

Hutton, Lawrence. "The Negro on the Stage." *Harper's Monthly*, LXXIX
   (1889), 131–45. Hutton offers a concise history of blackface entertainment before the rise of the minstrel show.

Keeler, Ralph. "Three Years as a Negro Minstrel." *Atlantic Monthly*, XXIV
   (1869), 71–85. Keeler's reminiscence is one of the liveliest firsthand accounts of life with touring minstrel troupes during the 1860s.

Logan, Olive, "The Ancestry of Brother Bones." *Harper's Monthly*, LVIII
   (1879), 687–98. Logan traces the parallels between minstrelsy and earlier European entertainment forms. The article is a representative example of the bemused respect with which journalists treated the subject.

Moody, Richard. *America Takes the Stage: Romanticism in American Drama and
   Theatre, 1750–1900.* Bloomington: Indiana University Press, 1955.
   Moody includes a discussion of minstrelsy's position in the context of
   American stage history.

———. *Dramas from the American Theatre: 1769–1909.* Bloomington: Indiana
   University Press, 1966. Moody's anthology includes eleven minstrel
   texts, eight of which are first-part pieces—burlesque lectures, stump
   speeches, interlocutor/end-men exchanges. The selections, along with
   Moody's brief historical essay, make a useful supplement to the materials in this volume.

Bibliography

New York *Clipper*, 1853–1924. A weekly theatrical newspaper that eventually became *Variety*, the *Clipper* is a valuable source of minstrel advertising. Editorials of the early years contain running commentary on the shifting currents in minstrelsy. Later issues contain a wealth of reminiscences and interviews with prominent figures in the art.

Nye, Russel. *The Unembarrassed Muse: The Popular Arts in America*. New York: Dial Press, 1970. Nye includes a brief discussion of minstrelsy that has the advantage of showing its position in the crowded history of American popular culture.

Odell, George C. D. *Annals of the New York Stage*. 15 vols. New York: Columbia University Press, 1927–49. This is the single best source of information on the performances and personnel of the major professional troupes during minstrelsy's golden age.

Paskman, Dailey, and Sigmund Spaeth. *Gentlemen Be Seated! A Parade of the Old Time Minstrels*. Garden City, New York: Doubleday, Doran and Company, 1928. A popular and superficial history of the subject, it is nevertheless valuable for its reprint of the text for an entire minstrel show including music. It serves as a useful supplement to the materials in this volume.

Rice, Edward Le Roy. *Monarchs of Minstrelsy*. New York: Kenny Publishing Company, 1911. Contains biographical sketches of the major nineteenth-century stars.

Rourke, Constance. *American Humor: A Study of the National Character*. New York: Harcourt Brace Jovanovich, 1931. Rourke includes a chapter on the minstrel clown. Her study, though provocative, is limited somewhat by her use of song lyrics rather than afterpieces as source material for her criticism.

Toll, Robert C. *Blacking Up: The Minstrel Show in Nineteenth-Century America*. New York: Oxford University Press, 1974. This is the best single critical study of the subject, discussing minstrelsy from a variety of perspectives including social, aesthetic, and historical. It contains much previously ignored information on specific black performers and all-black professional troupes; and the bibliography, though by no means exhaustive, is the most thorough one available on the subject.

Trux, J. J. "Negro Minstrelsy—Ancient and Modern." *Putnam's Monthly*, V (1885), 72–79. A quaint and entertaining rhapsody on minstrel music.

Wittke, Carl. *Tambo and Bones: A History of the Minstrel Stage*. Originally published in 1930. Westport, Connecticut: Greenwood Press, 1971. A delightfully readable and authoritative history of the art which includes a useful discussion of the economics of minstrelsy during the latter half of the nineteenth century.

ABOUT THE BOOK

The scene of action is the kitchen. The hero is an ant. The time is now.

> *"Teapot fell," said the dinner bell.*
> *"Broke her spout," said the trout.*
> *"Push her up," said the cup.*
> *"I can't," said the ant.*
> *"Please try," said the pie.*

The ant struggles in vain to lift Miss Teapot from the floor. Unable to do so by himself, he sets out for help, returning with an army of ants and two spiders.

> *"She'll die," said the fly.*
> *"She will not," said the pot.*
> *"Keep cool," said the stool.*
> *"I can't look," said the book.*
> *"I can't bear it," said the carrot.*

How Miss Teapot is finally saved, through the brilliant team-work of the rescue party—with the moral support of her fellow kitchen occupants, is the exciting climax of this uniquely told tale.

"I CAN'T"
SAID THE ANT

"I CAN'T" SAID THE ANT

SAID THE ANT

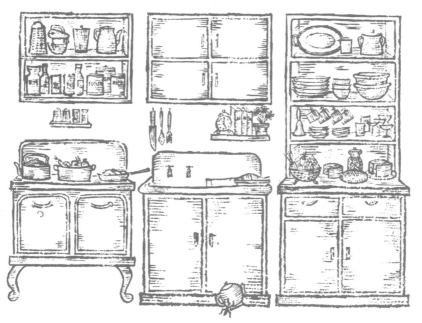

A SECOND BOOK OF NONSENSE
WORDS AND PICTURES BY POLLY CAMERON

Coward, McCann & Geoghegan, Inc. New York

ALSO BY POLLY CAMERON

THE CAT WHO THOUGHT HE WAS A TIGER

THE CAT WHO COULDN'T PURR

THE DOG WHO GREW TOO MUCH

THE BOY WHO DREW BIRDS

A CHILD'S BOOK OF NONSENSE

FOR
DONALD
CAMERON
McQUISTON

I was taking a walk...

I was taking a walk
When I heard a loud clatter!
I rushed into the kitchen
To see what was the matter.

There on the floor
With the tea pouring out
Was a cracked teapot
With a broken spout.

"Good heavens! What happened,
My poor Miss Teapot?"
She rolled over and murmured,
"The tea was too hot."

"What's all the clatter?" asked the platter.

"Teapot fell," said the dinner bell.

"Teapot broke," said the artichoke.

"She went kerplop!" said the mop.

"Is she dead?" asked the bread.

"Just a break," 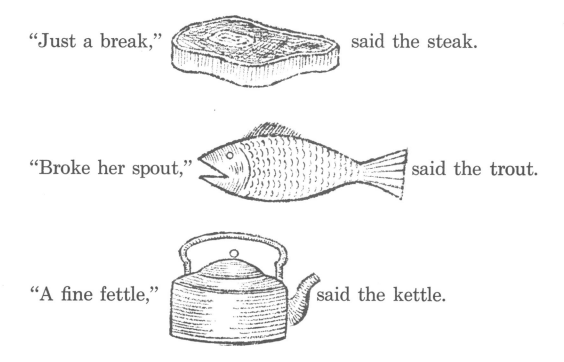 said the steak.

"Broke her spout," said the trout.

"A fine fettle," said the kettle.

"Alas," said the glass.

"What a life,"  said the knife.

"Push her up,"  said the cup.

"I can't," said the ant.

"You can,"  said the pan.

"You must," said the crust.

"Please try,"  said the pie.

"That's the way,"  said the tray.

"That's good!" 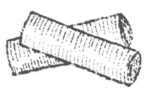 said the wood.

"Higher,"  said the fire.

"It's a breeze," said the cheese.

"You've gone far,"  said the jar.

"They slid," 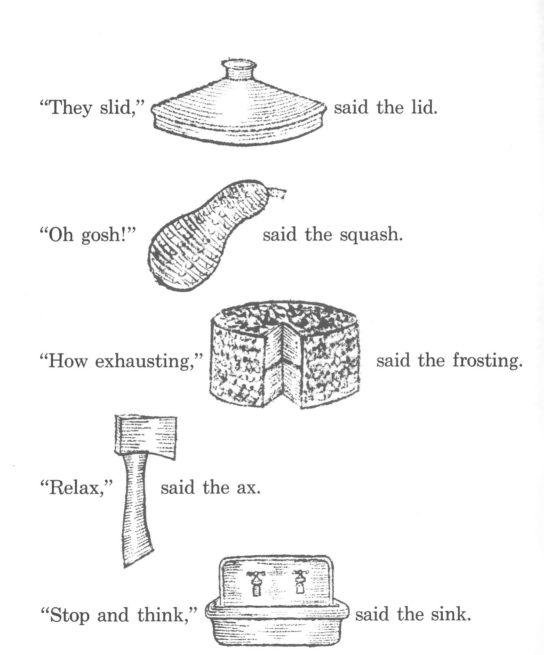 said the lid.

"Oh gosh!" said the squash.

"How exhausting," said the frosting.

"Relax," said the ax.

"Stop and think," said the sink.

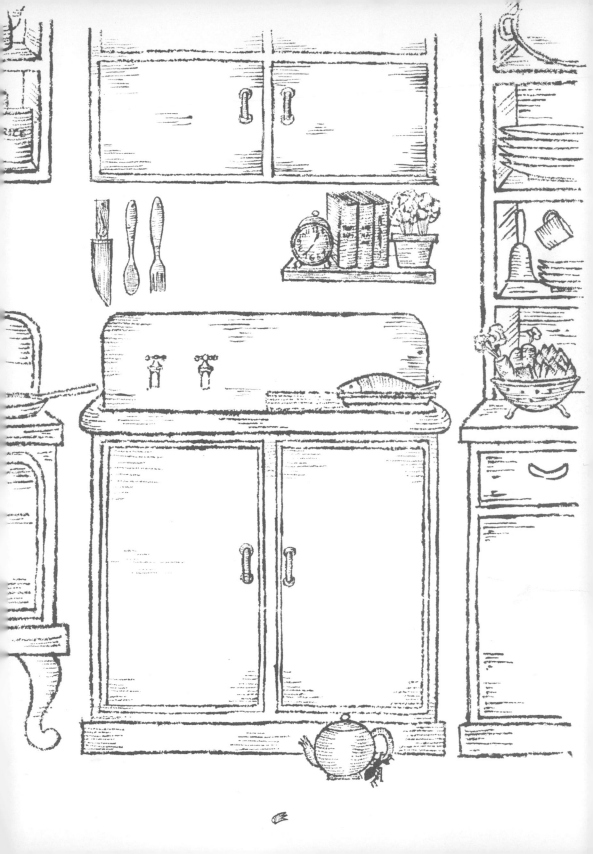

I rested her gently
Back on the floor.
"Fear not! Miss Teapot,
I'll be back for more."

I gathered my friends
And told them the trouble.
We spread the word
And came back on the double.

There was an army of ants
And a spider or two.
We quickly made plans
On just what to do.

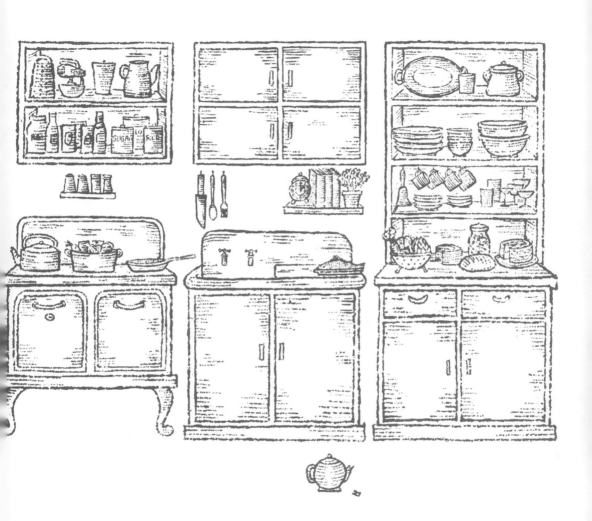

"How bleak," said the leak.

"She'll die," said the fly.

"She will not," said the pot.

"Don't be dumb," said the crumb.

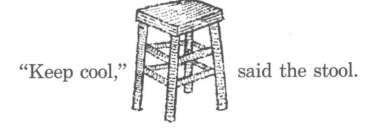

"Keep cool," said the stool.

"They'll fix her,"  said the mixer.

"We haven't lost yet,"  said the omelette.

"Give them time,"  said the lime.

"There's still hope,"  said the soap.

"They'll mend her,"  said the blender.

The spiders spun a splendid web
And wrapped it 'round her spout,
Making certain it was tight
So tea could never trickle out.

"Will you look at that!" said the cat.

"My word!"  said the bird.

"Aren't they nimble," said the thimble.

"Aren't they smart,"  said the tart.

"Rather rare," 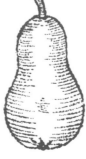 said the pear.

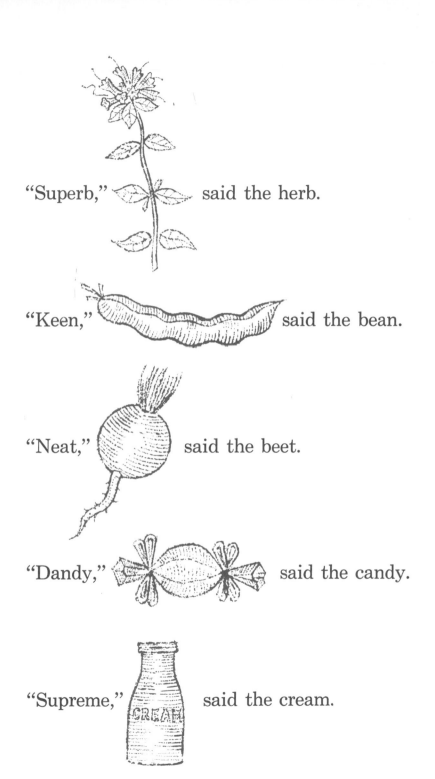

"Superb," said the herb.

"Keen," said the bean.

"Neat," said the beet.

"Dandy," said the candy.

"Supreme," said the cream.

From her spout to her handle
They spun a strong string,
And when they were finished
Her spout had a sling!

"That's the ticket," 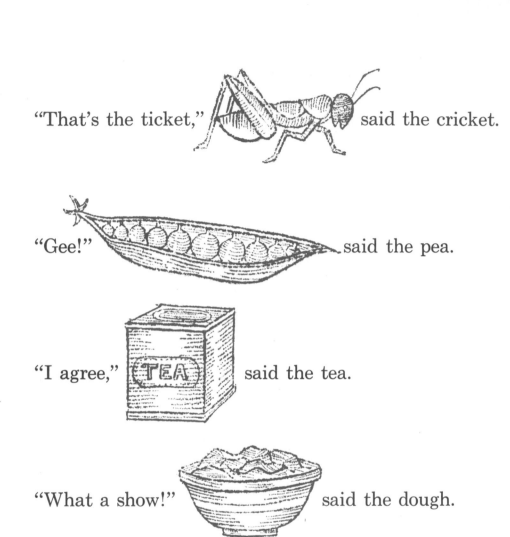 said the cricket.

"Gee!" said the pea.

"I agree," said the tea.

"What a show!" said the dough.

"Good cheer!"  said the root beer.

"She'll be all right,"  said the light.

"Take my advice,"  said the rice.

"She'll heal,"  said the peel.

"She's good as new,"  said the stew.

"What a blessing,"  said the dressing.

Miss Teapot's spout
Was nicely mended,
But we knew our job
Had not quite ended.

How do we get her
Back up on the sink?
To figure that out
We *all* had to think.

The spiders began
To spin and spin.
They spun up and over
And around and in.

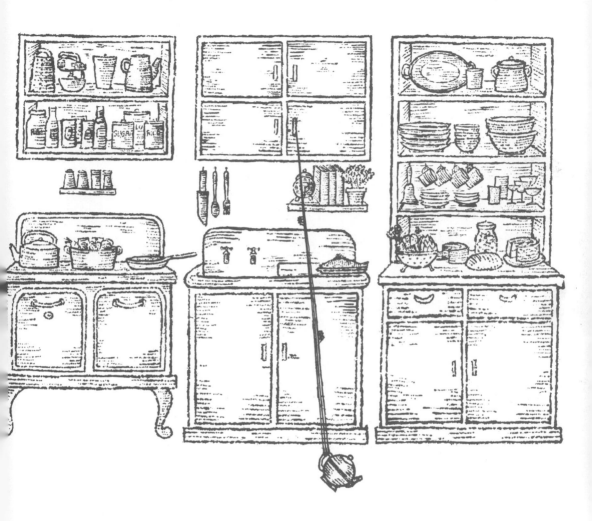

"Get her up to the top,"  said the chop.

"Some trick!"  said the candlestick.

"Some climb!" said the thyme.

"Give them room," said the broom.

"Keep alert,"  said the dessert.

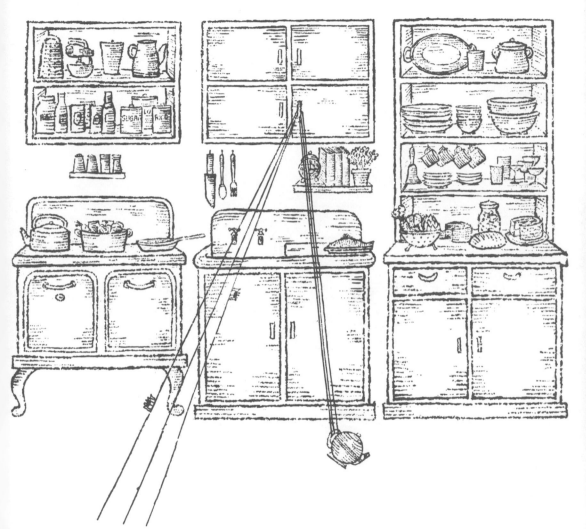

"Co-operate," 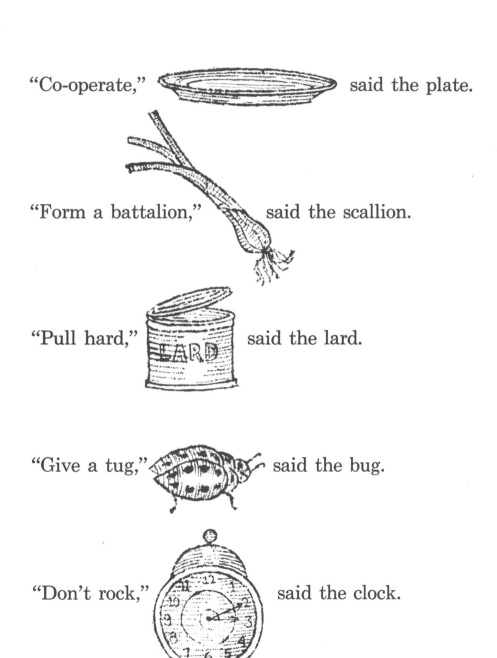 said the plate.

"Form a battalion," said the scallion.

"Pull hard," said the lard.

"Give a tug," said the bug.

"Don't rock," said the clock.

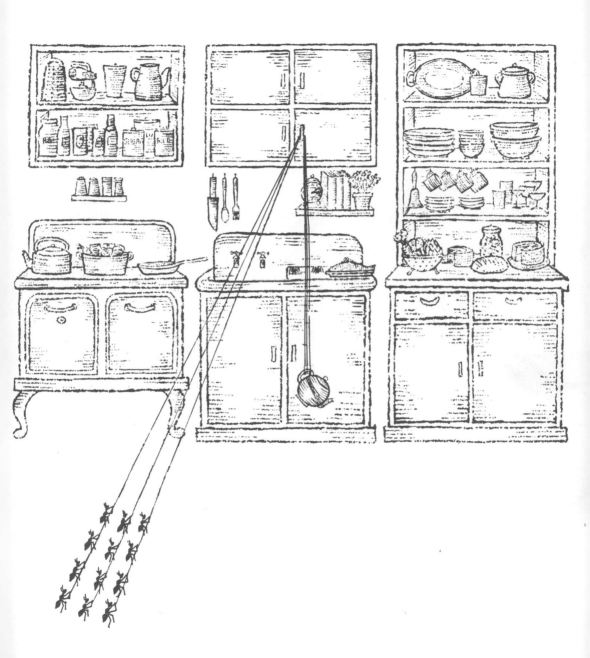

"Don't break her,"  said the shaker.

"Don't choke her," said the poker.

"She'll crash!"  said the trash.

"I can't look," said the book.

"I can't bear it,"  said the carrot.

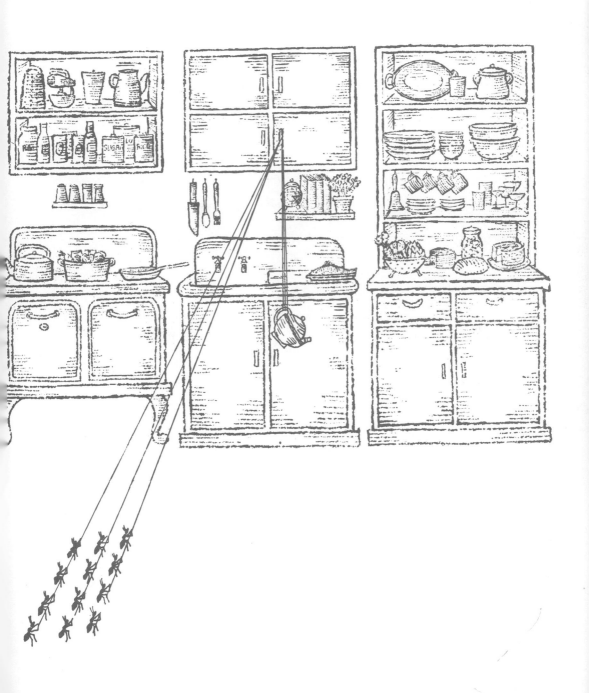

"Head her east,"  said the yeast.

"A close scrape,"  said the grape.

"What power,"  said the flower.

"We've WON!"  said the bun.

"What a relief," 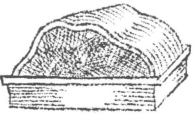 said the beef.

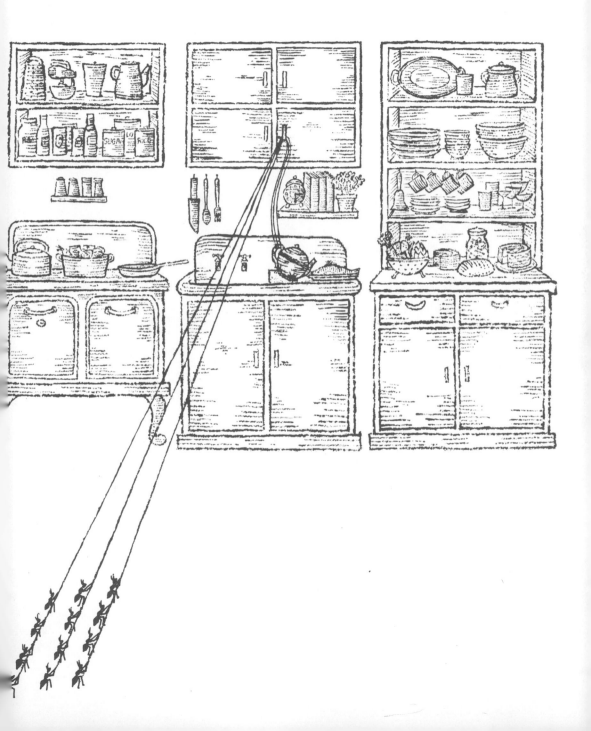

"Thank you," said Miss Teapot,
"You've been good to me.
 Polly, put the kettle on.
 We'll all have tea."

THE END

ABOUT THE AUTHOR

With the publication of her sixth children's book for Coward-McCann, Polly Cameron again demonstrates the successful combination of both her art and writing talents.

She has had much experience in both fields. When she was just 20 years old, she wrote and narrated a series of children's radio shows in her native California.

From there she worked in advertising and display in Arizona, managing to build a house in her spare time. In 1951 she began a three-year tour of Europe and North Africa, finally settling down to paint in Paris.

Polly Cameron now lives in a reconverted barn in Palisades, New York, where she works as writer, painter, sculptor and graphic designer.

She brings to her children's books a lively imagination and warm sense of humor.